Sustainable Communities and Green Lifestyles

Sustainable communities raise questions about the compatibility of capitalism and environmentalism and how we can green our way of life in a capitalist economy that values short-term production and consumption over long-term conservation and simple living. If capitalism and its drive towards consumption has produced social and environmental degradation, is it the best medium to identify solutions?

Sustainable Communities and Green Lifestyles examines one ecovillage as it attempts to create a sense of community while reducing its impact on the natural environment. Through extensive participant observation, the book demonstrates how ecovillages are immersed within a larger discourse of class, race, and lifestyle choices, highlighting the inseparability of environmental sustainability and social justice. Sustainable communities are confronted by the contradictions of green consumption and must address social inequality or risk focusing inward on personal green consumerism, creating mere green havens for the few who can afford to live in them. This book, cautious of redirecting environmentalist efforts away from structural solutions and onto personal environmentalism, offers a critical perspective on the challenges of an emerging green lifestyle.

This book offers a critical perspective on the direction of US environmentalism and contributes to debates in environmental studies, anthropology, and urban planning.

Tendai Chitewere is Associate Professor at San Francisco State University, USA.

Routledge Studies in Sustainability

www.routledge.com/Routledge-Studies-in-Sustainability/book-series/RSSTY

Democratic Sustainability in a New Era of Localism
John Stanton

Social Practices, Interventions and Sustainability
Beyond Behaviour Change
Edited by Yolande Strengers and Cecily Maller

The Politics of Sustainability
Philosophical Perspectives
Edited by Dieter Birnbacher and May Thorseth

Promoting Sustainable Living
Sustainability as an Object of Desire
Justyna Karakiewicz, with contributions from Audrey Yue and Angela Paladino

Rethinking the Green State
Environmental Governance Towards Climate and Sustainability Transitions
Edited by Karin Bäckstrand and Annica Kronsell

Energy and Transport in Green Transition
Perspectives on Ecomodernity
Edited by Atle Midttun and Nina Witoszek

Human Rights and Sustainability
Moral Responsibilities for the Future
Edited by Gerhard Bos and Marcus Düwell

Sustainability and the Art of Long Term Thinking
Edited by Bernd Klauer, Reiner Manstetten, Thomas Petersen and Johannes Schiller

Cities and Sustainability
A New Approach
Daniel Hoornweg

Transdisciplinary Research and Practice for Sustainability Outcomes
Edited by Dena Fam, Jane Palmer, Chris Riedy and Cynthia Mitchell

A Political Economy of Attention, Mindfulness and Consumerism
Reclaiming the Mindful Commons
Peter Doran

Sustainable Communities and Green Lifestyles
Consumption and Environmentalism
Tendai Chitewere

Sustainable Communities and Green Lifestyles

Consumption and Environmentalism

Tendai Chitewere

LONDON AND NEW YORK

from Routledge

First published 2018
by Routledge

2 Park Square, Milton Park, Abingdon, Oxfordshire OX14 4RN
52 Vanderbilt Avenue, New York, NY 10017

Routledge is an imprint of the Taylor & Francis Group, an informa business

First issued in paperback 2018

British Library Cataloguing in Publication Data
A catalogue record for this book is available from the British Library

Library of Congress Cataloging in Publication Data
A catalog record for this book has been requested

ISBN: 978-1-138-77540-4 (hbk)
ISBN: 978-0-367-19292-1 (pbk)

Typeset in Goudy
by Wearset Ltd, Boldon, Tyne and Wear

For my mother, Ruth Chengetai Chitewere, who taught me how to create community wherever I live.

Contents

List of figures		viii
List of tables		ix
Preface		x
Acknowledgments		xiii
List of abbreviations		xviii
1	Introduction	1
2	Community, environmentalism, consumption	8
3	A day in the life of the EcoVillage	30
4	Making community green	74
5	Emerging green lifestyles	109
6	Conclusion	133
	Appendices	145
	Index	154

Figures

3.1	EcoVillage at Ithaca organization structure 2001	40
3.2	EcoVillage at Ithaca organization structure 2015	41
3.3	Year residents were born	45
3.4	Distribution of neighborhood residents	64
4.1	Size of homes in EVI compared with previous residence	80
4.2	Highest rank of what residents see as their community boundary	84
4.3	Employment status	97
4.4	Income range	98
5.1	Number of cars per household	115

Tables

3.1	EcoVillage at Ithaca entities	42
3.2	EcoVillage at Ithaca neighborhoods at a glance	44
3.3	Social connections and EVI mission	47
3.4	Connection to others in the village and beyond	53
3.5	Ethnic/racial diversity	56
3.6	Gender identity	57
3.7	Sexual orientation	57
3.8	Community work	63
4.1	Activities that express commitment to social and ecological causes	76
4.2	Where residents moved from	86
4.3	Highest level of schooling	99
4.4	Religious practice	99
4.5	Political affiliation/party	100
5.1	Environmental goods	114

Preface

On New Year's Day 2016, my partner and I sat on our front porch with our new puppy, Kumi, the sun beaming down, warming us and the vegetable beds that replaced the lawn years ago. Shortly after we got comfortable with leftover New Year's Eve bread and cheese, guacamole and dips, our neighbor from five houses away, Misha, stopped by. He sat on the steps and we started to chat, then my next-door neighbor Marian and her dog Stormy walked by, stopped, and joined us. Although Misha had wanted to stay only briefly, we all enjoy Marian's company so we continued our conversations for another hour. Matthias made espresso and brought down the leftover chocolate cake. Shortly, Sandy and John from the end of the block stopped by on the way to their annual New Year's Day hike in Redwood Park. The porch is large and so we all sat in the sun and talked for another hour. We discussed the 109-mile bicycle ride some of us were doing from Oakland to Sacramento to raise money for Oakland public schools, a trip to see family for the holidays, what is growing in the front yard, and climate change—it was a warm, sunny day in the middle of California's worst drought, on the first day of January. As the sun gently reminded us that it would set, Sandy and John rushed off for their hike, and Stormy and Kumi had had enough of each other, so Marian walked Stormy home. Misha, two hours later than he initially planned to leave, collected his pots from the New Year's Eve potluck and went home across the street. This is what my partner and I now call an "ecovillage moment," a term we borrow from the EcoVillage at Ithaca project: the random meeting of neighbors, engaging in spontaneous conversation around the home.

My experience of living in an ecological cohousing community for over two years, and studying its development for over 14 years, helps me recognize these moments as precious. My years learning about the influence of a sense of community on social and environmental degradation leaves me well aware that these kinds of random conversations and meetings with neighbors represent something valuable to individuals and neighborhoods. Our Fairview Park community organizes itself around earthquake preparedness, random potlucks and outdoor parties, supporting an ill neighbor, and confronting social injustice. While not everyone participates all the time, there is a sense of community. This sense of community produces civic engagement through informal discussions about local and national politics, a healthy LISTSERV discussion on local needs and opportunities to address concerns for the natural environment, and a kind of neighborhood health and well-being that makes us aware of each other.

Yet the physical location of our neighborhood and the cultural context of this corner of the San Francisco Bay Area are significant. We are fortunate to live in Oakland, where sunny days in January mean we can still be visibly present to our neighbors, increasing the likelihood of a random encounter of people who live next door and have the resource of time to stop and visit. There is privilege that comes with living in a middle-to-upper-middle-class neighborhood with a mild climate and a large liberal contingent which proactively tries to create a sense of community and advocate for equality. The larger cultural context in which this exists is one of deep inequality, racial injustice, and environmental waste and degradation. How then do we address environmental sustainability without confronting social inequality? This book has grown out of my attempt to confront this dilemma; I believe our efforts will be fruitless if we fail to address social inequality while advocating for environmental sustainability.

I grew up in Mutare, Zimbabwe, and spent my school holidays in the rural villages of Chiramba and Nyamombe. Our community had a small footprint. We slept in mud and stick huts with grass roofs; we grew, harvested, and cooked vegan food on small fires (it happened to be organic because all we had was manure from the livestock that grazed on the land). On special occasions we killed a chicken or goat, or ate our sadza with sour milk. We gathered the wood from the nearby forests and used our heads to fetch water from a community well. If our embers had not survived the night, we would walk to the next village and get some. We had a composting toilet that was outside, and played with nearby relatives in the hills while watching goats or working in the fields. The women grew and cooked the food; as a young girl, I never spent time with the men, so cannot speak for their activities. We had a buzzing community with strict rules that varied depending on whether we were in my mother's village (Chiramba) or my father's (Nyamombe). Our lives were simple, at least during the holidays when we did not have electricity or electronic entertainment. As far as I recall, we all wanted to move out of this way of life. Moving into town, having access to a gas stove and water from a pipe, or a toilet that flushed was highly desirable and it propelled us all to study hard in school. Parents, relatives in the villages, all worked together to send the children to school in hopes that they would one day bring the entire family opportunities and resources for a better life. The community, the village, the family, was a powerful place to effect social change.

In writing this book I have hoped to contribute to the conversation on how communities are powerful places to effect social and ecological change. I do not believe there is an easy solution, but I strongly admire the effort to seek one. It is clear from ongoing social and environmental struggles that there is a need for change from the status quo. I hope this work helps to inspire us to build community where we live, get to know our neighbors, grow food and empathy, and organize to create lasting structural changes that are just and sustainable. The residents I got to know well during my stay in EcoVillage at Ithaca (EVI) are trying to rethink the way they live their everyday life. In this challenging effort, some felt their experiment was working, others not so much. But what I came to admire was the heartfelt ways residents engaged in conversations about how to create a sustainable community in the middle of a capitalist economy. Long and critical conversations with residents helped to uncover personal and structural barriers to a lifestyle that some felt was incompatible with living on a finite planet and enjoying the creature comforts. I have tried to share those conversations in this book.

What made the research data rich and meaningful was that participants in this study were promised anonymity. This makes sense in a small community that is experimenting with living together. Current and former residents were open and frank with me, and I appreciated their candor. But I also made a commitment to their privacy. This is hard to do in a community where families know each other well. Simply changing a name is not enough to disguise the individual's identity. After a year in EVI, I observed how easily residents could identify each other's opinion at meetings and in casual conversations. Therefore, in several places, I have used my own observations to describe a situation. It is my sincere hope that I have balanced this effort with minimal cost to the participant and the discipline.

Finally, as my friends, neighbors, and supportive colleagues will tell you, this book would not have been completed without the help of my various communities that I cherish dearly. Throughout the book I disguise the real names of current and former EcoVillage residents in order to protect their privacy; instead, you will see the names of my friends, neighbors, acupuncturist, hiking group, and all the people whose love and care represented a most valuable community in my life. For it is fitting to replace one set of good people with another.

Acknowledgments

This book has been a community effort. I am deeply grateful, indebted, to all the participants of the EcoVillage at Ithaca (EVI) project: the current residents, the individuals and families who moved out, the people who were part of the early planning stages, and the families who left before I arrived. I was warmly welcomed into the homes of every resident in the community and it was through their generosity of time and candid information that I was able to collect rich ethnographic data about their everyday lives. Residents were busy with community activities, neighborhood meetings, building new homes, working at their jobs, and caring for their families and friendships, yet they made time to meet with me. EVI receives a lot of visitors; I'm thankful for the time each participant took to give me depth and meaning in our long conversations. Although I can't mention them by name, I want them to know how much I appreciate our time together, not just as part of this research project, but in this life. Being part of the EVI community has been a humbling experience—thank you. I hope my work helps to answer the questions many had about their community and thus complement their ongoing process of creating a sustainable future. I am grateful to other members of the larger Ithaca community who talked with me about the project, including board members and neighbors to EVI.

Anonymous reviewers, colleagues, and my students gave me valuable feedback during conference presentations and in my classroom—thank you.

The editors at Routledge have been wonderful and I'm thankful for their contagious enthusiasm, timely feedback, and responses. Thank you.

In the fall of 2014, I spent a semester at the Freie Universität in Berlin as a Gastprofessorin. Colleagues from the Forschungszentrum für Umweltpolitik (Environmental Policy Research Centre) read early drafts and gave helpful feedback in seminars. I am indebted to Miranda Schreurs (formerly at the Freie Universität and now at Technische Universität München) for her support, encouragement, and wisdom. Our dinners and evening walks in Berlin after long hours in the office were much needed and refreshing.

I am most grateful to Linda Juang for our numerous stimulating conversations about women, people of color, and our role as teachers to students who find themselves in a culture so different from their own. Our joint research discussions on café terraces in Berlin and Potsdam have inspired a new direction in my sustainable communities research. Linda is the kind of colleague everyone who works on a long project needs. She and her family, Bodo, Tayo, and Keanu, hosted me for several weeks while I worked on the book, taking me on scenic bike rides around Berlin and its suburbs when I needed a break. I appreciated the lunch meetings at the mensa with enthusiastic graduate students and colleagues at both Universität Potsdam and the Freie Universität. Linda introduced me to Angela Ittel, who put me in touch with Sabina Hark, both from the Techniche Universität Berlin. I am grateful to have met these women leaders in their field. The wonderful dinner parties and stimulating conversations about sustainability, feminist theory, and European politics provided insight into German academic life—thank you. Sabina gave me an inspiring tour of her cohousing community—thank you. I appreciated Michael LaFond and his cohousing community for sharing a meal and conversation about creative ways Germany is building sustainable communities from the top–down and bottom–up. I'm part of a global community of friends and family, and throughout this project, these people have been oceans away, but always close at heart. Thank you to Mary Ellen Zuppan, Jean-Michel Jolly and Daniel, Evi Manger, Susanne Thoma, Jeanne Lätt, Susi Sauer and Michi Müller, Jochen Trumpf and Tanja Strive, Annegret and Gernot Schaal, Lewis Taylor, Karin Jöller, Miho Sato, Vanessa Kääb, Raman Sanyal and Konstantin.

In the spring of 2015 I was invited by Jill Schneidermann to join the Department of Earth Science and Geography at Vassar College. I'm incredibly grateful for my productive time with the faculty. One of the most helpful pieces of feedback I received was during a meeting among the faculty; they discussed three of my chapters while I listened. I learned a lot and it helped me develop my ideas. Thank you Jill, Joseph Nevins, Yu Zhou, and Mary Ann Cunningham. Jill welcomed me into her home and Poughkeepsie community with shared meals, gardening, and enriching conversations about meaning in life and work—thank you.

I have been fortunate in my academic career to have incredibly talented, kind, and dedicated mentors. I'm especially grateful to the late cultural anthropologist, Richard Antoun, for inspiring me to do qualitative research and for the small library of books he gave me in Binghamton. My graduate school advisors Carmen Ferradás and Susan Pollock challenged me to ask tough questions, look deep, and push my ideas further as a scholar. They both read numerous versions with great detail. I appreciated Laura Nader's support and insight at the early stages of the book. Dorceta Taylor warmly welcomed me to a conference at the University of Michigan in 2007 and enthusiastically supported my work as an innovative contribution to understanding environmental injustice. I'm grateful for her model of academic excellence and human goodness—thank you Dorceta.

I met Sally Fairfax through a mutual friend, Mark Spencer. We quickly became friends and colleagues. Sally and her wife, Monica, have not only encouraged and supported my work at various stages; they have enriched my life and become family. When not working through a complex scholarly problem or teaching me how to cope with the ills of academia, we applied our research skills to finding the best hamburger in the Bay Area as I finished each chapter. As foodies, we often stumbled upon some of the best restaurants in the United States, and I gained some of the best insights of a wise woman. Thank you.

There are a series of friends and colleagues who inspired me, pushed me, welcomed me, reminded me of the relevance and timeliness of my work, but also helped me stay grounded in the beauty of everyday life. A special thank you goes to Ginny and Nari Mistry, who were the first to tell me about the EcoVillage at Ithaca project, and opened their home to me on many occasions. I thank Nancy Tittler for long walks and deep conversation about personal life transitions and academic dreams. My Binghamton colleagues kept me intellectually fueled—thanks to Sofian Merabet, Constance Sullivan-Blum, Kari Colosi, Adam Flint, Marie Marley, Lynda Carroll, M. das Dores Cruz, Gaby Castro-Gessner, Maresi Starzmann, and Diane Enns. Several of my students, Maggie Chen, Sophia Rodriguez, Rosie Linares, Emily Feingold, and Nick Reeves, helped with different parts of data analysis. I thank my graduate students Misty McKinney, Heather Co, and Erika Poveda, whose enthusiasm for addressing social and environmental disparities, especially as they stem from racism and inequality, gives me hope.

In Washington, D.C., I have a group of friends I call family; Premila Mistry, my first US friend, has been unwavering in supporting me and makes sure I always have good music—thank you. I'm grateful to Gerlinda and John Boright, Laura Knapp, Sonnary Phongsawath, Darlene Arnold, Nancy and Tom Kelly, Garry Thomas, Sylvia Hemenway, Francine Montemurro, and Hilda Wilcox, who inspired me to write.

My life at SF State was especially challenging while I wrote the book. I'm grateful for the islands of inspiration and joy my friends provided through tasty potlucks, midday walks around campus, meditation on Monday nights, and the Oakland Museum on Friday nights. Avi Ben-Zeev and I connected over different kinds of communities in the Bay Area. I appreciated his support over meals at Crossroads and bay walks with Amos and Kumi. A big thank you to Dorothy Tsuruta, Brandee Marckmann, Lisa Lim, Lucia Volk, Irene Yen, Sheila Tully, Chris Bettinger, Darlene Franklin, Nancy Burke, Barbara Holzman, Xiao-Hang Liu, Jennifer Blecha, James Martel, Federico Ardilla, Mayli Khoe, Lisa White, Sheldon Axler, Carrie Heeter, Janet Shim, Laurie L. Meschke, Eric Hsu, Hope and Wyatt, Nilgun and Multu Ozer, Senem and Victor, and Lori Pottinger. Thanks to Nchale Anderson for sharing our love for Botswana and Zimbabwe and missing home together. Incredibly supportive women appeared in my life; we met weekly, monthly, or as needed. These women shared their experiences and taught resilience; we provided a solid intellectual foundation and a morally sound safety net for each other. My dentist invited me to join her Sunday hiking group of professional women of color. We conquered all the hiking trails in Tilden Park and across the Bay Area, lifting and supporting each other with every step. Nature is good medicine. I'm incredibly grateful to be part of this inspiring community of wise, brainy activists with large hearts: thank you Meeta Doshi, Tina Coles, Debbie Chan, Irma Herrera, Sandy Brumbaum, Kathleen Jimenez, Madeline Chun, Shoshana Rosenberg, Raphael Shannon Kraw for catching me. The bagel girls made it possible to stay grounded in turbulence—you know who you are—and I thank you.

My friends in the Fairview Park neighborhood of Oakland sustain me. My immediate neighbors Marian Hopping, Denny Dinwiddie, and Stormy, Laura Counts, Michael Mechanic, Maggie Newton, Nikko and Ruby, Jill, Jamey, and Rory, Rose Cahn and Jonathan Osler, and Noa and Aya deserve a special thank you. We took our fences down, raise backyard chickens together, borrow each other's car (well, actually, we mainly borrow theirs), grow food in our front and backyards, share long conversations about life transitions, freely unlock each other's doors when we need an extra cup of milk, an unusual spice, an extra oven, or help drinking a bottle of wine. We share meals; when I was sick they made me gourmet dinners. Their children run in and out of our house, play the piano, and wait for Matthias's fresh baked bread to come out of the oven. I'm grateful to these special neighbors for watching my puppy Kumi, for broadcasting that Black Lives Matter, caring about each other's families, for always being ready for a party and providing a shoulder to cry on in trying times, for being family in our small village—thank you. Other Bay Area friends and neighbors enrich my everyday life. Ellen Rigsby enthusiastically read several drafts and provided valuable comments; we also had an early habit of taking long neighborhood walks that made my transition to the Bay Area pleasant. Pam Long generously proof read with a keen eye, thank you. I'm grateful to Ingrid Mittermaier, with whom I tried every tiramisu café in North Beach and walked up every secret staircase in San Francisco while I bounced ideas around, Serkan Hosten for tasty BBQs, and Orhan. I appreciated the long bike rides I took with Irene Yen and Andy Stern as we prepared to complete a 109-mile bike ride to raise money for Oakland schools, providing much-needed breaks from sitting at my computer. Railey and Kai watched Kumi when needed. Carrie Lane has been a steadfast intellectual sounding board and compassionate friend—thanks to you and Matt and Frankie for fun visits to LA. A special gratitude goes to Susan Pollock and Reinhard Bernbeck, whose friendship in Binghamton and Berlin continues to be invaluable and long lasting. I very much appreciate our time together as we contemplate fears and hopes for our planet and its people. All these friends and their children are at the front of social justice rallies and anti-racism efforts; they model how to expand the borders of a community, how to fight for justice as far as we can reach. Thank you all.

Finally, I am blessed with a loving and supportive family. I thank my family in Germany for their support and treating me to endless servings of Rotweinkuchen, good dark chocolate, and Wildgerichte. Thank you to Hermann and Elisabeth Beck, Barbara and Thano Papadopoulos, Maria and Lukas (BvB Echte Liebe!), Johannes Beck, Günter and Renate Beck, Andreas Markert, and Katrin and Dirk Beschorner. I grew up in Zimbabwe during a time when the power of community transformed the country from colonial rule to independence. Although I have lived in the United States for over 30 years, I miss home.

My extended Zim family taught me to strive to be good to others and the resources we are privileged to use. I learned very early that life doesn't need material goods to be rich, but that without a community, we are all poor. How do we thank the ancestors who set this ethos in motion? My brother Kudzai and sister Chama, and their beautiful families, have remained steadfast supporters of my work; they keep me grounded with childhood memories and adult realities of living in community. As my brother says, "It can sometimes be a hot mess!" Thank you for being. My mother gave me strong values, the confidence to take a different path and to seek truth to affect justice. Her hard work and generosity to her community has inspired me throughout my life. Thank you, mum.

I am most grateful to my life companion, Matthias Beck. The research and writing of this work has been part of over half of our 23 years together. Matthias joined me in the field and followed me to Germany. In addition to reading numerous drafts, Matthias created an ideal writing retreat, complete with my favorite meals, regular supplies of fresh cups of tea, large bowls of fresh blueberries and papaya, and ample supplies of my favorite chocolate. More importantly, his unwavering support, steadfast love, patience, generous encouragement, and confidence in me and my work has been a beacon throughout our life together. Thank you, mein schatz.

Abbreviations

CRESP	Center for Religion, Ethics, and Social Policy
EVI	EcoVillage at Ithaca (the entire project)
EVI, Inc.	The EcoVillage at Ithaca nonprofit branch
EPA	Environmental Protection Agency
FROG	First Resident Group
GEN	Global Ecovillage Network
IC	Intentional Community
LEARN@ecovillage	The EVI, Inc. education branch
SONG	Second Resident Group
TREE	Third Residential EcoVillage Experience
VA	Village Association

1   Introduction

This book is an effort to engage in a conversation about one kind of sustainable community effort. Specifically, it examines how an ecovillage, an ecological cohousing community, like the early environmental movement in the United States, has focused myopically on environmental sustainability for an upper-middle-class, predominantly white community. This narrow focus makes confronting the myriad social and ecological problems difficult to integrate and easy to neglect. While the focus of this research is on one particular community culture, it is also about the way we as individuals and communities make decisions about how we live with each other and with nature, how the larger social and environmental structures where we live influence decisions we might take for granted, and how ultimately, if we are to effect the kind of change we desire, we need to critically examine the lifestyles we live. According to one of the founders of the EcoVillage at Ithaca cohousing project, "EcoVillage is answering what is perhaps the greatest challenge to the environmental movement today. It addresses the pressing need for people from wealthy countries to consume less: less land and fewer resources." This was further expanded by one of the residents, who remarked that the first of our goals for EcoVillage at Ithaca should be "beyond upper class white ghetto—diverse class and people. The second is that we're really doing something for the planet" (interview with Wilma 2001).

When we study another culture, we are not only interested in how others live; we are also curious about our own existence. What follows is a story about how a group of residents struggle to find the best way to live with each other and with the natural environment, while being deeply embedded in a capitalist culture, one that prioritizes the market over the needs of communities and the earth. Those of us with a commitment to reconcile our lifestyle with a finite planet struggle with how to do so. We struggle with confronting structural racism, inequality that manifests itself in homelessness, illness, crime, and other forms of neighborhood and environmental degradation. It is not easy. Decisions of whether to use paper or plastic can easily be answered by bringing our own bags to the grocery store. But what of the killing of unarmed black and brown men, women, and youth by police who go with impunity? Or the Spare the Air[1] days fueled by our increased air pollution? The effort and benefits to eating locally are well meaning but deeply complicated by the globalized nature of food production and labor in the United States. Is eating a local tomato grown by workers who have migrated great distances and earn little to no income while being exposed to poisons that will harm them for generations better than consuming fair trade organic tomatoes that are grown 3,000 miles away? An obvious answer might be to not eat tomatoes out of season, but many of us in the environmental movement still do, and this does not address the unfair labor practices that occur during the tomato season. There are no easy answers.

Creating ecovillages is not the most efficient way to address the ills of a growing consumer society. However, ecovillages present us with an opportunity to engage in a conversation to change, collectively reflect on the way a capitalist society has contributed to social and environmental degradation, and include space to critically explore our efforts to solve those ills. This book is a story of one community that is deeply engaged in such a dialogue. The EcoVillage at Ithaca project is unique in its architecture and social design of creating several cohousing neighborhoods within a village. Far from perfect, by the residents' own admission, it offers a unique opportunity to consider the reach of capitalism in our efforts to address social and environmental degradation.

This story of EcoVillage at Ithaca (EVI) also offers a unique opportunity to critically examine the growing ecovillage movement. The story presents a perspective of sustainable communities from inside a village where people are actively trying to create a way of life that is both socially and environmentally sustainable. Environmental sustainability and social justice are intricately linked, not just in places where pollution or polluting industries are visible, but in our experience of everyday life. In response, we need to engage in a deep conversation about what is right and just for the health and well-being of our communities and the ability of the earth to sustain the resources we need to thrive. We, especially in the United States, need to critically examine our lifestyle, be cautious of greenwashing,[2] and be committed to broadening the circle of who benefits from sustainability efforts to include the most vulnerable among us.

This research attempts to describe the ways residents in an ecovillage understand and respond to the growing concern for misguided suburban sprawl and the social and environmental disconnection that accompanies it in the United States. I explore how residents and participants in the EcoVillage at Ithaca project construct nature and community, and how ideas of nature and community are incorporated and negotiated in the everyday life of residents. A focus on the struggles, tensions, and contradictions that go into envisioning a lifestyle that is sustainable opens the door for constructive reflection. Unlike the other stories about ecovillages (Lockyer and Veteto 2013; Litfin 2014; Walker 2005), this work is critical of the exclusion of equity and justice from the discourse on sustainable communities, but optimistic that these projects can contribute to the ongoing debate on creating sustainable ways to live.

Too often the work and painful negotiations that go into ecovillage projects are glossed over—sometimes by those who are closest to their development—in an effort to show only the positive outcomes. In a conversation with Bryson, a resident at EVI, he expressed frustration at the lack of self-reflection within the project.

TENDAI: What do you think needs to change in order for you to think this is a place you could live for the rest of your life?

BRYSON: Well, um … I've also said, I also include the term "self-critique."

TENDAI: Mm'hmm

BRYSON: 'Cause one of the things that I think and that I'm hoping we can sort of get to, maybe if we do start some of these more deep discussions in the future, you know, just looking at what we're doing, what we're not doing, what we could be doing better. Um, and I get the impression from some people up here that they don't really talk about negative things, they don't like to get into negative things. Um, and you know, I can remember [a resident] always saying, "Oh, you know, if we try to do something like an accountability system in SONG for our work system, to make sure everybody's doing at least their two hours, you know, then that's judging and shaming and blaming people and they don't feel they should do that." But I have always maintained that, well, unless you take an honest look at yourself, how are you going to improve yourself? Um, and unless we figure out a way to improve ourselves, what hope is there for the world? Um, so to me, just um, just, you know, figuring out, you know, sometimes people say things that hurt other people's feelings, you figure out a way to deal with that and work through it. But I think avoiding, just avoiding any critiques because you're afraid of hurting somebody or making them angry is not how I want to live my life long term.

Bryson was not alone in this thought about wanting to stay in the community but disappointed that there was little or no self-reflection in the project and that this desire to only focus on what was positive hurt the project.

In doing so, these uncritical perspectives mask the very strength of the projects they attempt to celebrate. What I mean by this is that the successes that are often celebrated in EVI seem simplistic, privileged, and unrealistic at best: homes with small footprints because they include imported double- or triple-pane windows or easy access to several acres of fallow land. The benefits of living close to each other, sharing resources, and taking long walks on beautiful trails is appealing to those who live there, but other participants have left the project feeling irreconcilable tensions between trying to improve communities yet moving away from them, or the contradiction of being a model of sustainable living yet owning and using more resources than necessary. Indeed, the EVI project is complex; it presents discomfort as we face the entrapment of a capitalist society which prioritizes consumption, even if it is green, over human well-being. While we can appreciate the efforts to do something at a time when it is hard to know what to do, there is value in pushing ourselves to be inclusive in environmentalism. This book is a critical examination of the ecovillage model in order to identify realistic possibilities for sustainable futures for everyone. Growing research has emphasized the successes or the positive aspects of ecovillages by focusing narrowly on reduced consumption, increased social belonging amongst residents, and innovative uses of green technology. However, outside of those communities, we are seeing a growing gap between social classes, we continue to see environmental injustices amongst the most vulnerable, and we have made little structural progress towards improving the lives of those who are negatively affected by capitalist expansion. For ecovillages to be relevant, they need to be more than green gated communities for those who can afford them. The problems we face in 2017 cannot be solved by only celebrating what works for a small group and is out of reach for others. The energies that go into creating these eco-havens can be spent addressing structural and collective well-being that offers many people the benefits of social and environmental sustainability efforts.

To explore how to effect structural change, it is necessary to question the assumption that green consumerism and green technology are the appropriate mechanisms to address environmental and social degradation (Zehner 2012), rather than focusing on changing human behavior. Anthropological exploration is well suited to address these concerns as "cultural critique" because it places everyday practices within the context of larger social and cultural worlds (Marcus and Fischer 1986). By moving beyond simply describing the successes of EVI to analyzing green consumption and its relevance to lifestyles, this work examines the challenges of creating a sustainable lifestyle in the United States and why these challenges can be informative to the goal of creating a more ecologically sustainable and socially equitable community.

It is not my intention to disparage individual behavior or subject the EVI community to ill feelings amongst their neighbors. Like many of the people I have met in and outside of EVI, we all live with contradictions to our values and struggle to find balance. To the contrary, the contribution of ecovillages to that search for the right way to live within an overbearing culture of capitalism is recognized. What former and current residents have embarked on is public, brave, and challenging. All the EVI participants consistently opened their homes and their lives to anthropological inquiry and data collection for this book, knowing they were exposing themselves to the critical eye of an ethnographer. Over 80 percent of residents have a college degree, 66 percent had a graduate degree, making them well aware of the value of scientific research. This research offers an opportunity to "study up" (Nader 1969), a growing trend in anthropology to turn its gaze upon middle-class white communities in Western countries in general, and the United States in particular, especially with regards to environmentalism (Brosius 2001; Erickson 1997).

My "coming of age" in academia was at a time when non-US citizens were expected to study in their home country, in my case Zimbabwe, while my white US-born colleagues were encouraged to go abroad and study the "other." My inside knowledge was seen as an advantage to gaining access, while for my white classmates, their outsider status meant objectivity. I became aware of how race matters in the kind of questions we ask and the data we collect. A diverse research populace means we access varied research lenses, we can ask a diverse set of questions, and thus we contribute to new ways of thinking and innovative solutions that might otherwise be missed with homogeneous research teams.

Why was there so little critique of ecovillages by social scientists while the communities themselves struggled with diversity and inclusion? Residents themselves were curious to know what their neighbors *really* thought about the project. Several residents read an earlier version of this book and participated in a fruitful and open discussion about some of the findings. A small handful of residents are writing their own books in an effort to shed light on the complexity that is EVI.

The book is organized in six chapters. Chapter 2 outlines the multilayered ways community, environmentalism, and consumption have merged to create what I call a green lifestyle which at once provides an opportunity for residents to make social and ecological change and, at the same time, contribute to the very crisis that manifests itself in suburban sprawl and social isolation. The current US lifestyle is enshrined in a culture of consumption, while green capitalism, as a vehicle for environmentalism, is seldom scrutinized as problematic (Hawken et al. 1999; Miller 1997; O'Connor 1994; Smith 1998). This combination of consumption, community, and environmentalism has created a logical commodity—a green lifestyle, and an ecological cohousing one of its homes. This chapter sets the stage for the making of a green lifestyle. It also examines the trend of constructing new communities and the parallel efforts to respond to a global environmental crisis (Lee 1995). In Chapter 3, a typical day is described to illustrate how residents interact with each other, creating a sense of community in the process. This chapter also presents the history and structure of this unique ecovillage. Chapter 4, Making Community Green, continues to describe the EVI project by highlighting new neighborhoods, the growing village network, and the shifting demographics of the project. New data collected in 2014–2015 is also presented. Chapter 5, Emerging Green Lifestyles, is a discussion of green lifestyles, an explanation of how communities are spaces that symbolize our expressions of social and environmental relationships, increasingly ones that focus on individual environmentalism rather than community, national, or global efforts. I argue that communities embody the spaces through idealized or physical boundaries that represent how our lives are enmeshed within larger social processes, specifically, a capitalist world economy. Thus Chapter 5 explores how the EcoVillage at Ithaca project merges the goals of creating a sense of community and environmentalism through the choice, design, and designation of particular places and spaces for specific functions. It discusses how EVI attempts to create intentional spaces that foster community and that protect the environment through the consumption of green commodities, but also by the consumption of place, through purchasing homes that provide access to nature and construct a sense of community. I examine the meaning of consuming green, how constructions of nature influence what is conserved (James 1993), and how a green identity is created through a green lifestyle. Chapter 5 continues with a discussion of social and environmental justice as it relates to ecological cohousing communities and how a green lifestyle narrows who benefits from collective efforts. I ask if this form of environmentalism distracts us from addressing structural environmental injustice.

The book concludes with Chapter 6 and a discussion of how these communities might make significant contributions if moved into urban spaces, or integrated with neighbors in the larger cities in which they appear. There is interest in understanding the health benefits of a sense of community in neighborhoods, especially those places that are the most vulnerable to social and environmental degradation. Ecovillages may offer a unique perspective to this emerging research area.

A note on names

Except for public statements by the founders, all names and identifying information have been altered to ensure the privacy of the people who participated in this research. I edited quotes to remove identifiers that would expose a participant to an outside reader, but also to a reader who lives inside the community. While many participants expressed a willingness to be identified in the products of my research, several participants often expressed concern that they might be resented in the community if they openly criticized EVI, yet they also realized the importance of raising issues that continued to remain as "elephants in the room." While residents have the social capital and financial means to make green choices, many have chosen a lifestyle that is both public and open to observers from all over the world. Conscious of this lack of privacy, the identity of all participants is private. Thus, it is with the spirit of giving voice to the concerns and joys of residents who want the community to thrive, to address issues that have been left unsaid, and to continue to build on its strengths, that I present this work on EcoVillage at Ithaca.

Notes

1 Spare the Air is a designation in the San Francisco Bay Area that the air quality is unhealthy. This designation makes burning wood and other forms of solid fuel illegal because they are the largest source of harmful particulate matter in the air. Residents are also encouraged to drive less by taking public transportation. www.sparetheair.org/
2 Greenwashing is a term that refers to the use of disinformation or exaggerated information in order to suggest that practices are good for the environment when they may not be.

References

Brosius, Peter J. 2001. The Politics of Ethnographic Presence: Sites and Topologies in the Study of Transnational Environmental Movements. In: *New Directions in Anthropology and Environment*. C. Crumley, ed. pp. 150–176. Walnut Creek: AltaMira Press.

Erickson, Rita J. 1997. *"Paper or Plastic?": Energy, Environment, and Consumerism in Sweden and America*. Westport, CT: Praeger.

Hawken, Paul, Amory L. Lovins, and Hunter Lovins. 1999. *Natural Capitalism: Creating the Next Industrial Revolution*. Boston, New York, London: Little, Brown, and Co.

James, Allison. 1993. Eating Green(s): Discourses of Organic Food. In: *Environmentalism: The View from Anthropology*. K. Milton, ed. London: Routledge.

Lee, Martha F. 1995. *Earth First! Environmental Apocalypse*. Syracuse, NY: Syracuse University Press.

Litfin, K.T. 2014. *Ecovillages: Lessons for Sustainable Community*. Hoboken, NJ: John Wiley & Sons.

Lockyer, J., and J.R. Veteto, eds. 2013. *Environmental Anthropology Engaging Ecotopia: Bioregionalism, Permaculture, and Ecovillages* (Vol. 17). Oxford: Berghahn Books.

Marcus, George, and M. Fischer. 1986. *Anthropology as Cultural Critique: An Experiment in the Human Sciences*. Chicago: University of Chicago Press.

Miller, Daniel. 1997. *Capitalism: An Ethnographic Approach*. Oxford and Washington, D.C.: Berg.

Nader, Laura. 1969. 'Up the Anthropologist': Perspectives Gained from Studying Up. In: *Reinventing Anthropology*. D. Hymes, ed. pp. 284–311. New York: Random House.

O'Connor, Martin, ed. 1994. *Is Capitalism Sustainable? Political Economy and the Politics of Ecology*. New York and London: The Guilford Press.

Smith, Toby M. 1998. *The Myth of Green Marketing: Tending Our Goats at the Edge of Apocalypse*. Toronto, Buffalo, London: University of Toronto Press, Inc.

Walker, Liz. 2005. *EcoVillage at Ithaca: Pioneering a Sustainable Culture*. Gabriola Island, BC: New Society Publishers.

Zehner, O. 2012. *Green Illusions: The Dirty Secrets of Clean Energy and the Future of Environmentalism*. Lincoln: University of Nebraska Press.

2 Community, environmentalism, consumption

Leaving the city of Ithaca by car, an uphill ride past single-family homes, brings you to the top of West Hill. The road leading to EcoVillage is not paved with gold; it is paved with dirt. The turn onto the dirt road, only a short distance from the city, leads into a unique community. There is no welcome sign, no gate, no guard, only nature: meadows, wildflowers, trees, an occasional deer making its way across this wide dirt path, and a small green street sign that honors the late pioneer of US environmentalism—Rachel Carson Way. The view from the car is easy to take in because the speed limit is 15 miles per hour. Life seems to slow down; the long dirt road, sounds of lightly crushing gravel, seems to draw the traveler closer to nature as the fallow vegetation grows thick and dark green. The first turn to the left leads to an organic Community Supported Agriculture farm—West Haven Farm. A little further along, one sees the deer fence protecting a U-pick berry farm—Kestrel Perch Berries. Today, two women are out for a walk on a grassy path that winds its way around this 176-acre field that once was a small family farm. The traffic doesn't bother them; they look up briefly and wave. Smiling and random acts of kindness are just what people do up here. Next on the left is Gourdlandia, the first store at Eco-Village, which sells locally grown and artistically carved gourds used in magnificent lamp shades, piggy banks, night lights, and vases, as well as other handmade crafts by local residents. The handmade cards and bracelets by EVI entrepreneurial children are especially beautiful. After the half mile along this gently winding road past a fenced berry farm, the third neighborhood comes into view. It is fairly new and still looks like a construction zone. Thirty neat, light blue, solar-paneled homes are picturesque. Tall on the horizon is the Common House and four-story apartment complex. There is ample parking all around and the cars that meet your eye are a reminder that even in EcoVillage, we live in a car-dependent society. Look to the left and you'll see more dirt, grass, flowers, and butterflies. The first neighborhood Common House stands tall, towering over the clustered and orderly homes that are, by design, friendly and welcoming. Look to the right and the second neighborhood is tucked away behind car ports and young forest. The natural cedar siding on the majority of the homes makes the rustic, spontaneous design of the second neighborhood unique to the project.

On this warm summer afternoon, the neighborhood is buzzing: women chat with each other; young children run around and laugh, chasing each other between the houses, on the playground, and in the fields that surround them; some adults on the cook team prepare the Common House meal to be served later in the evening. It is easy to see why people move up here: the walkway between the two rows of houses in the first neighborhood is only for pedestrians, but if necessary, it can accommodate an emergency vehicle. The paths that run in the middle of each of the three neighborhoods are lined with beautiful perennial flower gardens, neat lawns, and small herb and vegetable beds. Each garden is designed by the respective household and reflects the diverse personality of the residents. The horticulturalist has a well-manicured ornamental garden, while the neighbor, known for her gourmet cooking, has vegetables and herbs. Another neighbor works as a naturalist writer and likes the "natural" look. She did not do anything to her garden, which is overgrown with wild grass and wildflowers, including what I've heard some neighbors grudgingly call weeds. Unlike some neighborhoods in the United States, this neighborhood is alive, active, and safe: everyone knows each other and makes an effort to create a friendly, welcoming environment.

In an "EcoVillage moment" I join two neighbors who spontaneously meet and start to talk about the changes that have taken place over the last decade. We talk about the new neighborhood and the rapid growth of the community's population; the physical design of TREE and the need to get to know a new set of residents is hard for some people. But there is new positive energy. It will soon be part of the landscape. Our conversation takes us into Lukas's home, where the now four of us share a cup of herbal tea in custom-fired pottery. It is easy to draw a passerby into conversations and then into homes; the neighborhood is designed that way. We spend the afternoon chatting about the past, the ongoing efforts to talk about inclusion and transparency. Despite significant turnover, several remain committed to effecting change in this experimental community, while others feel trapped and isolated.

By evening, we have dispersed, returning to what we were previously doing in our own homes: cleaning, reading, sending emails, and knitting. At 6:00 p.m. sharp, the Common House dinner bell (a large musical triangle) rings and neighbors pour out of their homes into the pedestrian-only walkway, chatting about the day, and asking about each other's families. Residents of all three cohousing neighborhoods stream into the first neighborhood Common House. Although we used to stand in a circle and acknowledge the cooks and their helpers, as well as introduce guests, there are just too many people and the cooks are too busy to continue this ritual. So we all join the queue and greet each other informally. Today's rice and beans meal is becoming a staple, but a growing number of residents have adopted the Paleo diet, and there is now a meat option that is one of the most popular choices. The residents attempt to be accommodating. The dining room is alive with chatter, children asking to sit with each other, and adults struggling to catch up with their neighbors. Twelve years ago, a gentle tapping on a table would turn into a loud rumbling of hands against wood, small voices would begin the once traditional chant, and we'd all join in … "YEAH COOKS!" Another "community moment" played out as we collectively expressed our gratitude to the shared community meal, a hallmark of cohousing. But in an effort to be accommodating, this ritual no longer exists; some felt the noisy rumbling was inappropriate and difficult for their children.

We return to our conversations, and the dish team is already cleaning up the empty serving dishes. By 9:00 p.m., the dining room is empty. The last resident in the Common House has been working late in the offices to the right of the dining room. While many things have changed since the EcoVillage at Ithaca project was envisioned over 20 years ago, the general atmosphere and overall philosophy have not. After everyone has gone home and the silence of night falls, the FROG night owl makes her way down the quiet neighborhood path, a short distance to get home.

The ways residents in an ecovillage understand and respond to the growing concern for misguided suburban sprawl in the United States are indicative of a kind of personal environmentalism. How residents and participants in the Eco-Village at Ithaca (EVI)[1] project construct nature and community, and how ideas of nature and community are incorporated and negotiated in the everyday life of residents, offers insight into this new environmental effort. Residents at EVI negotiate some of these tensions by consuming "green" commodities, rightfully pointing out that the average new home in the United States[2] is 1,000 square feet larger than the EcoVillage at Ithaca homes in the first neighborhood.

In this chapter, the assumption is that green consumerism and green technology are the appropriate mechanisms to address environmental and social degradation, over change in human behavior. The usefulness of situating ecovillages as models to create a sense of community and environmental sustainability is examined by applying anthropological analysis to understand how some US communities are attempting to create sustainable lifestyles—producing a kind of green lifestyle, one that provides a comfortable living while reducing environmental impact. Anthropological exploration is well suited to address these concerns as "cultural critique" because it places everyday practices within the context of larger social and cultural worlds (Marcus and Fischer 1986). What is needed is a critical perspective to complement the plethora of texts that successfully highlight what works for residents in these communities (Litfin 2014; Walker 2005, 2010). A critical eye to the subtle ways our capitalist economy impedes our best efforts to confront social and environmental degradation can help the environmentalist efforts consider and address its barriers to confronting social and environmental justice. Green consumption and its relevance to what I refer to as a green lifestyle provide a framework to discuss what is challenging about creating a sustainable lifestyle in the United States, and why these challenges can be informative to the goal of creating a more ecologically sustainable and socially equitable community.

The search for community

The search for a better place and way to live has been a preoccupation of the US middle class dating back to nineteenth-century European settlers (Durnbaugh 1997). Recent ideas of an ecovillage, the marriage between environmentalism and creating a sense of community, echo the work of twentieth-century city planners such as Lewis Mumford, Patrick Geddes, and Ebenezer Howard, who, instead of ecovillages, planned garden cities that emphasized designing the built environment in harmony with nature (Geddes 1979; Howard 1902; Mumford 1938). The EcoVillage at Ithaca is a design project that emerges out of a long history of creating intentional community and environmentalism in the United States.

The twentieth century saw a resurgence of groups of individuals responding to a concern for a loss of a sense of community and burgeoning environmental degradation in the form of resource depletion, toxic pollution, and waste, by creating utopias (Richter 1971), communes (Melville 1972), intentional communities (Bouvard 1975; Fellowship for Intentional Community 2000), and more recently, gated communities (Caldeira 2000; Low 2001), cohousing neighborhoods (McCamant and Durrett 1994), and ecovillages. Concurrently, the growing concern for the environment has increasingly been expressed through calls for climate change research and responses, policy-level initiatives such as the National Environmental Policy Act and related Clean Water Act and Clean Air Act. In academia, scholars examined environmentalism carefully, arguing that the constructions of nature informed activism, and criticized mainstream environmental groups for ignoring environmental justice. Taylor (2009) expands our understanding of US environmentalism by focusing on the shifting urban cultural landscape around race and class. In communities across the world, pockets of individuals are taking the initiative to change their lifestyle to one that actively brings them closer to others and uses this collective action to reduce their consumption and impact on natural resources. From voluntary simplicity (Elgin 1993) to transition towns (Hopkins 2008), growing groups of individuals are actively trying to create a sustainable way to live with each other and the natural environment.

Ecovillages trace their lineage to the Danish branch of cohousing, *bofællesskaber*, which addresses social isolation by creating intentional community. Unlike earlier efforts that emphasized communalism, however, cohousing encourages market-based private space and, at the same time, offers structured opportunities for community interactions. Ecovillages attempt to design living spaces that model ways to care and repair the environment through the sharing of resources that inspire a sense of community in the process. For example, in EVI, the energy-efficient houses are clustered around pedestrian-only walkways, bringing neighbors physically and socially close together, while protecting the surrounding land from development. The community design was inspired by images and experiences residents had of living in rural communities of non-Western countries, where villagers were perceived as being intricately connected to the environment around them, through living in mud huts, walking barefoot on the land, the absence of cars, and growing their food in small community gardens. The nostalgia for a better way to live with nature and each other reflects a broader concern within one form of US environmentalism that is critical of sub-urban sprawl, unplanned development, and the resulting environmental degradation and social isolation that is evident in abandoned downtown centers and the disappearance of open spaces.

Ecovillages emerge at the apex of intricate social phenomena that are at once an alternative way to engage with nature and, at the same time, constrained by market-driven exclusionary politics and practices. Influential works in the social sciences have explored ideas of environmentalism and constructions of nature, finding that environmentalism is diverse and multifaceted (Brosius 1999; Castree and Braun 1998; Crumley 2001; Descola 1996; Milton 1993; Taylor 2009). Not surprisingly, different actors use the discourse of environmentalism for personal, communal, political, and economic interests. Thus our ideas about sustainability are deeply rooted in larger cultural understanding of nature and the place of humans in the environment. Scholars have responded to this com-plexity by analyzing the environment in separate contexts. Escobar critiques development studies as a new form of Enlightenment discourse that substitutes Merchants' Enlightenment analysis of the "death of nature" with "the rise of environment," where he argues that sustainable development continues to impose Northern economic exploits of Southern "Nature" (Escobar 1995; Mer-chant 1980). Adams argues likewise that sustainable development is "firmly anchored within the existing economic paradigm of the industrial North" (Adams 1990). Feminist scholars have been effective in problematizing the ontological duality between nature/culture and human/non-human worlds (Soper 1996). Among feminist critiques of environmentalism is an argument that traces environmental destruction to the Enlightenment era, where male-dominated science and industrialization depended on the exclusion or exploita-tion of women and nature (Haraway 1991; Martin 1998; Shiva 1993). Critiques of sustainable development have begun to directly question the compatibility between capitalism and environmentalism (Foster 2002; O'Connor 1994; Smith 2013). The argument of the appropriateness of using a capitalist framework to achieve environmental sustainability is the subject of this book. I explore these themes through the lens of political ecology. Environmentalism, consumption, and community are intrinsically connected at multiple levels: through the expropriation of natural resources to produce commodities, and through creat-ing an identity with green commodities, and creating social relationships around objects and places that convey environmental sustainability (Appadurai 1986a; Douglas and Isherwood 1979; Lury 1996; Miller 1995a, 1995b). It is through this interconnected space of ecology, consumption, and community that EVI is situated within the larger cultural context of US environmentalism, capitalist consumption, and search for community. This work offers a Western case study of political ecology and green consumption to a growing body of literature on communities and environmentalism outside the United States (Caldeira 1996;

Carrier and Heyman 1997; Escobar 1996; Miller 1995b; O'Connor 1994; Peet and Watts 1996; Peluso 1992; Peluso and Watts 2001; Sponsel 1997; Wolf 1972).

Creating community and environmentalism is best understood through the study of consumption. The concept of green lifestyles evolves from ideas in consumption studies that address the importance of material goods in creating identity. Appadurai (1986b) argues that the practice of consumption is not a private or passive affair, but rather integral in forming social relations (Friedman 1994). If consumption helps to create identity, Bourdieu's (1984) seminal work on class, lifestyle, and tastes suggests that habitus makes reducing consumption patterns difficult, if not impossible, when it is the basis of creating class distinction. Miller (1995b) questions whether the social phenomenon of consumption, as it relates to identity, might come to replace kinship in the anthropological study of communities. Miller's assertion can be seen in the poignant way ecovillages create new social relations based on membership in the intentional village. As industrialization continues to reshape the social landscape, the social relations that once drew their meaning from biological ties are reconfigured through identity with commodities. The emphasis on commodities to create a green identity and green communities highlights the importance of goods as a central focus in the postmodern society (Douglas and Isherwood 1979). Natural capitalism and eco-capitalism embrace imposing a "green" tax on non-renewable commodities (Hawken et al. 1999). Sarkar (1999) argues for eco-socialism in opposition to eco-capitalism as a better means of confronting the contradictions of environmental protection, consumption, and personal identity that are influenced by political, economic, and ecological forces. Thus, in order to understand the ecological and social forces that are at play in the everyday practices of residents in EVI, it is necessary to examine the capitalist structure in which such communities are embedded.

Personal environmentalism

There has never been a globally adopted definition of what it means to be an environmentalist or environmentally "friendly" (Tsing 2001). Instead, environmentalism holds different meanings for different actors, at different points in time, and in different geographic regions. I use Milton's simplistic, elastic, and general definition of environmentalism as a quest for a viable future. The commonly used term in Western countries refers to a "concern that the environment should be protected … from the harmful effects of human activities" (Milton 1996: 27). This definition for a complex phenomenon is useful because it allows for multiple translations and interpretations. The fluidity is what makes environmentalism in Milton's "industrial society" challenging to identify as one concept, yet it also reflects the reality of an ambiguous environmentalism. Attempting to construct one unifying definition will result in the exclusion of a variety of important cultural constructs of human engagements with nature.

The recent preoccupation with personal commitments to the environment has been explained through Szasz's (2007) concept of inverted quarantine, where instead of confronting environmental problems that affect the public and public good, we see consumption used as a tool to self-quarantine people to protect themselves. This focus on individualism over public goods, as expressed in green lifestyles, overshadows concern for inequality and social injustice that disproportionately and acutely affect people of color, the poor, and recent immigrants, who continue to be impacted by polluted environments (Bullard 1994; Fortun 2001; Pellow 2002). The concern is that these communities become marginalized, or completely excluded from the sustainable community discourse. Thus, despite calls for a just sustainability (Agyeman and Evans 2003), we need a critical analysis of the emerging cultural trends which gain support from businesses that see a market niche for "green" commodities. Natural capitalism is less challenging to the structure of inequality than other forms of environmentalism that call for a shift in the way we live, away from our consumer culture to one that fights for human and environmental rights. Western consumption is at the heart of social and environmental degradation around the world, and the emphasis on green consumption is counter to aims of protecting, preserving, and regenerating our communities and the environment (Erickson 1997).

Athanasiou (1996) argues that the change in focus from public to private environmentalism occurred with the rise of public relations firms and a new form of environmentalism that is less confrontational and more cooperative with business. Ironically, the current trend that now embraces business-led environmentalism is contributing to misguided environmental strategies. This trend creates the illusion of sustainability, while drawing our attention away from important critiques of capitalist inequity, injustice, and environmental destruction—when being green distracts from being just. Much like the sustainable development rhetoric that functions primarily as a new means to continue unsustainable, often destructive, and neocolonial practices (Escobar 1996; Hobart 1993), the new market-driven environmentalism does little to change the global or local practices that are responsible for environmental degradation.

There is a disconnection between two distinct environmentalisms in the United States, one focused on conserving and preserving the natural environment, the other dedicated to remedying social injustice (Harvey 1996). These two groups are separated along racial, class, and geographic boundaries. The environmental justice efforts address the disproportionate exposure of people of color and the poor to polluted environments that result in poor health and dangerous employment (Bullard 1994). This is not the environmentalism of EVI, which designed their neighborhoods around open land, toxic-free spaces with access to healthful fresh food, nature, and beautiful views of hillsides, trees, and meadows.

Why have the two efforts taken such different paths? On one hand, US environmentalism has developed through the assumption that capitalism and environmental protection are compatible (Hawken et al. 1999). On the other hand, others argue that "natural capitalism" and the "eco-economy" merely distract from larger global social injustice and economic inequality (Sarkar 1999; Foster 2002), creating and perpetuating the same problems that capitalism and over-consumption have caused for people and nature the world over. The current trend in Western environmentalism of advocating the consumption of green commodities raises questions about the effectiveness of green consumption as a solution to environmental degradation. The debate between what Pepper (1993) identifies as eco-centrics (those who see humankind as part of the ecosystem and believe in ecologically constrained human action) and techno-centrics (those who believe that it is possible to reverse current environmental degradation through improved technology) is a useful tool to understand the debate in which US environmentalism is deeply entrenched.

Ecovillages raise interesting questions about the direction of US environmentalism. Five decades after Rachel Carson's, Lois Gibbs's, Robert Bullard's, and Grace Lee Bogg's outward-reaching demands that industry and government be held accountable for halting pollution in communities, we are witnessing an inward-reaching demand that empowers individuals to make choices for their own benefit.

Heavily influenced by businesses (Smith 1998b), a new environmentalism focuses inward and emphasizes personal lifestyle choices, such as consuming organic food, building green houses, and creating new socially and environmentally healthful communities away from industrial pollutants. Acknowledging the very different nature of these forms of environmentalism, I believe they have too often been separated artificially, when in fact they are related. That is, both forms of environmentalism are on the minds of the EVI participants; they expressed concern, discomfort, and sometimes indifference to the social injustice and environmental racism that surround the fringes of their community. As a result, residents expressed a level of dissatisfaction because of the contradictions of their actions (or non-actions). It is therefore useful to keep environmental justice in the discussion that follows because it is already there explicitly or implicitly. Nonetheless, if US environmentalism is to be sincere, it will require an open and realistic discussion of the two divergent views of nature and the human place within it. Many EVI residents are struggling with this effort, and their experiences shed light on some of those struggles as a way to encourage further dialogue.

Consumption in Western environmentalism

It is no secret that the United States consumes a disproportionate amount of the earth's resources (Erickson 1997; O'Connor 1994; Trainer 1997). This disparity in consumption contributes similarly to global resource depletion, environmental pollution, and social injustice in Western poor communities and non-Western communities (Bullard 1990). At the same time, environmentalism has become part of US popular culture (Kempton et al. 1996), where a prominent solution to address environmental degradation has come in the form of the consumer market (Smith 1998b). Advocates of using the market as a vehicle to improve the environment argue for natural capitalism (Brown 2001; Hawken et al. 1999), suggesting that the current rate of environmental degradation of the planet can be slowed, and reversed, through creating an economy of alternative energy and resource use. For example, by encouraging the construction of communities that are energy-efficient and reduce our dependence on cars, jobs are created, safe materials can be used, and natural resources are preserved. Natural capitalism also advocates for leasing commodities that would remain the responsibility of the manufacturer the same way apartment rentals are the responsibility of the landlord. Critics of natural capitalism make the central argument that because capitalism is itself the cause of environmental degradation, using a capitalist framework as a solution is problematic at best (Fotopoulos 2000; Sarkar 1999). Natural capitalism and green consumerism still encourage a culture of consumption. Hybrid cars still require vast amounts of energy to manufacture and run (Register 1996). Natural capitalism still offers a problematic model of production and consumption while we transition into a more sustainable lifestyle; by emphasizing technological solutions, natural capitalism skirts around the inevitable need for US-American culture to confront its obsession with consumption and waste (Shove 2003). In *Green Illusions*, Ozzie Zehner (2012) points out that as more alternative energy comes on the market, we see an increase in demand and use. Thus alternative energy sources are not curbing our wasteful consumption habits, but contributing to them. Recognizing this potential, Miller (1995a) called for anthropologists to explore the recent greening of commodities in Western consumption.

Certainly the effort to reduce consumption will not be easy or quickly implemented, yet there are projects that attempt to do just that. While EVI currently leans towards green consumption, the EVI concept has the potential to create a community that demonstrates a lifestyle where minimum consumption is possible. Because the central problems of environmental degradation are caused by polluting industries and the rampant depletion of non-renewable resources through production and consumption, as well as disposing the resulting byproducts of hazardous waste and toxic pollution, a model that demonstrates ways to reduce our dependence on these processes would be logical.

Well-meaning residents in EVI want to make choices and decisions that are good for the environment and that do the least harm to non-human nature. The vision statement of the EVI LEARN, the educational efforts of the community, is to create "a world in which people actively care for each other and the planet" (Vision of EcoVillage at Ithaca, Learn 2016). Some of the ways residents accomplish this are by consuming organic goods, if they can afford them, or by believing they are improving the environment simply by purchasing a "green" home in an ecovillage (a home that requires minimal energy to heat and cool). While EVI residents attempt to live a simple lifestyle, they are confronted with conflicts and tensions between living a comfortable lifestyle and protecting the environment. One resident confessed that he had to buy his first car when he moved into the first neighborhood because the community lacked public transportation and the mailboxes are located a quarter mile away from the houses.

If consuming green is part of the emerging view to improve the environment (Hawken et al. 1999; Smith 1998b), Bourdieu's (1984) concept of habitus and lifestyle is an appropriate framework to examine this practice because it emphasizes the broader structures in which residents are situated. In a culture that values mass consumption, greening that consumption can be a means of creating class distinction. By acknowledging distinction in lifestyle and taste, we see how for some families, living in EVI is a visible solution to a challenge many of us face every day: how to reduce our negative impact on the planet. Political ecology is a useful theoretical lens because it questions the relationship between land use, environmental degradation, and the influence of social, economic, and political power on environmental discourse (Peet and Watts 1996; Wolf 1972).

Athanasiou warns that while it is "easy to dismiss corporate environmentalism … in the end it may be as real a social movement as feminism or civil rights activism" (1996: 5). Corporate environmentalism may not have turned into a movement comparable to feminism or civil rights, but it has been successfully integrated into all forms of the US economy and socio-political sphere. Erickson (1997) demonstrates the rush of businesses to attach panda bears, whales, and the revolving arrows of the recycling symbol to as many commodities as possible because "being green" sells. There are now numerous books, magazines, and conferences that are geared to help businesses, and increasingly universities, make a profit with a green identity. We see little response from environmental groups that is critical of aligning with businesses that are more concerned with their "bottom line" than the state of the earth or the people their products make ill (Foster 2002). According to Taylor, "when people affected were poor or minorities, they received scant attention from environmental activists" (2009: 5). The Green 2.0 report, *The State of Diversity in Environmental Organizations*, rightly points out that despite years of effort, people of color are still missing from the decision-making table and on the board of directors of major environmental organizations (Taylor 2014). This leaves a gap in who contributes to the agendas of our environmental watchdogs.

The extent of the market's success in diverting attention away from the causes of environmental degradation and replacing it with a solution that is embedded in consumption of natural resources is not surprising. What is surprising is the idea that green consumption as a solution to ecological problems is embraced by well-meaning people concerned about the environment.

The intersection of community and environmentalism

> For me it's a bunch of people coming together to preserve resources, sharing and preserving, again, resources, and having minimal impact on the immediate environment around them—self-sustainability to a certain extent.… For example, you grow your own food, or you generate your own energy, or you reuse your garbage into compost, recycling.… That's what I mean. Cohousing is definitely closer to that than any other living situation I've been in so far.
>
> (Stan, EVI resident, 2001)

We walked around FROG and SONG, and we loved the sense of close-knit community. We read Liz Walker's books on EcoVillage and were attracted to the vision of cohousing. We attended TREE meetings and loved the collaborative feeling of the group. We were tired of living in suburbs and cities where we hardly knew our neighbors. We wanted to join a true neighborhood. At the same time, we were concerned about global climate change and we wanted to do more to shrink our footprint on the earth and increase our commitment to sustainability. We looked forward to joining neighbors who shared our commitment.

(Resident 2015)

The mid-twentieth century saw the exodus of upper-middle-class, predominantly white, families from city centers and into suburbs that contained homes surrounded by green lawns and ample yards. This exodus is mainly attributed to dissatisfaction with the city and a desire to return to older values "under conditions that threatened to destroy them." As cities became more congested, and commuter trains provided a reliable means to separate work from home, wealthier families moved into clustered suburbs connected to railway lines, forming communities such as Philadelphia's Mainline (Jackson 1985). The end of the Second World War, the Baby Boom, and the resulting increase in single-family homes saw the rise of the personal automobile. This meant that families could live further away from the city center. Those who could afford it were able to commute to work in socially and increasingly economically depressed cities (Gregory 1998). Race and racism as expressed in white flight also fueled the mass exodus of white city dwellers out of the core and into the periphery. Not long afterwards, city centers became more degraded as businesses and families moved to the outskirts, and this mass exodus resulted in more crime, abandoned buildings, and growing poverty, further contributing to a depressed social and economic environment, what Garreau (1991) calls "edge cities."

For these middle classes, the exodus out of the city and into the countryside, adjacent to farmland and forest, meant that the air was cleaner, and surrounding homes were filled, for the most part, with working families. Households had privacy and autonomy. Fear of crime, increasing social diversity, and an obsession with security resulted in some communities creating small neighborhood associations that governed the behavior and activities of the residents (Davis 1998; McKenzie 1994). These contemporary communities outside the city limits raised concerns and criticism from anti-sprawl groups, who called attention to the destruction of the land and the impact of an increased reliance on cars. Similarly, Setha Low argues that the new suburban developments lacked the infrastructure to bring people together the way city centers did with walkable access to schools, jobs, shops, and public plazas (Low 1996). Gated communities excluded people from their neighborhood altogether with walls and guarded gates (Caldeira 2000; Low 2001). These privately owned enclaves included streets, sidewalks, small parks, and recreation areas. They symbolized new forms of segregation that used surveillance and barriers to control behavior and exclude undesirable people from participating in the life of the community (Caldeira 1996). Unlike the ideas raised by city planners who called for garden cities and nature in cities as a way to improve the health of the city and the people who lived in them (Howard 1902; Mumford 1938), these new communities were intent on moving into places that already had "nature" or where they could create and enjoy it privately.

While communities were continuing to transform open space and farmland into post-war suburbia and gated communities, the environmental movement was spreading to all corners of the United States. Harmful effects of industrial pollutants on humans (Carson 1962) and ecological disasters such as Love Canal (Levine 1982) and Warren County (Bullard 1990) provided evidence of the vulnerability of communities to environmental hazards. This awareness, combined with growing political forces around civil rights and women's rights, gave momentum to an environmentalism largely focused on national public health. This environmentalism focused its lens outward on ensuring a healthful environment for the larger community. Activists worked to improve the broader environment, including a concern for public parks and public policy. The Environmental Protection Agency in the early 1970s became a public tool for protecting the country's natural resources and also ensuring the remediation of polluted spaces. Broadening its interest, US environmentalism began focusing on endangered species, wilderness preservation, and other global environmental problems (Cronon 1996; Guha 1989). The new focus on the global environment emphasized nature as needing protection from human destruction and often blamed "Third World" lifestyles for accelerating environmental problems through the neo-Malthusian focus on population growth, farming practices, and hunting of wild game (Ehrlich 1968; Harding 1968). Western nations responded by advocating for population control, conservation, and game parks, and by encouraging green and sustainable development (Adams 1990). By the mid-1990s, growing critique argued against narrowly focused criticism of non-Western and poor communities' practices. This critique raised concern over the advocacy of wilderness preservation while ignoring the poisoning of the human communities by Western industries (Di Chiro 1996; Fortun 2001; Harvey 1996).

Environmentalists in the United States did not gather under a single, unifying theme, but comprised diverse groups, including environmental justice (Bryant and Mohai 1991; Cole and Foster 2001; Cutter 1995; Di Chiro 2008; Sandler and Pezzullo 2007; Taylor 2009, 2014), anti-nuclear war activists (Gusterson 1996), anti-development, anti-World Bank, and anti-WTO activists (Adams 1990; Hobart 1993; Merchant 1980; Peet and Watts 1996; Shiva 1993), wilderness preservationists, deep ecologists (Naess 1988), and a variety of groups protecting endangered species such as the Sierra Club and World Wildlife Fund. Concurrent to the popular concern for the environment was the sudden increase of environmental studies programs across university campuses. In addition to new departments of environmental studies, established academic fields began including environmental sub-fields such as environmental law and environmental anthropology (Brosius 1999). These new foci deepened the debate to include discussions of power, access to resources, and social justice through fields of political economy, political ecology, and liberation ecologies. Common to all the debates is that over-consumption of the world's resources by the West is disproportionately impacting the global environment (Escobar 1996; Guha 1989; Merchant 1980; Peet and Watts 1996; Shiva 1993; Trainer 1997), yet there is little analysis of consumption patterns in the countries whose everyday practices and lifestyles significantly affect the global environment. In fact, we see just the opposite: instead of addressing over-consuming Western countries, environmental efforts often emphasize conservation and preservation in non-Western countries. The marketing of green products and conserving and preserving the environment have become a commodity, including as they apply to new ecological housing communities (James 1993). Efforts to unearth growing concern for environmental degradation and loss of community have come together through the creation of new ways of living green lifestyles.

Environmental cohousing communities

Ecovillage is a general term given to what is commonly known in communal studies and cohousing circles as an ecological cohousing community. Cohousing, a term coined by architects McCamant and Durrett (1994), describes a US-American version of the Danish *bofællesskaber*, where a neighborhood is intentionally constructed, usually with the participation of future residents, to encourage a sense of community. Members purchase homes that are built close together and that are deliberately designed to encourage and facilitate social interaction amongst neighbors. Although cohousing communities have different personalities, cohousing is generally defined as having 24–30 households and a shared common house where residents make collective decisions in a nonhierarchical process on issues that affect the neighborhood, share amenities such as laundry facilities and children's play areas, and have the option to participate in weekly common meals. Households remain financially independent of each other.

Cohousing communities are mushrooming around the US and, although they seldom identify themselves with a particular ideology or mission, generally aim to reduce their consumption of resources. McCamant and Durrett strongly recommend that for cohousing to work, it should not be attached to an ideology. However, several new cohousing communities call themselves ecovillages, a term that suggests a proactive stance towards living in harmony with nature and the environment. According to the Fellowship for Intentional Community (2000), an online directory of intentional communities around the world, there were approximately 536 cohousing communities and 545 ecovillages in December 2016. Most cohousing communities are located on the outskirts of cities; although there are some urban cohousing communities in larger cities in the United States, such as Swan's Market in the heart of downtown Oakland, California, and LA Ecovillage in the heart of downtown Los Angeles. Many cohousing communities view their lifestyle as an attempt to create both social and environmental sustainability (Meltzer 2000). Ecovillages, for the most part, have adapted the model of cohousing but take the concept a step further by embracing conservation and preservation of the environment as their primary mission. Many of these ecovillages are in suburbs with access to land, thus providing a way to model the sustainable use of the land they occupy.

Ecovillages in general, and EVI in particular, present themselves as communities where families who move into the neighborhood embrace both the desire to live in the community and the chance to participate in environmental protection and conservation. This intersection of environmentalism and community brings an assortment of competing actors together. According to Trainer (1997), those who are concerned for the fate of the planet and for the building of a sustainable world order should focus their energies on the establishment of example alternative communities that will illustrate the new values, arrangements, technologies, and economies that must eventually become the norm in rich and poor countries (1997: 1219). Concurrently, Fotopoulos (2000) points out that ecovillages prevent people from lower social classes from participating in these alternative communities. Environmental justice groups, working to improve the environment and social reality of communities that have been disproportionately targeted for waste incinerators and landfills (Di Chiro 1996), are largely ignored by these new community models. Fotopoulos makes the poignant argument that social change will not come about by "a plurality of groups ... operating within their own context and trying to bypass the political and economic power structures rather than confront them" (2000: 288). Fotopoulos's point becomes clear when these community projects are critically examined.

Cohousing communities are not an isolated housing phenomenon in the United States; on the contrary, they fit into a broader national discussion among planners on how to plan, build, and improve neighborhoods, communities, and cities (Joseph 2002; McKenzie 1994; Miller 1995a; Putnam 2000). Cohousing and ecovillage communities can be placed within the context of urban renewal and themed spaces. Tangentially, they react to interest in transforming spaces such as downtown shopping centers into privately owned shopping malls and office complexes (Garreau 1991). The rapid transformation of public spaces, from historical sites of political protests and democracy into private corporate-sponsored shopping malls, theme parks (Sorkin 1992), and neighborhoods (Ross 1999), is changing the political and ecological landscape of the United States.

The EVI project was established in order to create a space that would conserve and preserve land from development, for example, by creating easements. By building small homes, residents preserve the surrounding land for "nature," in a community that helps them, through guidelines and support networks within the neighborhood, recycle, compost, and reduce their reliance on automobiles[3] and material goods. The community itself becomes a commodity that residents are able to purchase and consume. Other forms of the consumption of community as a commodity can be seen in places such as Celebration, Florida, where families can live in a manufactured Disney city (Hannigan 1998;

Ross 1999). Residents in EVI are able to purchase a home where a sense of community (neighborliness) is built into the physical design and social mission of the place as well as the functionality of the everyday decision-making process of consensus. A resident of the First Resident Group (FROG) explained that while he knew many residents did not like the four-hour-long community meetings, he saw them as wonderful opportunities to get to know his neighbors and be in community with them.

Ecovillage as a solution to environmental and social problems

> The model that I'm interested in (EcoVillage) being, I do not know that we are (there) yet, but we might just be in process. [My vision] has to do with what I consider the cutting edge of human evolution. It has to do with learning. I think that on this planet with a population the way it is, we are going to have to learn how to live more closely together without fighting, without killing each other. And I mean animals in experiments and stuff. I think we have to change our chemistry. I think this [community] is a movement in that direction. And eventually there could be big disasters in our world, ecological disasters that require us to rely on each other more and live closely together. Maybe some places will be uninhabitable so it is just going to happen in some way or another, so we have to change how we relate to each other, how we are inside in order to do that; that is how we are being a model in our own little fledging way.
>
> (Joshua)

EcoVillage at Ithaca (EVI) is the first community of its kind. It is the first cohousing community that is creating a village with more than one cohousing neighborhood. The larger vision includes an education center to teach the general public about its model of sustainability, creating viable work opportunities for the village residents through cottage industries, as well as being self-sustaining by growing their own food and recycling waste water. EVI was conceived in response to the growing environmental and social problem its founders identified as suburban sprawl. Since its inception in 1991, the project has become internationally known and been profiled around the world. Unlike most cohousing communities that follow the recommended 24–30 household limit (McCamant and Durrett 1994), EVI initially intended to build a community that could accommodate 150 households divided into five cohousing neighborhoods. EVI is meant to model a new way for suburban developers to create neighborhoods that do not resemble sprawl. As a community that strives to create an environmentally friendly, comfortable lifestyle for US-Americans who could otherwise move to suburbia, EVI is an ideal opportunity to explore the intersection of community and environment in a small segment of the US population. As a contained community, the project is a convenient unit of analysis for ethnography.

EcoVillage also offers the opportunity to test anthropological methods for studying upper-middle-class white communities. In addition to studying "at home" in the United States (Di Leonardo 1998), it is also a study of those who have power instead of those who are affected by the powerful. Nader's call to study up asks what anthropological theories would look like if "anthropologists were to study the colonizers rather than the colonized, the culture of power rather than the culture of the powerless, the culture of affluence rather than the culture of poverty?" (1969: 289). At a time when environmental and community degradation focuses on poor urban communities or third world poverty, looking at the consumption habits of Western culture, which is responsible for much of the world's resource depletion, seems an appropriate area for anthropological exploration. Reversing this gaze might reveal larger questions about social and ecological power, a political ecology of US environmentalism. Eco-Village provides a context from which to view the US-American culture of consumption and the greening of this consumption culture.

Conclusion

> Lots of kids similar ages to mine, close to a great town, not too woo-woo, actual flush toilets, liked that many current residents had lived here for many years.
>
> (EVI Survey 2015)

Examining the intersection of environmentalism, community, and consumption in the context of the US environmental movement can reveal the impact of a capitalist model that relies on (and supports) production and consumption of goods as a means to conserve the environment and create community. In EVI, efforts to reduce consumption through calls for simplicity have been challenging for a variety of reasons, but primarily because of taste and lifestyle. Because it is not necessary to conserve environmental resources, the drastic changes needed to stop further degradation will be prolonged. Simplicity in EVI often occurred when residents had no alternative. Referring to the increased building cost of his new home, one resident said "our family is forced to live more simply because the house is getting too expensive, so that is a good thing" (Max). Consumption of resources was reduced only when they had to be, either by being required by law or, as in the above case, when residents were faced with financial limits. When given the choice, living comfortably takes precedence over the environment.

How can the environment be improved by consuming new green products, while the major problem in the environment is over-consumption itself? How does constructing new, green communities in undeveloped areas address social degradation? The collective, dedicated action that built the EVI project could also be applied to create sustainable communities that are inclusive and diverse. Capitalism and environmentalism are antithetical, and we need to critically examine the role of capitalism in creating degraded communities if we are to move towards greater environmental and social sustainability. This is not an easy task as it will require deep reflection, sacrifice, building community with people who are different from us, and learning to live with less, as more.

Solutions to environmental degradation and social isolation might best be found by changing the way we think and behave in relation to each other, what we consume, and how we relate to the natural environment. A cultural change in how we define the environment and community; a holistic definition that includes social justice, human rights, and an economic model that is not based on continuous growth, personal wealth, and the exploitation of the poor. Communities such as EVI attempt to facilitate a national dialogue on how we live by modeling an alternative to suburban sprawl. Yet in creating a new model it has itself become sprawl, a product, albeit a green one, of the culture in which it is deeply entrenched. EcoVillage for its part encourages voluntary simplicity at a personal and community level and some residents celebrate the mantra: "simplify, simplify, simplify." The community makes recycling, composting, and being a good steward to the environment easy. It showcases simple yet effective ways to live a lifestyle that puts nature and the environment in the conscience of residents on a daily basis. At the same time, residents acknowledge the limitations of environmental conservation and try to balance living a comfortable lifestyle while maintaining a commitment to environmental conservation and preservation. Green consumption has emerged as a way to negotiate the conflicting theory and practices of living comfortably and conserving the environment.

It is through the very things that EcoVillage encourages—communication, sharing, open debate about consumption and resource use—that we can begin to confront the larger problems of community and environmental degradation. EcoVillage offers a venue for middle-class families living in the United States to begin an honest dialogue about habits acquired from living in a country that puts individuality before community, capital accumulation before conservation, and consumption before preservation. Ecovillages raise questions that extend far beyond winding gravel roads, goldenrod-painted meadows and organic farming; they are an opportunity to seriously explore the absence of social justice and the existence of environmental racism at a time when communities across the United States are under immense environmental hazards, such as hydrologic fracking. This is the story of the efforts of a small village searching for a better way to live.

Notes

1 There are several entities that make up the entire EcoVillage at Ithaca project (the nonprofit that owns most of the land, the education nonprofit called LEARN@ecovillage, the three independent neighborhoods, the village association, the community-supported agriculture farm, the community-supported agriculture U-pick berry farm, and various other small businesses); it is sometimes confusing even to residents. For clarity and simplicity, I will use EVI to refer to the collection of all these entities. Residents in all three neighborhoods often used the term "EcoVillage" to refer to their community, or neighborhood; this can be seen in the data presented. When referring to the nonprofit, I will use EVI, Inc., or LEARN@ecovillage. I also use ecovillage as the generic term of the community in general as it is part of a much larger group of intentional green communities.

2 Average size of US single-family homes was obtained from the 2010 US census data.
3 One of the contradictions in EVI is that although opportunities to be less dependent on a car are celebrated, few residents actually reduce their car usage (see Figure 5.1).

References

Adams, William M. 1990. *Green Development: Environment and Sustainability in the Third World*. New York: Routledge.

Agyeman, J., and T. Evans. 2003. Toward Just Sustainability in Urban Communities: Building Equity Rights with Sustainable Solutions. *The ANNALS of the American Academy of Political and Social Science*, 590(1), 35–53.

Appadurai, Arjun. 1986a. Introduction: Commodities and the Politics of Value. In: *The Social Life of Things: Commodities in Cultural Perspective*. A. Appadurai, ed. pp. 3–63. Cambridge: Cambridge University Press.

Appadurai, Arjun. 1986b. *The Social Life of Things: Commodities in Cultural Perspective*. Cambridge: Cambridge University Press.

Athanasiou, Tom. 1996. The Age of Greenwashing. *Capitalism, Nature, Socialism*, 7(1), 1–37.

Bokaer, Joan. 1997. Intertwined Lives. *The EcoVillage Newsletter*, 7, 4.

Bourdieu, Pierre. 1984. *Distinction: A Social Critique of the Judgment of Taste*. Cambridge, MA: Harvard University Press.

Bouvard, Marguerite. 1975. *The Intentional Community Movement: Building a New Moral World*. Port Washington, NY: National University Publications Kennikat Press.

Brosius, Peter J. 1999. Analysis and Interventions: Anthropological Engagements with Environmentalism. *Current Anthropology*, 40(3), 277–309.

Brosius, Peter J. 2001. The Politics of Ethnographic Presence: Sites and Topologies in the Study of Transnational Environmental Movements. In: *New Directions in Anthropology and Environment*. L. Crumley, ed. pp. 150–176. Walnut Creek: AltaMira Press.

Brown, Lester R. 2001. *Eco-Economy: Building an Economy for the Earth*. New York and London: W.W. Norton.

Bryant, B., and P. Mohai, eds. 1991. *Environmental Racism: Issues and Dilemmas*. Ann Arbor, MI: University of Michigan Press.

Bullard, Robert D. 1990. *Dumping in Dixie: Race, Class, and Environmental Quality*. Boulder, CO: Westview Press.

Bullard, Robert D. 1994. *Unequal Protection: Environmental Justice and Communities of Color*. San Francisco, CA.

Caldeira, Teresa P.R. 1996. Fortified Enclaves: The New Urban Segregation. *Public Culture*, 8, 303–328.

Caldeira, Teresa P.R. 2000. *City of Walls: Crime, Segregation, and Citizenship in São Paulo*. Berkeley, Los Angeles, London: University of California Press.

Carrier, James, and Josiah McC. Heyman. 1997. Consumption and Political Economy. *Journal of the Royal Anthropological Institute*, 3, 355–373.

Carson, Rachel. 1962. *Silent Spring*. Boston, MA: Houghton Mifflin.

Castree, Noel, and Bruce Braun. 1998. *Remaking Reality: Nature at the Millennium*. London and New York: Routledge.

Cole, L.W., and S.R. Foster. 2001. *From the Ground Up: Environmental Racism and the Rise of the Environmental Justice Movement*. New York: NYU Press.

Cronon, William, ed. 1996. *Uncommon Ground: Toward Reinventing Nature*. New York and London: W.W. Norton & Co.

Crumley, Carole L. 2001. *New Directions in Anthropology and Environment: Intersections.* Walnut Creek, CA: Altamira Press.

Cutter, S.L. 1995. Race, Class and Environmental Justice. *Progress in Human Geography,* 19(1), 111–122.

Davis, Mike. 1998. *Ecology of Fear: Los Angeles and the Imagination of Disaster.* New York: Metropolitan Books.

Descola, Philippe. 1996. Constructing Natures: Symbolic Ecology and Social Practice. In: *Nature and Society: Anthropological Perspectives.* P. Descola, ed. pp. 82–102. London and New York: Routledge.

Di Chiro, G. 1996. Nature as Community: The Convergence of Environment and Social Justice. In: *Uncommon Ground: Toward Reinventing Nature.* W. Cronon, ed. pp. 298–320. New York: W.W. Norton & Co.

Di Chiro, G. 2008. Living Environmentalisms: Coalition Politics, Social Reproduction, and Environmental Justice. *Environmental Politics,* 17(2), 276–298.

Di Leonardo, M. 1998. *Exotics at Home: Anthropologies, Others, and American Modernity.* Chicago: University of Chicago Press.

Douglas, Mary, and Baron Isherwood. 1979. *The World of Goods.* New York: Routledge.

Durnbaugh, Donald F. 1997. Communitarian Societies in Colonial America. In: *America's Communal Utopias.* D.E. Pitzer, ed. pp. 14–36. Chapel Hill and London: University of North Carolina Press.

Elgin, D. 1993. *Voluntary Simplicity: Toward a Way of Life that is Outwardly Simple, Inwardly Rich (Vol. 25).* New York: Quill.

Erickson, Rita J. 1997. *"Paper or Plastic?": Energy, Environment, and Consumerism in Sweden and America.* Westport, CT: Praeger.

Escobar, Arturo. 1995. *Encountering Development: The Making and Unmaking of the Third World.* Princeton, NJ: Princeton University Press.

Escobar, Arturo. 1996. Constructing Nature: Elements for a Post-structural Political Ecology. In: *Liberation Ecologies.* pp. 46–68. London: Routledge.

Ehrlich, Paul R. 1968. *The Population Bomb.* New York: Ballantine Books.

FIC (Fellowship for Intentional Community). 2000. *Communities Directory: A Guide to Intentional Communities and Cooperative Living.* Ann Arbor: Sheridan Group.

Fortun, Kim. 2001. *Advocacy after Bhopal: Environmentalism, Disaster, New Global Orders.* Chicago: University of Chicago Press.

Foster, John Bellamy. 2002. *Ecology against Capitalism.* New York: Monthly Review Press.

Fotopoulos, Takis. 2000. The Limitations of Life-style Strategies: the Ecovillage "Movement" is NOT the Way towards a New Democratic Society. *Democracy & Nature,* 6(2), 287–308.

Friedman, Jonathan. 1994. *Consumption and Identity.* Chur, Switzerland: Harwood Academic Publishers.

Garreau, Joel. 1991. *Edge City: Life on the New Frontier.* New York: Doubleday.

Geddes, Patrick. 1979. *Civics as Applied Sociology.* London: Sociological Society by Macmillan.

Gregory, Steven. 1998. *Black Corona: Race and the Politics of Place in an Urban Community.* Princeton: Princeton University Press.

Guha, Ramachandra. 1989. Radical American Environmentalism and Wilderness Preservation: A Third World Critique. *Environmental Ethics,* 11(1), 71–83.

Gusterson, Hugh. 1996. *Nuclear Rites: A Weapons Laboratory at the End of the Cold War.* Berkeley and Los Angeles: University of California Press.

Hannigan, John. 1998. *Fantasy City: Pleasure and Profit in the Postmodern Metropolis*. London and New York: Routledge.

Haraway, Donna J. 1991. *Simians, Cyborgs, and Women: The Reinvention of Nature*. New York: Routledge.

Harding, Garrett. 1968. The Tragedy of the Commons. *Science, 162*, 1243–1248.

Harvey, David. 1996. *Justice, Nature and the Geography of Difference*. Cambridge, MA: Blackwell.

Hawken, Paul, Amory L. Lovins, and Hunter Lovins. 1999. *Natural Capitalism: Creating the Next Industrial Revolution*. Boston, New York, London: Little, Brown, and Co.

Hobart, Mark. 1993. *An Anthropological Critique of Development: The Growth of Ignorance*. New York: Routledge.

Hopkins, R. 2008. *The Transition Handbook. From Oil Dependency to Local Resilience*. Cambridge: Green Books.

Howard, Ebenezer. 1902. *Garden Cities of Tomorrow*. London: S. Sonnenschein and Co., Ltd.

Jackson, Kenneth T. 1985. *Crabgrass Frontier: The Suburbanization of the United States*. New York and Oxford: Oxford University Press.

James, A. 1993. Eating Green(s). *Environmentalism: The View from Anthropology*, (32), 203.

Joseph, Miranda. 2002. *Against the Romance of Community*. Minneapolis and London: University of Minnesota Press.

Kempton, Willett, James S. Boster, and Jennifer A. Hartley. 1996. *Environmental Values in American Culture*. Boston: Massachusetts Institute of Technology.

Levine, Adeline. 1982. *Love Canal: Science, Politics and People*. Lexington, MA: Lexington Books.

Litfin, K.T. 2014. *Ecovillages: Lessons for Sustainable Community*. John Wiley & Sons.

Low, Setha M. 1996. The Anthropology of Cities: Imagining and Theorizing the City. *Annual Review of Anthropology, 25*, 383–409.

Low, Setha M. 2001. The Edge and the Center: Gated Communities and the Discourse of Urban Fear. *American Anthropologist, 103*(1), 45–58.

Lury, C. 1996. *Consumer Culture*. Cambridge: Polity.

Mapes, J., and J. Wolch. 2011. 'Living Green': The Promise and Pitfalls of New Sustainable Communities. *Journal of Urban Design, 16*(1), 105–126.

Marcus, George, and M. Fischer. 1986. *Anthropology as Cultural Critique: An Experiment in the Human Sciences*. Chicago: University of Chicago Press.

Martin, Emily. 1998. Fluid Bodies, Managed Nature. In: *Remaking Reality: Nature at the Millennium*. B. Braun and N. Castree, eds. New York: Routledge.

McCamant, Kathryn, and Charles Durrett. 1994. *Cohousing: A Contemporary Approach to Housing Ourselves*. Berkeley, CA: Ten Speed Press.

McKenzie, Evan. 1994. *Privatopia: Homeowner Associations and the Rise of Residential Private Government*. New Haven and London: Yale University Press.

Meltzer, Graham. 2000. *Cohousing: Toward Social and Environmental Sustainability*. Dissertation, University of Queensland.

Melville, Keith. 1972. *Communes in the Counter Culture: Origins, Theories, Styles of Life*. New York: Morrow.

Merchant, Carolyn. 1980. *The Death of Nature*. San Francisco: Harper Row.

Miller, Daniel. 1995a. *Acknowledging Consumption: A Review of New Studies*. London and New York: Routledge.

Miller, Daniel. 1995b. Consumption and Commodities. *Annual Review of Anthropology, 24*, 141–161.

Milton, Kay, ed. 1993. *Environmentalism: The View from Anthropology*. London and New York: Routledge.

Milton, Kay, ed. 1996. *Environmentalism and Cultural Theory: Exploring the Role of Anthropology in Environmental Discourse*. New York: Routledge.

Mumford, Lewis. 1938. *The Culture of Cities*. New York: Harcourt, Brace, Jovanovich.

Nader, Laura. 1969. 'Up the Anthropologist': Perspectives Gained from Studying Up. In: *Reinventing Anthropology*. D. Hymes, ed. pp. 284–311. New York: Random House.

Naess, A. 1988. *Ecology, Community and Lifestyle*. Cambridge: Cambridge University Press.

O'Connor, Martin, ed. 1994. *Is Capitalism Sustainable? Political Economy and the Politics of Ecology*. New York and London: The Guilford Press.

Peet, Richard, and Michael Watts. 1996. *Liberation Ecologies: Environment, Development, Social Movements*. London and New York: Routledge.

Pellow, D.N. 2002. *Garbage Wars: The Struggle for Environmental Justice in Chicago*. Cambridge, MA: MIT Press.

Peluso, N.L. 1992. *Rich Forests, Poor People: Resource Control and Resistance in Java*. Berkeley, CA: University of California Press.

Peluso, N.L., and M. Watts. 2001. *Violent Environments*. Ithaca, NY: Cornell University Press.

Pepper, David. 1993. *Eco-Socialism: From Deep Ecology to Social Justice*. London and New York: Routledge.

Putnam, Robert D. 2000. *Bowling Alone: The Collapse and Revival of American Community*. New York: Touchstone.

Register, Richard. 1996. An Encounter with Tomorrow's Auto-crats: Ecological Cities "Yes"; Electric Cars "No." In: *Culture Change*. www.culturechange.org/issue9/electric carsno.html: Auto-Free Times.

Richter, Peyton E. 1971. *Utopias: Social Ideals and Communal Experiments*. Boston: Holbrook Press.

Ross, Andrew. 1999. *The Celebration Chronicles: Life, Liberty, and the Pursuit of Property Value in Disney's New Town*. New York: Ballantine Books.

Sandler, R.D., and P.C. Pezzullo. 2007. *Environmental Justice and Environmentalism: The Social Justice Challenge to the Environmental Movement*. Boston: MIT Press.

Sarkar, Saral. 1999. *Eco-Socialism or Eco-Capitalism? A Critical Analysis of Humanity's Fundamental Choices*. New York: Zed Books.

Shiva, Vandana. 1993. *Staying Alive: Women, Ecology, and Development*. London: Zed Books.

Shove, Elizabeth. 2003. *Comfort, Cleanliness and Convenience: The Social Organization of Normality*. Oxford and New York: Berg.

Smith, Neil. 1998a. Nature at the Millennium: Production and Re-Enchantment. In: *Remaking Reality: Nature at the Millennium*. B. Castree, ed. pp. 271–286. London and New York: Routledge.

Smith, R. 2013. Capitalism and the Destruction of Life on Earth: Six Theses on Saving the Humans. *Real-World Economics Review*, 64, 125–150.

Smith, Toby M. 1998b. *The Myth of Green Marketing: Tending Our Goats at the Edge of Apocalypse*. Toronto, Buffalo, London: University of Toronto Press, Inc.

Soper, Kate. 1996. Nature/'nature'. In: *FutureNatural: Nature, Science, Culture*. G. Robertson, et al., eds. London and New York: Routledge.

Sorkin, Michael, ed. 1992. *Variations on a Theme Park: The New American City and the End of Public Space*. New York: Hill and Wang.

Sponsel, Leslie E. 1997. The Master Thief: Gold Mining and Mercury Contamination in the Amazon. In: *Life and Death Matters: Human Rights and the Environment at the End of the Millennium*. B.R. Johnston, ed. pp. 99–127. Walnut Creek: AltaMira Press.

Szasz, A. 2007. *Shopping Our Way to Safety: How We Changed from Protecting the Environment to Protecting Ourselves*. Minneapolis: University of Minnesota Press.

Taylor, D.E. 2009. *The Environment and the People in American Cities, 1600s–1900s: Disorder, Inequality, and Social Change*. Durham, NC: Duke University Press.

Taylor, D. 2014. *The State of Diversity in Environmental Organizations*. A report for Green 2.0. www.diversegreen.org/.

Trainer, Ted. 1997. The Global Sustainability Crisis: Implications for Community. *International Journal of Social Economics*, 24(11), 1219–1240.

Tsing, Anna Lowenhaupt. 2001. Nature in the Making. In: *New Directions in Anthropology and Environment: Intersections*. C.L. Crumley, ed. pp. 3–23. Walnut Creek: Altamira.

Walker, Liz. 2005. *EcoVillage at Ithaca: Pioneering a Sustainable Culture*. Gabriola Island, BC: New Society Publishers.

Walker, L. 2010. *Choosing a Sustainable Future: Ideas and Inspiration from Ithaca, NY*. Gabriola Island, BC: New Society Publishers.

Wolf, Eric. 1972. Ownership and Political Ecology. *Anthropology Quarterly*, 45, 201–205.

Zehner, O. 2012. *Green Illusions: The Dirty Secrets of Clean Energy and the Future of Environmentalism*. Lincoln: University of Nebraska Press.

3 A day in the life of the EcoVillage

The EVI project is, and continues to be, a complex project. It is complex in its efforts to create an ideal village that aims to simultaneously solve both degraded environments and disconnected communities. This chapter introduces the EcoVillage at Ithaca project through a thick description of a day in the community. This could be any day; it is a reflection of real events that happened throughout my 545-day participant observation in the neighborhoods. It is by no means a typical day; there are no typical days. Each day is unique in what it presents, from the blizzard-like weather that results in long conversations over hot chocolate, to a family crisis where neighbors spend their time helping each other, to an explosive email that raises difficult questions and can lead to hurt feelings that require the help of the mediation team. The chapter illustrates the way people in the community traverse the concern for the environment and community within the larger context of US-American culture.

The chapter is an account of my experience, as a researcher and member of the community. I attempt to demonstrate the joys, ironies, paradoxes, efforts, conflicts, cooperation, love, and friendship that individuals display while trying to protect the environment and connect with each other. It is a description of the EVI case study. This day is from 2001, a time when FROG residents had been settled in the community for five years and the SONG was in the early stages of construction. The TREE did not exist—that would come more than ten years later.

A day in the life of the EcoVillage

A Friday in August 2001

Although most people are asleep, Hannah begins her day at 5:30 a.m. with a quick snack. She puts on her walking shoes, and along with her daughter, she heads down the hill in her Honda Civic, about two miles from EVI. Her family occupies four of the 30 houses of the first neighborhood in EcoVillage. She tells me how she started the EVI project as she parks her car at the bottom of the hill and we begin her morning exercise routine. Her daughter will go for a swim in the pond today before she leaves to teach at the local elementary school. The long hike up Elm Street Extension's gradual, then steep, slope is great for getting one's heart rate up, she says, then goes on to describe the moment she discovered the land where EVI is located. (She was pivotal in deciding where the community would be built.) She often struggles with the consequences of the decisions she made almost ten years earlier. "Someone had to make the decision," she says, and she made the best ones she could. She knows that not everyone agreed with her, but she believes that if she hadn't acted quickly, the project would have fallen apart and might never have been realized. Although many people love the project, she wishes people could see her side of the conflicts. She accepts being the target of disgruntled residents and former residents as part of her role as a pioneer. After breakfast, she leaves and walks a quarter mile down the long winding dirt road. She catches the 7:00 a.m. bus that runs down the busy State Highway 79. She will take the bus down the hill to where she parked her car earlier this morning, and then drive the rest of the way to work. In 2001, she was one of only three residents who regularly rode the city bus from EVI. We talk about alternative transport and I'm told that early in the project, free land 10 miles away from the center of town was offered to the group. The generous offer was turned down because it would have meant residents would have to drive too far and early planners did not see that image fitting into their model of ecological living. A few residents have made the effort to use alternative transportation; I observed two people who regularly bike to work throughout the summer and on warm winter and spring days.

At 7:30 a.m. Francine and I meet for a morning hike. We've become friends and because we both work at home, we often call each other to take a walk when we need a break from the community. We pass Lenny, Tanya, and Carol, who are on their way to meditate in the Common House. On our way to West Haven Road, Francine and I pass the chickens, which run to greet us in hopes of getting leftover bread or lettuce. None of the chickens are killed and eaten, at least not by residents. There were a few instances of an animal attacking the chickens; it was rumored to be one of the neighborhood dogs, but as far as I know, nothing was ever proven. We walk down the emergency access road and head towards Route 13A. The three-mile round-trip hike is very hilly, which is the primary reason why many residents do not bike often. It gives Francine and me a good workout, allows us to chat about the weekly happenings in our personal lives, and is an opportunity to vent our gripes about community meetings, emails, and workloads. Although we enjoy walking around the perimeter of the land, we gradually become tired of the mid-August mud and trade a scenic hike on the EVI land for a mud-free walk on blacktop. When things dry up, we'll resume our picturesque hikes along the boundary of the 176-acre former farmland that EVI sits on.

By the time we get back, the kids are off to a variety of schools in their various carpooling teams. Not all the children attend the local elementary school, thus they do not have free public buses that take them to school. Instead parents drive several children across town to a more diverse and popular school. It's Howard's turn to take a van full of kids to Bell Sherman Elementary School.

Many of the older kids go to an alternative high school just down the hill from EVI. Wesley hops on his bike and rides down the hill to the Alternatives Community School (ACS), passing up a chance to get a lift with the other young adults going to ACS. Beatrice stays home along with her brother Peter and a couple of other children who are either ill, homeschooled, or unschooled. Beatrice is one of two children who is "unschooled"; that is, she learns what she wants at her own pace. No textbooks, no assignments, no bedtime or designated playtime. A mother of an unschooled child tells me that she finally decided to purchase a math textbook, as her daughter really wanted one. From my conversations with her, she does not appear to be behind any of the kids her age. But that isn't the point; in fact, her parents discourage competitiveness and emphasize personal achievement. There are several mothers who stay and work at home; they've preferred to quit high-paying, highly qualified jobs to be fulltime parents. Some are doctors, computer engineers, and teachers.

Rikki has returned from putting her many loads of laundry in the community laundry room. Although it is cloudy now, she hopes it will clear up soon so she can hang her cloth diapers on the clothesline. Not everyone likes to hang laundry on the line, but it is certainly widespread here. Rikki and I chat about the joy she finds in doing her daily chores as 18-month-old Maya gives passersby a "high five." After our brief conversation, Rikki collects last night's kitchen chicken scraps and heads down the middle of the neighborhood with Maya on one hip and a bucket of salad scraps on another. Just as she approaches the far end of the neighborhood, the chickens will run up to meet her and she'll probably collect half a dozen eggs. Feeding the chickens kitchen and leftover food scraps is just one of the ways EVI recycles.

The community LISTSERV, a voluntary email list managed by the "geek team" (computer specialists in the neighborhood), is almost always active. Every family has opted to be electronically connected to each other; the LISTSERV includes some participants who were part of the EVI project at some point in the past. For many residents, especially households with children or busy jobs, checking email is a love/hate relationship. It is a great way to know what is happening in the neighborhood to the minute, but it easily gets overwhelming. Today the topics include:

> Whoever folded our laundry? Thank you and thank you. Ruth and Alexander

> We will be meeting this Sat. at 9:30 a.m. at Vivian's house.

> This is a notice to the FROG [First Residents Group] neighborhood for people who may wish to attend or may have concerns to bring up with the Process Steering Committee.

It is turning out to be a warm day as the sun peeks out from behind the thick August clouds. Amy is working in the Common House garden. An amateur yet avid gardener, she works on the outdoor team to keep the EcoVillage grounds in top working condition. Her garden, and the one she maintains for the Common House, is full of colorful, ever-changing perennials. She grows herbs and vegetables alongside marigolds, Echinacea, and columbines. Her garden is only one of many flower gardens that will burst to life every spring and throughout the summer. Aside from putting in more than the required three to four hours per week of community work, Amy volunteers hundreds of unseen hours calculating the cooperative's complicated finances.

The 200-foot walk from the beginning of the neighborhood to the end takes a good four hours. I run into Peter and Lilian, who are on their way to a political rally to protest the US foreign policy in the Middle East. After a ten-minute conversation and a quick glance at my Palm Pilot™ to make sure I don't have an interview scheduled, I'm grabbing my notebook and going along with them and another resident, Cecilia, who saw us from her window and had a feeling of what we were planning. We drive down, across the valley and uphill to the Cornell University campus. We meet other Ithacans we know from other teach-ins. I'm introduced to a protester as the EcoVillage anthropologist. He briefly tells me that he often wonders how ecological EVI really is; being up on the hill and needing a car really makes him suspicious of what the place is all about. I encourage him to visit.

Back on the hill, Max, a SONG resident and one of the construction management team members, is finishing up the loft he recently installed in his self-built house. He is one of the residents who are paid by SONG members to manage part of their housing development project. Unlike in the FROG's construction process, the SONGs have welcomed the chance to employ people from within the group. Some future residents of SONG tell me that it seems like a conflict of interest to hire some of their members to work by the hour and not by the job. Some residents in both neighborhoods also found it confusing that some workers were paid and others volunteered for various community tasks. It is a hard topic for residents to talk about and my interviewee would rather not elaborate. With trust in the process and good intentions, he tries not to worry about these feelings of mistrust and doubt that otherwise would seriously be of concern to him.

I stop by the Common House to see who is "around." Heather from SONG and her son are playing. She likes to visit the Common House just to be near her future home. I ask her how her house is coming along. She is frustrated that the houses are getting bigger at the same time that her finances are getting thinner. But she is confident that it will all work out; she trusts the process. The benefits far outweigh the losses and she has already become very close to some of the people who will be her future neighbors. The whole process has been a big change for her family. They both left good jobs and careers to be part of an innovative community, and they risked everything, including selling their previous home in a depressed market.

Families like Heather's have moved across the country with, in many cases, a home on the market and a lot of trust in strangers. Without jobs, some have volunteered hundreds of hours to run meetings, provide childcare, and organize community finances. I am inspired by the generosity of time that is freely given to see the community thrive.

I'm off for another walk, this time with Vivian, a resident of FROG. We brave the mud and walk into what is affectionately called mudvillage—the SONG site. The second neighborhood is designed differently from the first. About one-third of the houses in SONG have a wooden shell and are looking rather large. The profile is pronounced because there is no landscaping, and siding has not been installed. Clearly the houses on the south side are wider, longer, and higher than the ones on the north side. Most of the houses are built to the Architectural Review Committee (ARC) recommended maximum, which happens to be larger than the FROG maximums. Several things make walking through the second neighborhood unique. Each house is designed differently, a feature which apparently was very attractive to the people joining SONG. At the same time, it meant households could build as individuals with less concern for the group product. Vivian comments that she wishes she could have designed a bigger home in FROG. The cohousing philosophy is to build small houses with minimal basic needs; the shared Common House would provide the space and amenities that are used less frequently such as a large kitchen and dining room, guest room, office spaces, libraries, and so on. Many of the houses in SONG have private office spaces, extra rooms for guests, attached apartments, full kitchens, and especially on the south side, livable basements— all amenities that make their price and stature high.

My companion comments on how important it is to be out in nature, to see the seasons change and watch the wildlife. The fields are turning bright yellow from the goldenrod towering over the spent blackberry and black raspberry plants. She is worried about the dogs running free and chasing deer. An email went out recently encouraging children (and adults) to help chase the Canadian geese away from the pond to prevent them from nesting there. According to a resident "they poop everywhere and are a pest to this region." Some residents are very concerned about non-native species (plants and animals) in this region.

The EVI land is relaxing and pleasing. There is no noise from cars and buses, no loud music, and it is easy to hear the sounds of nature that we often only find at The Nature Store. It feels safe. Kids have returned home from school. They run up a large gravel pile left for the day by workers repairing the road. Tiny pebbles slide down the pile like flowing water. The older boys are fast; they stake claims to the top while the younger ones struggle to climb the sinking sand of stones. The girls seem less impressed and look for adventure further in the woods. A parent comes out to help supervise and joins our conversation. Eric is a programmer and works three days a week out of his EVI office.

In the current global climate it is hard to have a conversation longer than 30 minutes without the subject of Palestine and Israel coming up, or the state of US politics and the rise of what one woman calls an emerging Christian theocracy. My companion's political views are more conservative than mine; Eric's interruption gives us both a chance to pause.

EcoVillage is not politically homogenous, though most of the residents tend to be liberal Democrats or greens, like the rest of Ithaca. When the boys have exhausted their enthusiasm for the gravel pile, they collect long sticks and run around. An older resident returning from work looks at us and shakes her head. She's both irritated and annoyed that the kids are so wild and that the parent doesn't seem to react the way she did as a parent. Of course this is why many of the residents moved here; the young, old, playful, serious, shy, and politically motivated all find a sense of community in an ever-changing day. The sun was out just long enough to dry the diapers on the line, and now Sandra asks her husband to help her carry the loads home. His "see you later" is genuine; we'll have many opportunities to spend time together.

Today is one of the three evenings a week when we can share a community meal, and the cook team meets at 4:00 p.m. to begin preparing the evening's Common House meal. Maisy is making her famous fried tofu. Her two assistants, Tanya and Katrin, begin chopping tofu, preparing organic brown basmati rice, and washing fresh farm lettuce for a salad. We run out of nutritional yeast, but it is not a problem—one of the assistants begins walking through the neighborhood asking neighbors if they have any we can borrow.

She returns with more than enough. This is a great meal for the cooks because it is wheat-free, dairy-free, and doesn't have mushrooms; there is no need to make a special dish for vegans and vegetarians. In an earlier discussion with a member of the cook team it was suggested that, like the vegetarian options at every meal, there should be a meat option available. (Although Misty moved out in the mid-2000s, she would be surprised that 14 years after her comment, the Common House meals often have meat.) About 30 adults and 20 children have signed up before yesterday, giving the shopper enough time to go to regional chain market, Wegmans, or the local cooperative market, Greenstar, and purchase the right amount of items requested by the cook. The head cook adds about ten more people to count for the late sign-ups and potential visitors; the team of three will prepare a delicious meal for 60 people in two hours. Preparing the meals together is a great time to catch up on each other's lives. The recent exchange of email messages about the Common House guidelines and the problem of the overflowing garbage dumpster are the topics of discussion. The general consensus is that we should encourage residents to throw away less stuff and not get a second dumpster, but the reality is that the dumpster overflows and attracts undesirable animals. A small group discussion like this allows us to get to know each other's views and feelings between slicing carrots and seasoning the tofu. Empathy is a good characteristic to have in cohousing and moments like these help us understand each other later during long neighborhood meetings.

There will be a team of journalists from a Spanish magazine at dinner tonight. A lot of different groups come to EcoVillage throughout the year: journalists, city planners, potential residents, and students like myself. It makes the place feel like being in a fish bowl. Some residents complain that after a full day of work, the last thing they want to do at dinner is talk about why they live in

EcoVillage. "It's my chance to wind down and not engage in some research project; as a result, people must think we are a rude bunch, but we are just too tired to be interviewed at dinner" (Helen). It is rush time, 5:50p.m. A total of six residents have asked if there is enough food for them to sign up at the last minute—no problem. Joshua has set up the dining room for a buffet-style meal.

Various children gather and check out the kids' table; it usually contains a bland version of what the adults eat. Not all families are happy about a separate meal for the children. Today's serving table has tamari-marinated baked tofu, brown rice, salad, and sliced oranges. Josiah rings the dinner bell and soon residents who have been congregating on the steps to the Common House stop their conversations about West Haven Farm's new deer fence and come into the dining room.

In a large circle that fills the room we hold hands. Lots of smiles send greetings as we face a neighbor on the other side of the circle. Maisy welcomes everyone and describes the meal. After thanking the assistants, including two younger girls who helped cut oranges for the kids' table, she asks if there are any announcements. The Spanish magazine folks are introduced and a friend of Susi's from downtown has come for dinner. A few residents who do not like being part of the circle stand patiently outside and wait until Maisy gives the "ok" to begin. I ask a resident why they don't like the circle and they say it seems too cultish.

One can't help but overhear evening greetings among neighbors: "how was your day?", "isn't it great weather?", "could we meet after dinner?" fill the food line. Although there are plenty of tables, it is not always easy to decide where to sit, once you have your food. The largest table seats ten and usually fills quickly; this is the place to sit if one is worried about eating alone. Based on your mood, some people talk too much, some people don't talk enough; the table might be joyous, full of laughter, and lift your spirit, or depressing or boring. An interesting visitor might share stories from their cohousing community, or a visiting parent might share funny childhood memories of a shy neighbor. Sometimes the kids are too loud, and at other times the topic is so interesting you stay long at the table, the sky darkens, and we forget how we got here. The noise level is especially high tonight and a resident at my table is complaining that this is not what they had expected when they moved to EcoVillage. He had imagined dinner to be a quiet, peaceful time to catch up with neighbors and get to know each other. Instead he feels exhausted and irritated by the kids running around, children calling for their parents, and babies impatient from sitting. He rushes to finish his meal and leaves. The rest of us completely understand the occasionally frustrating dinner, but we don't mind it tonight. Our table is lively and we talk about how exciting the SONG site is looking and the free vegetables the farmers left for residents outside the Common House. Claire plans to make zucchini bread and freeze it, giving us all a great idea. She tells a story that happened two years ago. Neighbors got together and collected the pounds of surplus tomatoes from the farm, built a huge bonfire, and canned several jars of tomatoes. Claire doesn't have the energy to organize the canning this year and fears that it might not happen. We are all excited at the thought of tons of good organic tomatoes left on the field that we can collect and can. The magazine journalists are looking for people to interview and a few residents talk with them. Those remaining at our table dread them coming to us and we try not to be noticed.

Brian rings a small bell hanging from the kitchen island, signaling an announcement. Some kids from ACS are selling chocolate for a class trip and they ask if anyone is interested in buying some. Cohousing is a good market for social fundraisers. Three more announcements are made: a group is going to see the film *Together*, a comedy about life on a commune in Sweden; a meeting of anyone interested in building a sauna; and the "Tune Café" gathering after the sauna meeting. Our table continues to talk about the Spanish TV crew. A resident makes the comment that they had no idea they would be under such a microscope by moving into EcoVillage. Lenny jumps in and says it is a wonderful thing—last week EVI was featured in a Japanese magazine. It is a chance to model the many good things we have here and possibly influence how other communities are developed, although he realizes that we still have a long way to go with meeting the mission of the community.

We continue chatting over empty plates full of leftover salad dressing and juicy tomato seeds. A member of the dish team asks if he can take them—our plates. Concentrated on our conversation, we haven't noticed the dining room emptying and a small group gathering for the sauna meeting. The dish team has turned up their music and is hurriedly gathering the remaining plates from our table. Most people have bused their own table, scraping their leftover tofu snippets and lettuce into red tubs for the chickens and compost piles. Very little food is wasted. It is too distracting to continue the conversation as someone has come to the table to ask if one of us is attending the meeting. The meeting heads downstairs to the recreation room. It is not a big deal to end our conversation, as we know we can pick up where we left off another time. We agree that being such close neighbors means there is always another time. Living at EVI can feel like putting on a thick pair of warm socks on a snowy winter day—bulky enough to notice the source that warms your body and soul.

I pass Eleanor's house on my way to the Tune Café and stop in for tea—another EcoVillage moment. Her house is warm from the afternoon sun. With large south-facing windows, the passive solar design allows the houses to receive maximum sunshine all winter. Triple panes of glass in the windows keep the warm air in, save energy, and provide spectacular views of deer playing in the open field and residents chatting by the pond. I ask if she is planning to go to the café, but after a long week of teaching she needs to unwind with a small crowd. She'll go to the movies with the regular group of young women whose husbands will stay home and watch the kids. After the movie they'll probably head to a downtown café and splurge on dessert and great conversation.

A bunch of us head to Adam's house. We bring our favorite CDs with songs picked out to share with the group. There is a dessert potluck of a variety of cookies, cake, fruit, tea, and coffee. Although some desserts are homemade, many come from Greenstar, the local health food store, and Wegmans, the large regional grocery chain. Garrison says a brief welcome and we are introduced to his friends from the greater Ithaca community. About one third of the guests are not residents and Francine comments that it is nice to mix with local community members. Vanessa puts in Tracy Chapman's "Give Me One Reason" and says that it reflects the way she is feeling this evening. Everyone gets a turn to play a tune and we hum, sway, and laugh about the memories the songs invoke in us. Garrison has been hosting Tune Cafés for several years. He has a large collection of Putumayo World music CDs and plays a tune from the South American collection. Like many of his neighbors, he has traveled outside the United States quite a bit. He recently came home from a bike tour in Canada with his wife and stepchildren. A member of the SONG group has just come in; we chat, and she tells me that her family is struggling with the decision to continue to be a part of the second neighborhood. The costs continue to rise and the houses continue to get larger; their income is fixed and limited and the financial strain is causing problems in her relationship with her partner. It is no secret that many current, soon-to-be, and former residents are disappointed and discouraged by the high cost of living at EcoVillage. Some soon-to-be residents are ashamed to admit that things are rolling out of control and they don't know how to have a discussion about these uncomfortable situations. A new song is played and we are distracted by Cat Stevens's lyrics of collecting bags, bringing good friends, and taking the peace train home.

The ongoing conflicts around the world are depressing. Hilda, a former member who could not afford to build in the SONG, but who tries to stay connected to the group while living in downtown Ithaca, comments that her small tribulations seem insignificant when compared with larger global problems such as war and AIDS. She and a couple of other residents are planning to attend an upcoming political rally in Washington, D.C.

People come and go from the Tune Café; by 9:30 p.m. the group is quickly dispersing. As people leave, I stay and help the hosts clean up; it is a chance to observe their home and learn more about their lifestyle. Most houses were designed without full ovens and with an electric range, although this household made a special request to have a gas stove and a full oven—they prefer to use gas over electric. There are other households that made an exception to the community guidelines. These exceptions are aimed at meeting people's personal practical and comfort needs, and yet few of these minor changes are publicly known, helping to give the community a sense of unity. Some residents who do not have a dishwasher in their home commented to me, with disappointment, that one or two households went ahead without group permission to install dishwashers and other appliances the group had decided not to acquire, like full ovens. We end the evening with a hug and I make my way across the neighborhood to the house where I rent a small room.

I don't think twice about walking alone past 20 homes at 10:30 p.m. Although there are a few lights on in the homes of EVI's night owls, the sky is dark and so is my way. Without glaring streetlights, cars parked away from the neighborhood, and no automatic lights, one can see bright stars in the sky. The evening is still except for the sound of water gently splashing at the pond. I walk south along a narrow stone path separating two duplexes and see that there are some residents swimming. The swimmers have their clothes laid across the picnic table.

I'm greeted and encouraged to join the small group of skinny-dippers at the pond. Treading water, Jonathon reflects on why he moved to the community: it is for moments like this that brought him here. Swimming with his neighbors in a relaxed environment was something he did not, and knew he would not, find in his former suburban neighborhood. There is a meteor shower and we stare desperately to spot the next shooting star. We only get out and go home when our toes and fingers are shriveled and pruned. We quietly walk back to the neighborhood and say hi to a late-night neighbor who is leaving her office in the Common House and heading home. We talk for a minute or two. She asks who was at the pond and I tell her. She wishes she had known as she was stuck on a problem at work and could have used the company and downtime. But like many things at EcoVillage, things just happen, and if not this time, there will always be another.

When I ask residents what community means, they struggle to find the right order of words to express their definitions, but a "sense of community" becomes clear to me after observing daily life in EcoVillage. This is the kind of day many residents moved here for; it is what community means; it is the sense of community that is so hard to define in a couple of words because it is a day, a week, a month, years of living together and knowing each other and changing together.

Creating a "sense of community" for many residents means knowing that a conversation can be interrupted because it can be picked up again soon. It is feeling safe and having the opportunity to give and receive simple acts of kindness on a regular basis. It is a lifestyle that civically engages residents in the everyday management of their community, all while caring for the natural world around them.

Although the initial focus of research was on the first neighborhood and the daily practices of residents within the village, this idea changed quickly after I became familiar with the multiple competing agents of the project and the various components that contributed to both creating a sense of community and working to become an ecological model of neighborhood development. During the ten years that it took to build the FROG, many participants came and went; approximately half of the neighborhood was not part of the original planning group in the summer of 2001. The community attracted families and individuals with a diverse set of ideas that would work together to achieve the ambitious goal set forth in the EVI mission. For many residents, the ecovillage concept and the cohousing model it is based on were unfamiliar until they joined the community. This book is meant to give useful insight into the community that I hope will encourage residents, and the broader audience, to continue to pursue ways to simplify their lifestyle. As a resource into the celebrations and struggles of individuals and the community, I hope the reader is motivated to pursue a deep dialogue on how to improve our communities and our environments through critical reflection and collaboration.

Social and physical structure of EcoVillage at Ithaca

EcoVillage at Ithaca is a complex organization dedicated to improving the way communities are built, advocating that they be constructed in ways that enhance social interaction and protect the natural environment. Joan Bokaer and Liz Walker founded the organization in 1991 after their return from what was called "A Global Walk for a Livable Planet," although Joan and Liz, and most of the walkers, only walked across the United States, from Los Angeles to New York;[1] the goal of the walk was to engage in a national dialogue about creating sustainable neighborhoods that provided a sense of community and preserved the natural environment.

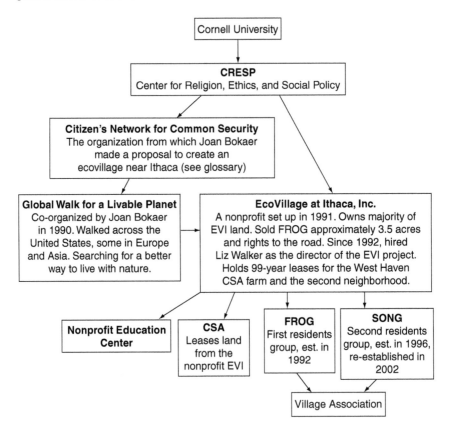

Figure 3.1 EcoVillage at Ithaca organization structure 2001.

Source: Author.

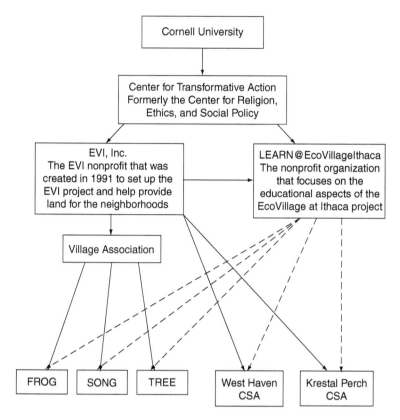

Figure 3.2 EcoVillage at Ithaca organization structure 2015.
Source: Author.

In March, Joan wrote:

> I propose that we build a demonstration ecological and cooperative village near Ithaca, N.Y. The EcoVillage will draw from and integrate the vast amount of work already done in the areas of appropriate technology, design, and social ecology while creating an experiment that will open up new ways of thinking and being.

The end of the Global Walk culminated in finding a place to create this ideal ecological community that would define the way new neighborhoods would be developed. Ithaca was selected as the site for the first multi-neighborhood cohousing community; it would model sustainable agriculture, energy-efficient homes, and a built-in sense of community. In September 1991, a proposal called EcoVillage at Ithaca: A Model for Land Conservation and Sustainable Neighborhood Development was prepared (Bokaer 1991).

Table 3.1 EcoVillage at Ithaca entities

Name	Description	Legal status	Land	Participants
EcoVillage at Ithaca Incorporated (EVI, Inc.)	Overarching organization that created the project and purchased the 176-acre parcel	Educational Nonprofit 501(c)(3)	176 acres 55 acres held in a conservation easement (Finger Lakes Land Trust)	Open to membership from inside and outside of EVI. Membership dues were $35 per individual and $50 per household in 2016
Learn @EcoVillageIthaca	Uses EVI as a laboratory to showcase sustainability and applications of green technology as part of its education mission. Runs tours, media relations, local and global outreach	A nonprofit education organization arm of EVI, Inc. A program of Cornell University's Transformative Action, a 501(c)(3) nonprofit	Uses the EVI, Inc. land as well as the resident homes and common houses to model sustainable living	Resident instructors and tour guides, teachers, researchers, students, and visitors
First Resident Group (FROG)	Residential community since 1997	Cohousing cooperative	Purchased 5 acres for $1 from EVI, Inc.	Owners and renters of homes in FROG
Second Neighborhood Group (SONG)	Residential community since 2003, completed construction in 2006	Cohousing cooperative	Leases 5 acres from EVI, Inc.	Owners and renters of homes in SONG
Third Resident EcoVillage Experience (TREE)	Residential community since 2014	Cohousing cooperative	Purchased 5 acres for $40,000 from EVI, Inc.	Owners and renters of homes in TREE
Village Association (VA)	Association of residents from FROG, SONG, and TREE	Nonprofit 501(c)(3)	Road, village crux	Owners of homes in FROG, SONG, and TREE
West Haven Farm	An organic community-supported agriculture farm owned by a FROG family	CSA farm	10 acres of EVI land is leased	Local and regional community
Krestal Perch Berry Farm	A U-pick berry farm owned by a SONG resident	CSA farm	5 acres of EVI land is leased	Local and regional community

The EcoVillage at Ithaca project consists of several parts (see Table 3.1), including: a nonprofit 501(c)(3) called EVI, Inc., and three independent and private residences that are set up as three distinct cohousing cooperatives. Together, the three cohousing cooperatives form the Village Association to oversee the resources shared by all neighborhoods, such as the basic infrastructure of water and sewage, the road, and the village electronic LISTSERV. Other primary features of the EVI project include an organic community-supported agriculture (CSA) farm and U-pick berry farm. All these components are legally and financially independent, but they overlap by staff, membership,[2] and mission.

The nonprofit EVI was incorporated in January 1992 as part of the Center for Religion, Ethics, and Social Policy (CRESP), now called Center for Transformative Action,[3] an affiliate organization of Cornell University. The original mission of EVI, Inc. was to demonstrate sustainability through education, outreach, affordable housing, and the creation of a model village of 500+ residents. This model would illustrate how families can live sustainably and comfortably through integrating clustered cohousing neighborhoods and at the same time preserving most of the land as open space.

EcoVillage at Ithaca, Inc.

One of the first priorities of the nonprofit EVI, Inc. was to be an education center with the FROG, SONG, and TREE as the demonstration sustainable resident neighborhoods. The education center is intended to teach the general public about successful methods of preserving and conserving open space and ways to live in community. The original vision of the ecological village included a village center, an education center, organic farm, various orchards, meadows, and forested land, five separate neighborhoods, and a waste treatment center. An appointed board of directors manages the EVI nonprofit.

The EVI, Inc. board and residents groups were and have remained separate legal entities for practical and financial reasons. A founding resident with legal training explained that this was necessary to ensure that if one entity failed, it would not cause the other entities to fail. Thus the nonprofit EVI, Inc. owns the greater part of the land; the VA owns the only road that leads into the community and some additional land, the FROG and TREE own the land they live on, while SONG leases their land from the nonprofit. To guarantee that the land that surrounds the neighborhoods is preserved and protected from development if the nonprofit needs to sell it, the FROG encouraged and the nonprofit adopted various easements on the land. These easements are one way the FROG influences what happens to the remaining nonprofit land. This separation of public land and privatized homes in the middle places the EVI project in a complex web of private/public space. Through the nonprofit, residents have exclusive access to the public lands of EVI, Inc. Adding to the complication is that the money raised to pay for the land debt of the nonprofit was raised in part through the construction of the neighborhoods.

Some residents are not aware of their connection to the larger EVI project and especially the role of the neighborhoods in being a model for sustainable housing. This tension usually expressed itself when a community facility like the Common House was requested for an academic class that was hosted by a neighbor. Some residents complained that while the instructor was paid to lead classes through the Common House, these instructors were not required to pay rental fees for the space. Nor was it easy to be paid to host visitors. Also, other residents were unclear about who was paid to give tours (others volunteered) and how they had agreed to be a model community. In addition to demonstrating sustainable neighborhoods, the nonprofit plans to construct an education center, hostel, and village center to support the educational mission of the organization. Although the 2016–2021 Strategic Plan no longer mentioned these original goals, tensions between the nonprofit mission and the residents' homes continued to be a concern for those who left and remain.

The design of the privately owned homes in the middle of the nonprofit land means the two groups are subtly dependent on each other. The reality is more complex and important to emphasize; the majority of meetings I attended during fieldwork had some relation to this complexity. In order to build the project, the nonprofit needed to repay the land loan, and residents who would move into the project were seen as the source of funding to repay the lenders. This was not always explained to new residents. The cost of living in community is often mixed with the value of the land, pond, forest, farm, and so on, and the ability to preserve 90 percent of the land from development, yet this land is not explicitly owned by the neighborhood. In fact, EVI, Inc., which owns the undeveloped land, is a tax-exempt nonprofit with its own board of directors. This means that the residents themselves do not necessarily own that land, but nor do they have the burden of paying taxes on it. For example, if you owned a home in the

Table 3.2 EcoVillage at Ithaca neighborhoods at a glance[4]

Neighborhood	FROG	SONG	TREE
Year completed	1997	2003	2014
No. of structures	30 houses	30 houses	40 houses
House size	900–1650 sq. ft.	750–2500 sq. ft.	425–1440 sq. ft.
Approx. cost in 2011	$150,000–$270,000	$200,000–$350,000	$80,000–$235,000
Legal structure	Cohousing cooperative community	Cohousing cooperative community	Cohousing cooperative community
Land	Bought 5 acres from EVI, Inc.	Leases for 99 years, 5 acres from EVI, Inc.	5 acres
Accessibility	Multilevel duplex	Multilevel duplex	Common House with single-level condos and an elevator

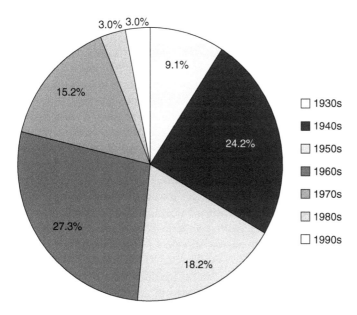

3.0% 3.0%

9.1%

15.2%

24.2%

27.3%

18.2%

□ 1930s
■ 1940s
□ 1950s
■ 1960s
▨ 1970s
□ 1980s
□ 1990s

Figure 3.3 Year residents were born.
Source: Author.

city of Ithaca, you would be responsible for paying taxes on your owned property. But what about the park next door? Or the gorges and lake that provide
educational opportunities or the area schools? In fact, as a resident of the city,
your taxes pay to maintain those amenities. In EVI, it is not clear who pays the
nonprofit assets that own and legally maintain the land that surrounds the
households. The cohousing communities want access to the land, or at least that
it not be developed into something they do not like, so they support EVI, Inc.'s
education effort, even though residents sometimes resent the fishbowl experience of being the laboratory for sustainability studies. This is the tension that I
heard from current and former residents: that they have access to an amenity
that is privileged. The question that could help us understand this relationship
is whether EVI, Inc. and the cohousing communities attached to it are the best
models for sustainable living. And whether the lessons they teach are impactful
to the growing social and environmental problems, specifically as they relate to
access, equality, and justice.

A significant factor in the exclusive nature of EVI relates to the idea of creating a village of more than one neighborhood. EVI is unique because of its
mission to create several cohousing communities in a village. An early version
of the community plan included six to eight clustered neighborhoods of 15 to
25 families. McCamant and Durret (1994) recommend that one neighborhood
of 20 to 25 households is the best way to create a sense of community and make
decision-making manageable. Also, most cohousing communities in Denmark,

where the housing model traces its roots, recommend one neighborhood with up to 30 households.

The planners of EVI felt that a larger community was a better option for being a model because it would demonstrate an alternative to the generally held belief that if EVI did not build, a typical developer would have built 150 houses on one-acre lots. This image helped to promote EVI as a more sustainable option than the typical development. A large EVI project supported efforts by residents to create a themed community that would demonstrate sustainable living by having a critical mass to create car-sharing, fund gray-water recycling, and create small cottage industries (amongst other project ideas) and a green lifestyle. More people meant more opportunity to share, thus reducing the need to consume, but also, more people meant there would be more opportunity to connect with each other. During my research, however, it became clear that bigger is not always better. As SONG began to organize, some residents complained that there were already too many people in EcoVillage. The construction of the SONG meant that new people, strangers in some ways, were being added to the freshly settled FROG. One resident of FROG complained that the SONG neighborhood brought younger, "cooler" residents to the community and her neighbors in FROG were more interested in getting to know the new families than maintaining and being interested in deeper friendships with her and other FROG neighbors. Some felt the point of creating a community where neighbors knew each other well was being diluted by additional neighborhoods. More people meant that the beautiful open land would start to become congested. These attitudes reflected the fact that the original purpose and vision of the EVI project was not well known.

> The purpose of EcoVillage at Ithaca is to redesign the human habitat by building a model village for up to 500 residents that will carefully integrate design for human needs (shelter, food production, social interaction, energy, work) with land and water conservation and ecosystem preservation. As a living laboratory associated with an internationally prestigious university, EcoVillage will become a teaching center with a global audience. As a national and international model, it will showcase systems and methods that are sustainable, practical and replicable.

However, it also revealed the fact that not everyone wanted more neighbors, and to some extent they were concerned that their peaceful backyard would be inundated with a lot of people—one of the reasons they left the city to begin with. It also highlighted the tension between the nonprofit, which decided what was built on the land they owned, and the residents who used the land every day. On October 28, 2009, a new mission was adopted by the EVI board.

> To promote experiential learning about ways of meeting human needs for shelter, food, energy, livelihood, and social connectedness that are aligned with the long-term health and viability of Earth and all its inhabitants.

Table 3.3 Social connections and EVI mission (%)

Question	Very well	Well	Somewhat	Not that well	Not well at all
How well connected do you feel to residents in your immediate (FROG/SONG/TREE) neighborhood?	33.3	35.0	28.3	1.7	1.7
How well connected do you feel to residents in other EVI neighborhoods?	6.7	30.0	50.0	11.7	1.7
How well do you feel you can share your personal needs with the community (disability, family concerns, need for privacy, etc.)?	16.7	45.0	26.7	8.3	3.3
How well does EVI meet visible and invisible (mental illness, hearing loss, ADHD, chemical sensitivity, etc.) disability needs?	6.7	35.0	45.0	13.3	0.0
How well does consensus decision-making work at EVI?	5.0	41.7	35.0	11.7	6.7
How well do you understand the EVI mission?	18.3	53.3	21.7	5.0	1.7
How well does EVI meet its mission?	1.8	40.4	45.6	10.5	1.8
How well do you comprehend the various parts of the EVI project?	13.3	30.0	45.0	10.0	1.7
How well do you understand the goals/mission of EVI LEARN?	11.7	33.3	28.3	20.0	6.7
How satisfied are you overall with life at EVI?	31.0	41.4	22.4	5.2	0.0
How engaged are you in social, political, or other activities in the town/city of Ithaca? Include the ways you are engaged below.	18.6	25.4	22.0	25.4	8.5

When asked a series of questions on how residents experience life at EVI and understand the mission, and various parts of the organization, residents expressed mixed understanding. Those who completed the survey generally felt that they understood the mission; more than half felt the project met its mission "somewhat" or "not at all."

The question of how large the community should be relates to several contradictions that EVI faces on a regular basis. One such contradiction is the desire to create community by leaving established communities and building new homes as a way to prevent development. Yet the community was developed in a way that emphasizes personal benefits, such as views, over ecological options, such as creating access for children and adults to use public transportation and easily pick up their mail. In an effort to encourage membership, the project did little to discourage larger homes in SONG and, as many participants confessed, they preferred that only two neighborhoods were built on the land, and only if absolutely necessary, a third.

First Residents Group

The FROG is a community cooperation with a board of directors from among the resident neighbors. Residents of FROG buy shares[5] in exchange for a house and an optional carport if one is available; each household, based on its square footage, owns proportional shares of the Common House, including the guest room, recreation rooms, large kitchen, and children's play areas. Individual community members own the private office spaces within the Common House.

The cooperative collectively owns the Common House, the outside of duplexes, and the 2.5 acres it purchased from the nonprofit EVI, Inc. The decision to build FROG in the middle, rather than near the road that provided easy access to public transportation along Route 79, was disappointing to some participants because it meant residents would drive to pick up their mail, decide not to take the bus because there was no shelter, and it was inconvenient to walk the half mile in cold weather. Others argued that the space near the road was marshland and not geologically suitable for construction. The current location in the middle of the land also provided views and the sense of being immersed in nature.

In addition to purchasing home shares (a house) in FROG, residents pay a monthly maintenance fee based on the number of shares owned (approximately $400 to $600). The monthly fees pay for such things as EVI, Inc. (prior to 2014 all residents were charged a fee for the nonprofit), a savings account for home repairs,[6] and Common House utilities. Because the community owns the outside of the houses, residents need to seek permission from neighbors to install anything that affects the structural integrity of the outside, such as TV satellite dishes and solar panels. Although the houses and energy centers are designed to accommodate solar panels, they had not been installed because some households couldn't afford them and blocked the idea. However, when tours of the neighborhood were conducted, the ability of the houses to accommodate solar panels was touted as an ecological feature. I often felt that explaining the reason there were no solar panels would point out the reality that solar panels are expensive, even for families who believe they are a good source for alternative energy.

The physical design of the homes brings neighbors together. A north- and south-facing row of duplexes ensures that adjacent neighbors and those across the pedestrian-only walkway run into each other regularly. The north-facing homes have an additional back room attached to compensate for facing carports and their limited view of the countryside that the south-facing homes enjoy. According to the architects, there was

> a lot of tension around views … and people needing to reconcile conflicting values, their own conflicting values. On one hand saying, we believe in tight spaces and facing each other and being in community, but damn it, I want my view.

Residents also struggled over home sizes: at first, during the planning stage the group preferred a 700-square-foot house size, but in the end no one wanted to build the smaller home and the average size became 1,300 square feet. Acknowledging that FROG still created a small footprint, one of the architects commented, "… at the same time, the average new home in the United States is over 2,200 square feet."

The homes are built vertically to minimize the footprint of the building; all but three of the 30 houses have five separate living levels, with five sets of stairs. Although residents imagined growing old in the neighborhood, and thus contributing to the natural diversity of the new model community, they admit that the stairs that separate five levels per house will make the homes inaccessible to the elderly and people dependent on a wheelchair. The internal spaces are open and simple.

All the interior features of the FROG are similar: the countertops, the cabinets, the convection ovens, and the built-in bookshelves. This was done to save money and maintain simplicity. Small changes were made by some residents to create more comfortable living than the simplicity model offered. For example, some households installed dishwashers, private laundry machines, and air conditioners, while others have gas stoves, and custom counters and ceilings. The architecture included large south-facing windows that allow maximum sunlight in the winter while wooden awnings are designed to grow vines that shade the homes in the hot summer months.

The windows facing into the community are large and the doors are glass; this design allows residents to stay visually connected to each other. Flower and vegetable beds border the pedestrian walkway that runs through the two rows of houses; in two locations the path diverges, creating a recreation space in the middle. One half has a picnic table where adults gather for impromptu conversations and an occasional light breakfast. The table is adjacent to a large sandbox, where children frequently gather to bury construction trucks and watch the grapes grow on the natural canopy above them. The other half of the neighborhood has a larger picnic table, a small vegetable garden, and a cherry tree.

The FROG Common House is designed to be the heart of the community. It was meant to bring people together, to be a place to hang out, read, cook, work, and play. Most neighbors complain that it is seldom used. Residents prefer to stay in their houses or go downtown for an afternoon outing with friends rather than sit in the Common House. My early attempts to meet people by sitting in the Common House were unsuccessful. Some of the residents who work from home, such as computer programmers and therapists, own office spaces in the Common House. The availability of such office space is supposed to reduce the need to drive to work, and allow employees to stay connected to their families. Ironically, a part-time telecommuter decided to move their office downtown in order to be more connected to other people. Another resident, a therapist who used the surrounding nature as part of her sessions, was happy that she did not have to drive to town, an eco-option for her, but not her clients, who had to drive up the hill to EVI. She was happy about bringing her clients to the open land. Echoing Lewis Mumford's sentiment, she told me that part of the therapy is being in nature.

Second Neighborhood Group

The Second Neighborhood Group is also arranged as a cooperative cohousing community with its own board of directors from within the neighborhood. Unlike the FROG, the SONG has a 99-year lease on three and a half acres of land from EVI, Inc. to build individually designed homes. While the FROG hired an architect team, the SONG hired what some complained were inexperienced designers and project managers. The design and management team was made up of two residents of FROG. As I explore later in this section, a culture of trust in the process prevented members—who otherwise would be critical and at least request résumés and references were they building outside of EcoVillage—from hiring a more qualified team. Although in interviews some residents were concerned about the doubling of housing costs in SONG, participants did not want to appear untrusting of their neighbors; therefore, no one was held accountable for what often put a financial strain on some families. Some families volunteered sweat equity in the community to keep costs down. At the same time, the group paid other residents. This distinction was never clear and few households dared to raise questions at meetings. When a mistake was made on the site, the cost to fix it was absorbed by the entire neighborhood. Eventually the group hired a builder and several subcontractors, and construction began on the homes. There were several entities working on different houses and it was therefore hard to keep track of individual work, neighborhood work, sweat equity, and who was and was not paid for work. Residents raised the questions during our interviews and we engaged in long discussions about why it was hard to raise them in the community.

The physical design of the SONG neighborhood is noticeably dissimilar to the FROG; this difference might be due to the planning and construction process of the group. The SONG houses represent a diverse set of ideas about community and nature, and express personal taste for comfort and luxury. The homes also reflect more individualism, with less emphasis on the simplicity and community on which the FROG is based. A closer look suggests class divisions from north to south. The neighborhood has tall homes on the south-facing side and smaller houses located behind them on the northern side. Houses on the south side are built larger and, for the most part, resemble typical suburban homes in that many have basements for recreation space, large kitchens and dining areas, guest rooms and office space, as well as individual laundry spaces. The cohousing model of the FROG takes these extra spaces and designs them into the Common House, with the argument that they are used infrequently and therefore can be shared.

The SONG version of cohousing includes all the basic ingredients of a Common House with shared dining space, guest room, living room, children's play space, a recreation room, and a few offices upstairs. While many families designed their home with amenities normally reserved for the Common House, individual houses included in-law apartments or bed and breakfast spaces to earn an extra income. In 2002, some families in SONG suggested that they not build a Common House because, outside of the three common meals a week, the large and expensive Common House in the FROG was seldom used, and because cost overruns were making the SONG project expensive. During a few neighborhood meetings, some households argued that they preferred to have smaller shared dinners in individual homes. The decision not to prioritize a Common House was in part because the group was rushed to construct homes and pay back the EVI, Inc. land debt. Some participants felt that the development team paid little attention to explaining cohousing (the FROG residents were all required to read McCamant and Durret's cohousing book before joining), and little effort went into explaining the larger mission of the EVI project. This lack of communication and understanding was evident at village-wide meetings and in my random conversations with frustrated SONG families. There was pressure to get the neighborhood built.

The planning process for the design and construction of SONG was not as well carried out as in the FROG. While the FROG spent years planning their neighborhood, most residents in SONG had spent less than six months as part of the group or joined shortly before construction began. Few new residents understood the cohousing concept or the ecovillage model of small footprints and shared resources. Many homes feature custom trimmings and green technology such as composting toilets, solar panels, masonry stoves, and straw-bale insulation. During the sunny months, some households sell electricity back to the city. A member of the SONG planning team commented that this neighborhood was a good model in EVI, while another member felt sad that given the choice, most households chose the maximum house size and thus decreased what some felt was an important green option: a small footprint and affordability. This experience supports the argument that improved green technology risks increasing consumption (Erickson 1997; Fotopoulos 2000; Zehner 2012).

Compared with the FROG neighborhood design, the houses in SONG are farther apart, creating a less clustered style with larger areas for pedestrians. The pedestrian-only walkway through the middle creates a central location for children and adults to gather. Although a community garden was initially planned for the middle, allergies of some residents meant it had to be moved away from the homes. However, a small Common House garden just outside of the kitchen makes it easy to harvest onions and herbs for shared meals. The SONG Common House is in the middle of the neighborhood instead of at one end. Unlike the FROG, who put their playground away from the houses, there is a large play structure in the middle of the neighborhood where parents at home or in the Common House can keep watch. The duplex houses are spread apart, giving families more privacy. Windows and doors are not collectively open to the community so one can see who is home. During a SONG Architectural Review Committee meeting, a resident who built a south-facing house argued that having a north window into the community was not energy-efficient.

Third residential EcoVillage experience

The third resident group was completed in 2015 and is a unique cohousing cooperative. Like FROG, TREE bought its land from EVI, Inc. for $40,000. The FROG architect was again hired to design the neighborhood and thus it resembles the FROG. The community features a uniform style with three different housing models, but unlike most cohousing communities that have 24–30 households, TREE has 40. A large Common House that sits at the top of the community has 15 units built on top. This tall structure represents EVI's first apartment building and includes units on one level, making them accessible via an elevator. The accessibility feature made TREE attractive to older, retired residents who imagine being able to stay in the community.

Each neighborhood's construction represents an opportunity to explore architecture that enhances a sense of community and advance energy-efficiency. All the homes in EVI are designed to actively reduce the energy needs to heat and cool the buildings; this strategy usually involves tight insulation in walls, floors, ceilings, and windows, allowing for passive solar heat, and the purchase of energy-efficient appliances. Dequaire (2012) reminds us that there are no standard definitions for "low-energy building," passive houses, or what counts as energy-efficient. Is a building energy-efficient if the windows are built and shipped from a different continent, or built using an energy-intensive process? At what point does the efficiency count? In TREE, the architects adopted a formalized passive house standard design that is presented by the Passivhaus Institut in Darmstadt, Germany. Passivhaus "provides a universally applicable set of requirements for energy efficiency, including its own certification scheme" (378). Widely adopted in Germany and Austria, it is a widely used standard across the European Union. TREE contains seven houses that meet the strict Passivhaus Certification.

One of the driving forces in EVI history was the need to raise money to pay for various aspects of the project, such as the land debt and cost overruns during various construction phases. In the case of TREE, ten additional households were added to the project in order to make the neighborhood affordable. This last-minute deviation from the standard 24–30 households because of financial shortcomings created new challenges for TREE, including changes in building codes and last-minute decision-making during an already stressful period. In the midst of these rapid changes, some families felt the project was getting too big, too fast, and despite the emphasis in cohousing that participants are active in the construction of their community, some felt that they were powerless in the face of the community expansion. At the same time, several TREE families expressed enthusiasm for their new homes and the opportunity to create a sense of community at EVI.

The Village Association

The Village Association (VA) is another legal cooperative that consists of board members from the neighborhoods. It is designed to accommodate the sharing of resources between the three separate cohousing cooperatives; for

Table 3.4 Connection to others in the village and beyond (%)

	Very often	Often	Half the time	Occasionally	Seldom
How often do you attend your neighborhood meetings?	49.2	18.0	8.2	14.8	9.8
How often do you attend the Village Association meetings?	21.7	11.7	21.7	23.3	21.7
How often do you participate in leadership at EVI (e.g., process steering, finance committee, etc.)?	27.1	13.6	5.1	11.9	42.4
How often do you attend EVI board meetings?	3.4	1.7	3.4	8.5	83.1
How often do you attend other miscellaneous meetings? Describe the meetings below.	22.8	26.3	8.8	17.5	24.6
How often do you participate in your neighborhood meals?	20.0	28.3	11.7	21.7	18.3
How often do you participate in village meals?	17.0	22.0	20.3	22.0	18.6
How often do you participate in general neighborhood or community work?	11.7	40.0	23.3	20.0	5.0

example, after the SONG incorporated, the VA assumed joint ownership of the road, the pond, and a small piece of land between the two neighborhoods called the Crux. The VA functions as an umbrella group to facilitate the sharing and billing of common expenses as well as to create guidelines and bylaws for the three neighborhoods. Some residents find the VA to be bureaucratic and represent one more set of meetings to attend, while others argue that the Village Association will be the glue that holds together the original envisioned five planned neighborhoods.

Growing food at EcoVillage at Ithaca

Growing food was a central theme of the ecological village, and the ability to grow food for itself continues to be highlighted in the project. Thus West Haven Farm and Kestrel Perch Berry Farm are two signature features of EVI.

The organic West Haven Farm on the land has a 99-year lease on ten acres from the EVI, Inc. nonprofit and is operated by a FROG household. The farm is organized as a community-supported agriculture (CSA), where residents and members of the larger Ithaca community can purchase a summer vegetable "share" at the beginning of the season. A share consists of a quantity of fruits and vegetables that are harvested from the farm during share pick-up day. Throughout the summer, shareholders are able to pick up their ration of vegetables from the farm. The advantage of a CSA is that participants share the risks and benefits of farming during the season: if there is a good year, participants pick up more vegetables; if the season is less productive, shareholders receive fewer vegetables. The farm grows organic vegetables such as kale, spinach, carrots, beets, potatoes, onions, leeks, peppers, eggplants, and tomatoes. They grow herbs, flowers, and organic strawberries and raspberries. By 2014, organic apples and peaches were grown at the farm. The CSA vegetable boxes are picked up at two locations: West Haven Barn on Tuesdays and Fall Creek on Wednesdays. A full share (or standard share) can be bought for $600 or on a sliding scale between $504 and $696 for the 2016 season. Half shares cost $348, or on a sliding scale between $300 to $396. This is one of the many ways West Haven Farm makes its resources available to a wide range of community members. In fact, I volunteered at the farm throughout my fieldwork and witnessed the backbreaking work of growing organic food on a small family farm. And despite the real physical exhaustion and financial uncertainty inherent in farming, I observed the West Haven farmers to be dedicated, compassionate, and generous in the Ithaca and EcoVillage community. West Haven Food is literally grown with love.

The farm also serves as one of the educational components of the nonprofit. For many residents the organic farm represents an ecological feature of the EVI project, though many families still purchased their groceries at the local chain grocery store. Nonetheless, many households are proud of the farm and the opportunity it presents for residents to feel connected to nature. The farm is privately owned, but neighbors treat it as their own, and the farmers generously supply the community with bushels of zucchinis and beets. During one of the farm's early summers, excess tomatoes about to be lost to the first winter frost were canned in the FROG Common House by a group of residents. The canned tomatoes supplied the Common House meals with organic tomatoes for the winter. The farmers also rely on volunteer residents to help during busy times of the summer, or when one of the farmers is injured. During a season when deer were ravaging the vegetables, the farm obtained permission to shoot the deer; the meat was distributed to those who wanted it. Afterwards, a fundraiser was organized by a neighbor to raise money for a large fence. The sense of community that EVI creates fosters neighbors to generously give their time and money to each other.

Kestrel Perch Berry Farm is a U-pick CSA owned and farmed by a SONG resident. U-pick farms allow participating members to pick their own berries from the bushes, then pay for them as they leave the field. As a CSA, Kestrel Perch Berry Farm offers shares they call "flex" shares. For $175 members can pick a variety of berries for 12–13 weeks from June through September. The farm includes strawberries, raspberries, red and black currants, gooseberries, blueberries, and elderberries. Like West Haven, the berry farm offers low-income households a discounted membership; individuals can share their CSA membership and the berry-picking. In addition, working memberships allow individuals or teams to volunteer for 17 hours before picking season in lieu of paying for a full membership. The farm offers residents and non-residents an opportunity to learn about berry farming, volunteer, and support a local farmer. In return, the berry farmer cheerfully shares the bounty of her work with the wider Ithaca community.

Peoples and cultures of EcoVillage

The community (FROG, SONG, and TREE) is primarily white and upper-middle class. A survey in 2014 was distributed electronically to 151 residents of the project; only 74 responses were received. The continuous flow of residents moving out or new families joining the project means it is hard to keep track of the specific demographics of the community. As far as I know, there has never been a systematic tracking of who has been a member of the community, why they joined, and why people leave. As I scheduled an interview with a family who had lived in one of the neighborhoods for more than ten years, but was now moving out, I was invited to join an exit interview. This, to my knowledge, was the first wave of exit interviews being conducted in the project. I determined that most residents were upper-middle class from an internal survey of residents that was conducted during my stay in the community as well as data from the 74 surveys completed in 2014. Income was perhaps the hardest data to collect. The community is diverse in many areas except race and ethnicity. According to a report, in 2012 there were

> … 15 percent people of color, with 10 adults and 16 kids who identify as other than Anglo. This is in contrast to the overall Tompkins County

population, which has 20 percent non-White population (although the city of Ithaca has 33 percent non-White residents.) Interestingly, couples tend to be mixed-race, and there are some adopted children of color. Most people of color come from an Asian or Latino background, with very few African Americans. **Pros:** Diversity of various sorts is considered a plus at EVI, and it has been well achieved in some areas, such as age range, spiritual background, disabilities, and range of jobs. Overall there is a culture of acceptance, and interest in embracing differences, although of course this is not always practiced as well as it could be. **Cons:** It has been harder to achieve a range of income levels and racial diversity, with especially few African Americans. Representation of different sexual preferences is also lower currently than in the general population. **Lessons Learned:** Creating a well-functioning, diverse community is quite difficult. Use of the self-development model has meant that the village is primarily accessible to people who can afford to purchase a market-rate house. This tends to exclude not only low-income people, but some racial minorities who have less access to capital. There are also long-standing tensions in some circles between people who are seen as "environmentalists" and people who are seen as promoting social justice. There is an active study circle in the village that is working to bridge this gap. In the future, it is hoped that some rental housing in TREE (both at market-rate and subsidized) will help to encourage more diversity. At the same time, diversity is generally embraced by the village as a worthy goal, and this value helps to build a high level of acceptance.

(Walker 2012: 23)

Other forms of diversity exist. There are lesbian and gay members; the ages of residents range from over 80 years to newborn; Jewish and Christian festivals such as Hanukkah and Easter are celebrated, as well as summer solstice. Some home gardens are adorned with miniature Buddha statues. A variety of professionals have lived in the neighborhood, ranging from elementary and high school teachers, lawyers, doctors, university professors, as well as full-time parents, writers, and programmers. There are also retired households, and at least one household where the adult was supported by her family and did not need to work.

Table 3.5 Ethnic/racial diversity (%)

Asian	1	1.35
African American	0	0
Caucasian	53	71.62
Hispanic	0	0
South Asian	0	0
Mixed Race	"Irish/Pakistani," "Puerto Rican/Caucasian"	2.70
Other	"Russian Jew," "European," "identify as 'human' only"	
No response	15	20.27

Several of the early participants from the Global Walk, and the first planning stages of EVI, envisioned a community that would address concerns of class, social, and environmental injustice. Those households left early in the project when it became clear that affordability would not be a priority. Early participants thought the project would be an effort to change the way we think about democracy, cooperation, power, and material needs. They wanted the project to be multicultural because that would make living there more holistic in the sense that all walks of life would be included. Having a community with a mix of different ages, races, ethnic backgrounds, and abilities was desirable. This ideal was reflective of the national trend for multicultural programs that sprang up in university departments, business-training programs, and in community centers during the early 1990s. Participants did not want EcoVillage to be an upper-middle-class white community on a hill overlooking the urban center. Some potential residents were concerned about being perceived as a gated community, a model that also became fashionable in the 1990s in the US and abroad (Caldeira 2000).

The demographics of EVI impacted how the community functioned. For example, families where two adults had to work outside the home did not have as much discretionary time to attend meetings and participate in community functions as families where one person worked part-time. At the same time, residents who did not work, either because they were retired or were supported by other means, expressed that they did not want the expectation to be the caregiver to their neighbors' children or do unequal community work just because they stayed home and did not have children. The influence of work is a significant factor to understand how the community functions. For example, if decisions about spending are made at a meeting and you are unable to attend, your missing input could have a real impact on your comfort level. I observed

Table 3.6 Gender identity (%)

Female	61.7
Gender-neutral	0.0
Male	36.7
Trans-gender	0.0
Gender non-conforming, biological female	1.7

Table 3.7 Sexual orientation (%)

Bisexual	6.7
Gay	1.7
Heterosexual	81.7
Lesbian	3.3
Other	6.7

"Under different socialization, who knows?", "I am in a committed heterosexual relationship. I believe all human beings are pansexual", Queer, pansexual

meetings where families with less wealth felt pressured to be silent, or humiliated because raising concerns of affordability would "out" their economic status and, in some incidences, breed long-lasting resentment.

The community

> Neighborhood Symbols: a place forming a circle around the central fountain where each neighborhood could contribute a statue, which symbolizes the essence of their presence in the village (for example, the Iroquois used various animals such as the bear and turtle as symbols for the different clans within the tribe). This circle of symbols would provide a garland of mascots, and symbolize the unique unity made from the diversity of each neighborhood (EcoVillage Planning Council).

Apart from the physical features of the neighborhood, a multitude of experiences and concepts were observed that exemplified ways that residents felt a sense of community. Two prominent concepts include the prevalence of trust among neighbors and the practice of creating rituals.

Trust is a powerful motivation in EVI. In a variety of situations residents trust "the process" and believe in the goodwill of their neighbors and leaders such that few neighbors asked for qualifications, or an application, when agreeing to hire a fellow neighbor for an important paid community job. The open-ended questions I posed during interviews often reflected my curiosity about hired positions and the payment of salaries, to which residents responded that they either had not thought about it or were not concerned with such issues. Often residents in SONG said they did not have time or energy to raise questions, or do the required work that would provide alternatives.

During two separate interviews participants were critical of my curiosity. Few residents questioned how certain paid neighbors continued to be employed by the community, or that the community failed to monitor obvious conflicts of interest that often involved large sums of money. Many residents were unaware of where their monthly fees to the neighborhood were deposited and how the money was used. When I asked about this silence over money management, participants either declined to answer, or felt that those who were paid worked hard and they did not want to criticize them or appear suspicious of their neighbors.

Extensive observation revealed that most residents shied away from doubting and questioning decisions made by the community or its informal leaders. A few people I interviewed, however, were willing to share their thoughts, but only unofficially. Participants asked me to stop recording when they mentioned sensitive issues that related to directly criticizing or pointing out a neighbor's shortcomings. With the recorder turned off and my notebook set aside, participants would continue to tell me, in a hushed secretive tone, of things that were left unsaid. When asked why they were hesitant to speak openly about these conflicts and tensions, those participants confessed that there was an unspoken rule against it and that they did not want to either hurt their neighbor's feelings or be ostracized from the community. Ironically, although residents often felt they were alone in this opinion, several of their neighbors shared similar sentiments, but almost always off the record. This counters the claim that the community fosters openness and participatory democracy because residents often felt hesitant to voice their opinions or question the status quo.

Another example of the lack of public objection and trusting "the process" occurred during the development of the SONG. Initially the FROG residents who offered to develop the construction process refused to do so, stating that they did not feel qualified. Later, however, they came back with a proposal that was readily accepted by the SONG, despite the lack of qualifications and experience to be development managers. At a meeting soon after the proposal was accepted, a pay increase was requested and granted with little resistance. As a group, the community supported their neighbors; yet during interviews individuals voiced concerns that they felt isolated in their discomfort, but said that perhaps they needed to have more trust in their neighbors and trust in the ability of the group to make wise decisions. I often heard that the wisdom of the group is greater than that of an individual, or that the sum of the whole is greater than any of its parts. However, a few prospective members dropped out of the group because they did not like the unspoken inability to voice concerns about neighbors.

A second observable pattern in the community that was an integral part of creating a sense of community was the prevalence of rituals. Several events, from birthing to birthday parties, and job transitions to seasonal changes, are celebrated through rituals. These were often joyous occasions: my favorite was the mid-meal thanking of the cook team that began with a light tapping on the table and ended with a loud "yay cooks!" Each meeting in the community— FROG, SONG, Board, or VA[7]—often began with some form of personal sharing. The most common and simplest form of personal sharing is by passing a "talking" stick. Hilda, an enthusiastic member of the SONG and an avid supporter of the talking stick, maintains that the talking stick is a Native American tradition that allows the holder of the stick to speak while others in the circle listen.

> The neighborhood meeting is about to start. Two volunteer facilitators, who always seem to volunteer, begin reading the agenda: item one, personal sharing. A standard ritual in FROG and more so in SONG, personal sharing is a chance for residents to talk about "where they are at" in life, in the day, wherever. Wherever more than three are gathered, there is personal sharing. It is a ritual that reinforces the communal effort to get to know each other. During personal sharing we say more than simply make an announcement; it is about sharing a part of our day or life that lets our neighbors know something special about us or something deeper and more private than is easily accessible. A variety of topics are raised: coming out as bisexual, exhaustion with cranky children, dissatisfaction with a new job,

excitement about the upcoming spring, anxiety about a medical exam, relationship breakups, etc. We nod and show non-verbal signs of understanding, compassion, and solidarity. It is humbling to share someone's tribulations or to be trusted with personal details. When a neighbor takes a disproportionate amount of time and sounds whiny, we wait patiently as our flexibility is stretched. Awkwardly, but what most of us admit understandably, the openness and generosity of our listening and nodding seems strained and nearing the artificial. Some are genuinely concerned and show signs of encouragement to the speaker, the rest are becoming impatient. Finally, one of the facilitators, in his position of power, announces the need to watch our time in order to complete the three-hour meeting—a polite way to silence the speaker and move the talking stick along. The tension in the room is thick; it is hard to know what the community is all about. Should we give more time and really listen to each other's lives, or be satisfied with small sound bites of acceptable daily struggles? What about the meeting agenda? Why is personal sharing so necessary when we meet to talk about neighborhood business? But isn't it important to know where each of us is "at" before we try to come to a consensus? Isn't the fact that we care about each other what makes the community rich, special, and different than most neighborhoods?

In a spontaneous informal interview, Emil, who is retired, tells me that he likes the meetings and the personal sharing; it is a great way to get to know neighbors. Amy, a busy woman who works at home, doesn't like personal sharing and refuses to attend the first part of meetings. She'd prefer to get down to business and not take time away from her already full schedule to listen to someone talk about their "issues." Another resident found the occasional crying and outbursts at meetings irritating: "these meetings should not be psychotherapy; they should just stick to the issues." Halfway through my research I discovered that several residents practiced Harvey Jankins's Re-evaluative Counseling (or co-counseling), a practice that encourages discharging emotional energy with a partner (Jackins 1983). A few other residents found the decision-making process undemocratic, arguing that consensus is the tyranny of the minority (see Nader 1969, and Table 3.4). According to one resident, "there have been times when I have felt the group was held hostage by consensus."

The third way I observed how residents create a sense of community was through the use of leisure. Much of the data used in the analysis that follows came from my observations and conversations about leisure and personal growth. The emphasis on consumption of leisure is in contrast to the emphasis on the production of the community. That is, many residents are not actively engaged in producing an ecovillage on a daily basis; rather, they create community through consuming the spaces (walking trails, buildings, etc.) and experiences (community meals, meetings, work teams) that create community and connect them to nature. The weekly Saturday morning, 5:50 a.m. trip to the CSA I made with a neighbor to harvest vegetables on the farm is an exception to the disconnection between creating an ecovillage and merely enjoying the built-in structures. An active resident and I spent our Saturday mornings picking beets and washing spinach, which helped the farmers prepare for market, but also gave us a chance to get to know each other.

Leisure in EVI was described to me in ways that made the concept synonymous with creating community. A middle-aged resident of FROG described the land debt and its impact on the neighborhoods in terms of leisure.

> One was the costs of the land debt have been crippling to people's leisure and to their creativity. And that is a big cloud that has drained energy daily, every day of the project. There isn't a meeting that isn't overshadowed by how driven we are to build neighborhoods to pay off debts and to pay off our mortgages and whatever. I mean people just don't have very much leisure, that makes it very hard to build an ecovillage. So the cost of the land and the fact that it had to be borrowed to do, is devastating to the project.
>
> (Christopher)

While only occasionally mentioned publicly, several residents admitted that they hire housecleaners to clean their home and gardeners to maintain their small yards. The women, who did not live in the community, drive up the hill to work; they can be glimpsed walking from one house to the next cleaning their usual houses. Occasionally, an email is sent out asking if other neighbors would like their house cleaned so the women can get more work when they come to the village.

According to archived documents, in the summer of 1993 several board members resigned because affordability was removed from the bylaws and it became clear that comfort and leisure would take priority over affordability. This division represents what Harvey (1996) describes as the separation between the environmental justice movement and the "Big Ten" environmental groups such as the Sierra Club and Friends of the Earth. In theory some residents want the connection to nature, but a very specific nature that is often manicured and maintained by someone else.

Members of an earlier board of EVI who represented environmental justice activists rejected the idea of working within the status quo to achieve their goal. They envisioned EVI as an attempt to radically change the social and political structure of community and environment. They disagreed with "broadly 'bourgeois' attempts at co-optation and absorption into a middle-class and professional-based resistance to that impeccable economic logic of environmental hazards that the circulation of capital defines" (Harvey 1996: 159). For these earlier participants and some current residents who struggle to raise these questions within the confines of the community, the ideas of living a middle-class lifestyle and fighting for the environment are thought of as antithetical. Yet, for others, EVI demonstrates that a middle-class lifestyle where the environment is enhanced is possible. The initial proposal of EVI explained that "even those who know there are solutions to the environmental crises we face tend to think they are going to be enormously costly, unimaginably difficult, and require extreme personal sacrifice" (Bokaer 1991: 1).

Participants appreciated that EVI made recycling, composting, and sharing in the village easy and convenient. They also expressed gratitude for the surrounding land that the EVI, Inc. board gives them exclusive access to use. These were the things that residents felt connected them to each other and to nature. Neighborhood places that create a sense of community do not necessarily need to be actively produced by residents; these spaces are predesigned. It is not necessary to be involved in the production of the CSA farm by working with the resident farmers; the community is designed to allow residents to consume farm-fresh fruits and vegetables, by purchasing a CSA share or simply buying a home in a community that comes with a CSA. I often worked on Saturday mornings on the farm and felt good about watching my food grow and talking with some of the farm workers, many of whom did not live in EVI. A sense of community, connection with nature, and growing food thrive inside and outside of EVI.

Methodology

I came to study EcoVillage at Ithaca in part to protest the assumption that as a Zimbabwean national studying anthropology in the United States, I would study at home—my home. While there is nothing wrong with Zimbabweans doing fieldwork in Zimbabwe (something we desperately need), like other colleagues, I was interested in a culture different from my own. Laura Nader's (1969) "studying up" inspired me to explore a different side of sustainability and US environmentalism. EVI embodied three interconnected sites of inquiry: first, the community is an upper-middle-class white community, a group seldom explored in anthropology. Second, the community is attempting to create a village, as described in early anthropological ethnography. If the community was using anthropological work in non-Western countries to create a "village" in the US, perhaps a study of EcoVillage would reveal how anthropology has contributed to romanticizing village life. Upon meeting me on my first day, a resident excitedly said, "I never thought of us as natives, but I guess we are" (Karin). Third, the physical location apart from the larger Ithaca community served as a natural physical and social boundary. Initially this somewhat bounded community represented a manageable group; those who lived within the boundary would define the limits of my research. It also reminded me of a green gated community where trees and meadows replaced concrete barriers and iron gates.

Participant observation[8]

I moved into the home of one of the first EVI residents in May 2001 and immediately attended a community dinner in the Common House, where I was introduced as the village anthropologist. I joined the cook team[9] as a way to

Table 3.8 Community work (%)

Question	<2 hrs	2–4 hrs	4–6 hrs	6–8 hrs	>8 hrs
How many hours per week does your neighborhood expect you to work in the community?	3.3	95.0	0.0	1.7	0.0
How many hours do you estimate you actually work each week?	25.9	53.5	10.3	3.5	6.9

informally meet residents. I attended a variety of meetings, including neighborhood FROG meetings, EVI, Inc., board meetings, various work team meetings, SONG meetings, the Village Association, and a number of small committee meetings, such as the walkways improvement committee, sauna committee, and Common House sharing committee. Residents did not contribute evenly to the required two to four work hours per week, leaving some overworked, upset, or resentful.

My attendance at the meetings was to get to know residents, observe how the community is structured and functions, how consensus is achieved, and who participates in the decision-making process. I took detailed scratch notes (Sanjek 1990) during the meetings on the agenda, but also on people's reaction. I also identified follow-up questions to be posed during a later interview with an individual. When I returned in 2014, I once again moved into FROG, then later SONG. During both stays I volunteered at West Haven Farm. I harvested vegetables, prepared produce for market—polishing red peppers and washing spinach—and helped with miscellaneous projects when volunteers were solicited. I babysat when it was more important that a parent participate in a meeting than for me to observe it (sometimes the parent only wanted to stay until consensus was reached, then return to their children while I returned to the meeting), and I conducted background research for various community projects. Occasionally, I substituted for a resident who was unable to do their weekly work team responsibility. I helped organize the tenth anniversary celebration and served as an occasional community mediator.[10] During the planning and building of the SONG, I attended town board meetings and hearings in the city of Ithaca. As the SONG was beginning to take form, I attended the meetings of the planning, architecture review, alternative energy, Common House design, and finance committees, as well as the meetings of the newly forming Village Association. My goal was not simply to observe, but to be an active contributing member of the community. Residents shared many hours of their time with me, and I appreciated the chance to give back to them.

Survey

In 2014 I returned to EVI and conducted participant observation as well as designed and distributed a survey with the help of residents. We called the survey the EcoVillage Cultural, Demographic Survey and Census, recognizing

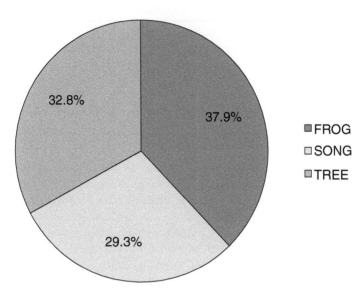

Figure 3.4 Distribution of neighborhood residents.
Source: Author.

the need for the community to conduct a regular census so residents can identify patterns and trends. It is hard to know how much turnover exists in the community and at what rate families move in and out. The census was tested then distributed to an email list of 151 names. Appropriately 50 percent ($n = 74$) of people responded. The respondents were almost equally from each of the three neighborhoods.

Archival data

Information on the history of the project was gleaned by reading hundreds of pages of archived data. This data was often unorganized and amorphous. I volunteered to archive some of the early documents, including the first meeting minutes of the community. Although the recorded history was abundant, it contained holes that proved hard to fill. These holes resulted in more unanswered questions than answers.[11] Specifically, financial details such as who was paid and where funds originated were difficult to trace. I found it especially difficult to garner information on how the neighborhoods were legally structured, how property was purchased, and the relationship between the nonprofit and specific individuals. How original decisions were made was also not available in the documents gleaned.

Interviews

Formal interviews began in June 2001. Through snowball sampling I was referred to various residents and former residents, most of whom were eager to talk to me about their positive and negative experiences. Some participants explicitly wanted to tell me of their disappointments and bitterness towards the project. Many participants wanted to be a "fly on the wall" during my interviews with their neighbors, hoping to get a glimpse of what other community members thought, but did not discuss openly at community meetings. Others wanted to know if they were the only ones. Frequently participants wanted to know what I thought of the community. This was surprisingly complicated to answer; by mid-June my comfort level in the community was increasing—I had fallen in love with the place and the people. I could see why it was attractive to families as well as singles. But, at the same time, I was critical and observant. I needed more time to answer this basic question, and as I later discovered, distance. I tried to answer these questions as honestly and openly as I could.

I began the interview process with my immediate neighbors, and as other residents saw me interviewing, they asked to be included in my research. The succession of the interviews was random and I made an effort to interview as many community members as were willing to talk with me. In 2001–2003 I interviewed every adult member of the FROG. Before each interview I asked participants to sign an informed consent form; we each kept a copy. The interviews were primarily audio-recorded (cassettes in 2001 and digital in 2014). Some were not recorded, either because the participant preferred not to be recorded or because it was a rare conversation where the recorder was not with me. I asked a variety of open-ended questions about the environment and the community, specifically why they moved to EVI, what they saw as the project mission, how they expressed concern for the environment while living in EVI, and how they experienced a sense of community. Finally, participants were asked what they found rewarding and challenging. The interviews themselves were open-ended; they evolved over time and would resume after hours or days of interruptions, or they transpired randomly when a participant had something interesting they wanted to share with me. Open-ended questions also allowed residents to talk about the aspects of the ecovillage project that were important to them. When they did not know what to talk about, I posed my prepared questions. Residents often deviated from these and directed the conversation to what they wanted me to know about the project and about their daily life in the community.

The interviews took place in people's homes, in the Common House sitting room, on long morning hikes, while preparing a Common House meal, while relaxing by the pond, or at a restaurant or café in Ithaca. Because most residents were very busy with community and family obligations, the interviews were generally conducted while we did something else together. They lasted anywhere from 30 minutes to over six hours in some cases, the average being two and a half hours. Informal group interviews occurred when neighbors or friends spontaneously sat together and talked about the community: I would ask if I could record the conversation, take out my recorder, and we would continue the conversation. The majority of the people I interviewed between 2001 and 2014 lived, or used to live, in one of the EVI neighborhoods. I interviewed the two architects of FROG, two West Hill neighbors, and three local community members. Altogether I gathered over 120 audio recordings on 90-minute cassettes or digital files of interviews, residents' stories, community meetings, informal discussion sessions, and ritual ceremonies.

I had not intended to focus on consumption and how it relates to environmentalism; these were topics that my data revealed. Residents frequently talked about the importance of being surrounded by nature not because they identified themselves as environmentalists, but because they liked nature. They also talked about the community in terms of its contradictions and mentioned the difficulty of being a model when their own behavior did not reflect that model. Participants who left talked about anger and deception, while those who lived in the community described their struggle to negotiate and explain their daily practices of consumption in light of trying to live simply. In general, residents were happy with their decision to live in EVI and emphasized the many positive experiences of the community, most noticeably that they were living a less wasteful and less isolated lifestyle than they would have otherwise.

Role of the anthropologist

I consider myself an environmentalist and try to live a lifestyle that is both simple and politically engaged. I am an avid cyclist and use my bike primarily for transportation. I recycle neurotically and have composted for many years. Some of the furniture in my 800-square-foot apartment in North Oakland was picked up from the curb in my Westside Binghamton neighborhood during graduate school. I find it easy to become overwhelmed with global environmental problems and often feel, like many residents in EVI, that composting is an insignificant act; yet it is a small contribution and every little bit counts. I am an "outdoorsy" person and enjoy being in nature for picnics, hikes, and cross-country skiing. I try to consume less, would buy all organic food if I could afford it, and prefer to support small local businesses, although I admit that this is not always possible. I now live in a city that allows me to walk, bike, and live without a car, although many residents in my community drive frequently and generously let me use their car when I need one. Like residents in EVI, I value community, knowing my neighbors, and sharing meals. My neighbors and I grow food in our front and backyards, took the fences down between us, and raise chickens together. I seek a wide range of multinational friendships as part of what makes my life rich.

Although I have spent over 20 years in the United States, I grew up on what might be described as a small family farm in Zimbabwe, just outside the city of Mutare. Before going to Hartzell boarding school, my parents drove my siblings and me into town for work or school. I grew up in a modern home surrounded by beautiful tropical, edible landscape which my mother planted and worked at tirelessly. We, my mother mainly, grew most of our own food: staples like corn for mealie-meal, sweet potatoes, peanuts, squash and pumpkin, fresh vegetables and herbs. As children, my siblings and I spent many hours plowing with oxen, picking stones from the field, and husking maize. We had many fruit trees and often sold the excess mangos, bananas, papaya, guavas, passion fruit, or citrus at a local market, or by the side of the road. My parents raised chickens, which we slaughtered on Sundays, ducks, and occasionally a few turkeys. On special holidays we slaughtered one of the many goats or sheep. We had two oxen and a cow, and during my childhood, a small calf we named "America" was born. I grew up with a few neighbors half a mile down the road from whom we occasionally borrowed butter, and with whom we carpooled, or shared heavy equipment. I felt safe and had a lot of opportunity to play in nature.

My grandmother and her family had much less. Mbuya lived in a rural village, without electricity or running water, with a genuine composting toilet, and she works hard to produce the food she needs for survival. I can imagine her disbelief if I were to tell her that families in the US spend up to $4,000 to purchase a toilet that does not flush. After carrying water on my head from a well, I know the luxury of running water. I have also experienced the need to compost, not because it is trendy, but because it is necessary to grow food one cannot buy at a local chain store, and where else would you put unneeded vegetation? I know that living simply is not always a choice, but in many parts of the world, it is the result of inadequate resources such as decent shelter, food, and medical care.

In some ways, I am an outsider to a community like EVI. I planned to live in the community for only a brief period of time and had no intention of purchasing a home there. Except for an adopted child who moved out soon after I arrived, there were no other African Americans living in EVI. Just before I left, another adopted African American child became part of the SONG. I believe strongly in public access, public transportation, public education, affordable housing, and socialized medicine, and I question the sustainability of capitalism. Yet I share the love of nature and have an appreciation for what participants in EVI are trying to create. My experience of, and belief in, combining nature and community are often conflicted and challenged in the same ways that residents of EVI are challenged.

I fell in love with EVI when I arrived and continued to enjoy living there. During my 21-month stay, my participants became my friends and I treasure those friendships still. Many residents asked what I felt about the community and if I would consider moving in. Occasionally a participant would tell me how important diversity was to her and that I would make living in EVI more diverse.

My race played a prominent role in my research simply because I offered the community the much desired diversity they sought. Rosalyn, a retired resident, expressed her concern for diversity.

I was really happy when [an Asian male] moved here. At least we have a Chinese person. I was delighted when [an Asian female] moved here. But somehow or other we have not been able to attract a Spanish family, an Afro-American family, an Indian family ... not Indian from India, but a Native American Indian family. Both of those [Asians] are in interracial marriages.... So obviously they're saying it's safe. I would imagine that we could attract an Afro-American-white Caucasian couple if we could find one ...

Rosalyn felt that non-white families did not move to the community because they felt it was not safe and because these families did not want to be diversity tokens. She felt strongly that the high cost of living was not a limiting factor to non-white families in the neighborhood.

ROSALYN: I can't even say [living in EVI presents] an economic barrier, because there are a lot of Afro-American professionals who can afford (EcoVillage), but they choose not to take it.

TENDAI: A lot of people say the reason we don't have more minorities is because the housing is too expensive.

ROSALYN: That's bullshit. Afro-American people, by and large, are not poor. There are a greater number of people among them that are poor. But hey! They are my professors. They're my doctors, they're my lawyers, and they're my accountants. They can afford to live here. Easily. And the same goes for the Spanish and the Native American. They're the psychologists. They're the teachers. We have teachers here.

I did not verify that in fact Rosalyn's accountant, professors, and doctor were African American. Aside from adopted children, I met very few African Americans in EVI throughout my fieldwork. Occasionally in public presentations, my presence represented the African American diversity that many residents felt was missing and perhaps made them feel exclusive. I often resented what felt like tokenism and attempted to either remove myself from those instances (by making it clear that I was a resident researcher) or I made a note to raise the issue in my writing. One participant complained that

the community is not diverse enough, there are virtually no minorities here, except people's adopted children.... I think there is plenty of diversity of religions from Jewish to Hindu to Buddhist to Christian, there is plenty of diversity. But not having blacks like you, not having equal access to this financially and in other ways is simply not fair.

(Lucy)

Many residents mentored and encouraged me with my fieldwork. Several participants who either had PhDs or considered themselves intellectuals gave me tips and practical advice on which themes would be good topics to write about, and where to publish articles about the community. At times I felt residents saw my work as a way to advertise the community to a broader audience and occasionally residents were apprehensive about how I would present the community. In other instances participants wanted me to tell their side of the EVI story. I tried to leave out the gossip, rumors, and sensational topics and focus on constructive data, both from those within and without the project. I attempted to make it very clear at the beginning of each interview that my intention was to write a book and to produce scholarly work from the data they gave me. I gained informed consent and assured each participant that I would do my best to keep their identity confidential. I have tried to be informative and critical in areas residents suggested and I felt would help the community realize their goals of ecological and community sustainability.

The majority of participants encouraged me to be critical; after all, they wanted an outsider's view of the neighborhoods and appreciated the extensive time I stayed in the community to try to understand how it really functioned, compared with other scholars who merely presented interview questions or visited only occasionally. They also appreciated the fact that I was giving back to the community through volunteering and working as a regular member.

Notes

1 I was only aware of one couple at EVI who went on to walk across Europe and Asia.
2 For example, every owner-resident of FROG, SONG, and TREE is automatically a member of the VA, and residents of the cohousing communities were automatically charged an annual membership to EVI, Inc. This mandatory charge was made voluntary in 2015.
3 www.centerfortransformativeaction.org/.
4 Data for this estimate was gleaned from Walker (2012).
5 Residents purchase shares of the community instead of a house per se because the community collectively owns the physical structure of the house. Residents own the inside but need to consult the community if they want to change any permanent features of the home or do renovations or install major changes such as dishwashers and air conditioners. I was aware of only a handful of residents who did not consult the community when they made changes to their home.
6 Because the EVCC co-op owns the outside of the homes, it is also responsible for upkeep and maintenance.
7 I did not attend a TREE meeting and thus have no observed data.
8 During my 2001–2003 fieldwork, the first of five planned neighborhoods had been completed. While residents of the first neighborhood had lived in their homes for approximately five years, the second neighborhood was being developed and constructed. Although I attempt to include as many experiences from both the first and second neighborhoods, the majority of my data comes from residents in the first neighborhood.
9 The cook team is one of five official work teams that is recognized by the FROG. The other work teams include: outdoor, maintenance, dish washing, network or geek and the finance team. While almost everyone (I noticed four adults who did not work on an official work team, although two of those adults did other things to help the community) does the required two to four hours per week, there is no penalty for not

participating. Some residents proposed hiring neighbors to do their share of the required community work.

10 As a trained mediator at the Community Dispute Resolution Center (CDRC), I occasionally filled in when one of the regular mediation partners was absent.

11 Former residents gave me their collected files on the history of EVI development.

References

Adams, William M. 1990. *Green Development: Environment and Sustainability in the Third World*. New York: Routledge.

Appadurai, Arjun. 1986a. Introduction: Commodities and the Politics of Value. In: *The Social Life of Things: Commodities in Cultural Perspective*. A. Appadurai, ed. pp. 3–63. Cambridge: Cambridge University Press.

Appadurai, Arjun. 1986b. *The Social Life of Things: Commodities in Cultural Perspective*. Cambridge: Cambridge University Press.

Athanasiou, Tom. 1996. The Age of Greenwashing. *Capitalism, Nature, Socialism*, 7(1), 1–37.

Bokaer, J. 1991. *A proposal called EcoVillage at Ithaca: A Model for Land Conservation and Sustainable Neighborhood Development*. EVI website.

Bokaer, Joan. 1997. Intertwined Lives. *The EcoVillage Newsletter*, 7, 4.

Bourdieu, Pierre. 1984. *Distinction: A Social Critique of the Judgment of Taste*. Cambridge, MA: Harvard University Press.

Brosius, Peter J. 1999. Analysis and Interventions: Anthropological Engagements with Environmentalism. *Current Anthropology*, 40(3), 277–309.

Brown, Lester R. 2001. *Eco-Economy: Building an Economy for the Earth*. New York and London: W.W. Norton.

Bullard, Robert D. 1990. *Dumping in Dixie: Race, Class, and Environmental Quality*. Boulder, CO: Westview Press.

Bullard, Robert D. 1994. *Unequal Protection: Environmental Justice and Communities of Color*. San Francisco, CA.

Caldeira, Teresa P.R. 1996. Fortified Enclaves: The New Urban Segregation. *Public Culture*, 8, 303–328.

Caldeira, Teresa P.R. 2000. *City of Walls: Crime, Segregation, and Citizenship in São Paulo*. Berkeley, Los Angeles, London: University of California Press.

Carrier, James, and Josiah McC. Heyman. 1997. Consumption and Political Economy. *Journal of the Royal Anthropological Institute*, 3, 355–73.

Castree, Noel, and Bruce Braun. 1998. *Remaking Reality: Nature at the Millennium*. London and New York: Routledge.

Cronon, William, ed. 1996. *Uncommon Ground: Toward Reinventing Nature*. New York and London: W.W. Norton & Co.

Crumley, Carole L. 2001. *New Directions in Anthropology and Environment: Intersections*. Walnut Creek, CA: Altamira Press.

Davis, Mike. 1998. *Ecology of Fear: Los Angeles and the Imagination of Disaster*. New York: Metropolitan Books.

Dequaire, X. 2012. Passivhaus as a Low-Energy Building Standard: Contribution to a Typology. *Energy Efficiency*, 5(3), 377–391.

Descola, Philippe. 1996. Constructing Natures: Symbolic Ecology and Social Practice. In: *Nature and Society: Anthropological Perspectives*. P. Descola, ed. pp. 82–102. London and New York: Routledge.

Di Chiro, G. 1996. Nature as Community: The Convergence of Environment and Social Justice. In: *Uncommon Ground: Toward Reinventing Nature*. W. Cronon, ed. pp. 298–320. New York: W.W. Norton & Co.

Douglas, Mary, and Baron Isherwood. 1979. *The World of Goods*. New York: Routledge.

Durnbaugh, Donald F. 1997. Communitarian Societies in Colonial America. In: *America's Communal Utopias*. D.E. Pitzer, ed. pp. 14–36. Chapel Hill and London: University of North Carolina Press.

Erickson, Rita J. 1997. *"Paper or Plastic?": Energy, Environment, and Consumerism in Sweden and America*. Westport, CT: Praeger.

Escobar, Arturo. 1995. *Encountering Development: The Making and Unmaking of the Third World*. Princeton, NJ: Princeton University Press.

Escobar, Arturo. 1996. Constructing Nature: Elements for a Post-structural Political Ecology. In: *Liberation Ecologies*. pp. 46–68. London: Routledge.

Ehrlich, Paul R. 1968. *The Population Bomb*. New York: Ballantine Books.

FIC (Fellowship for Intentional Community). 2000. *Communities Directory: A Guide to Intentional Communities and Cooperative Living*. Ann Arbor: Sheridan Group.

Fortun, Kim. 2001. *Advocacy after Bhopal: Environmentalism, Disaster, New Global Orders*. Chicago: University of Chicago Press.

Foster, John Bellamy. 2002. *Ecology against Capitalism*. New York: Monthly Review Press.

Fotopoulos, Takis. 2000. The Limitations of Life-style Strategies: the Ecovillage "Movement" is NOT the Way towards a New Democratic Society. *Democracy & Nature*, 6(2), 287–308.

Friedman, Jonathan. 1994. *Consumption and Identity*. Chur, Switzerland: Harwood Academic Publishers.

Garreau, Joel. 1991. *Edge City: Life on the New Frontier*. New York: Doubleday.

Geddes, Patrick. 1979. *Civics as Applied Sociology*. London: Sociological Society by Macmillan.

Gregory, Steven. 1998. *Black Corona: Race and the Politics of Place in an Urban Community*. Princeton: Princeton University Press.

Guha, Ramachandra. 1989. Radical American Environmentalism and Wilderness Preservation: A Third World Critique. *Environmental Ethics*, 11(1), 71–83.

Gusterson, Hugh. 1996. *Nuclear Rites: A Weapons Laboratory at the End of the Cold War*. Berkeley and Los Angeles: University of California Press.

Hannigan, John. 1998. *Fantasy City: Pleasure and Profit in the Postmodern Metropolis*. London and New York: Routledge.

Haraway, Donna J. 1991. *Simians, Cyborgs, and Women: The Reinvention of Nature*. New York: Routledge.

Harding, Garrett. 1968. The Tragedy of the Commons. *Science*, 162, 1243–1248.

Harvey, David. 1996. *Justice, Nature and the Geography of Difference*. Cambridge, MA: Blackwell.

Hawken, Paul, Amory L. Lovins, and Hunter Lovins. 1999. *Natural Capitalism: Creating the Next Industrial Revolution*. Boston, New York, London: Little, Brown, and Co.

Hobart, Mark. 1993. *An Anthropological Critique of Development: The Growth of Ignorance*. New York: Routledge.

Howard, Ebenezer. 1902. *Garden Cities of Tomorrow*. London: S. Sonnenschein and Co., Ltd.

Jackins, Harvey. 1983. *The Reclaiming of Power*. Seattle: Rational Island Publishers.

Jackson, Kenneth T. 1985. *Crabgrass Frontier: The Suburbanization of the United States*. New York and Oxford: Oxford University Press.

Joseph, Miranda. 2002. *Against the Romance of Community*. Minneapolis and London: University of Minnesota Press.

Kempton, Willett, James S. Boster, and Jennifer A. Hartley. 1996. *Environmental Values in American Culture*. Boston: Massachusetts Institute of Technology.

Litfin, K.T. 2014. *Ecovillages: Lessons for Sustainable Community*. John Wiley & Sons.

Low, Setha M. 1996. The Anthropology of Cities: Imagining and Theorizing the City. *Annual Review of Anthropology*, 25, 383–409.

Low, Setha M. 2001. The Edge and the Center: Gated Communities and the Discourse of Urban Fear. *American Anthropologist*, 103(1), 45–58.

Lury, C. 1996. *Consumer Culture*. Cambridge: Polity.

Marcus, George, and M. Fischer. 1986. *Anthropology as Cultural Critique: An Experiment in the Human Sciences*. Chicago: University of Chicago Press.

Martin, Emily. 1998. Fluid Bodies, Managed Nature. In: *Remaking Reality: Nature at the Millennium*. B. Braun and N. Castree, eds. New York: Routledge.

McCamant, Kathryn, and Charles Durrett. 1994. *Cohousing: A Contemporary Approach to Housing Ourselves*. Berkeley, CA: Ten Speed Press.

McKenzie, Evan. 1994. *Privatopia: Homeowner Associations and the Rise of Residential Private Government*. New Haven and London: Yale University Press.

Meltzer, Graham. 2000. *Cohousing: Toward Social and Environmental Sustainability*. Dissertation, University of Queensland.

Melville, Keith. 1972. *Communes in the Counter Culture: Origins, Theories, Styles of Life*. New York: Morrow.

Merchant, Carolyn. 1980. The Death of Nature. San Francisco: Harper Row.

Miller, Daniel. 1995a. *Acknowledging Consumption: A Review of New Studies*. London and New York: Routledge.

Miller, Daniel. 1995b. Consumption and Commodities. *Annual Review of Anthropology*, 24, 141–161.

Milton, Kay, ed. 1996. *Environmentalism and Cultural Theory: Exploring the Role of Anthropology in Environmental Discourse*. New York: Routledge.

Mumford, Lewis. 1938. *The Culture of Cities*. New York: Harcourt, Brace, Jovanovich.

Nader, Laura. 1969. 'Up the Anthropologist': Perspectives Gained from Studying Up. In: *Reinventing Anthropology*. D. Hymes, ed. pp. 284–311. New York: Random House.

Naess, A. 1988. *Ecology, Community and Lifestyle*. Cambridge: Cambridge University Press.

O'Connor, Martin, ed. 1994. *Is Capitalism Sustainable? Political Economy and the Politics of Ecology*. New York and London: The Guilford Press.

Peet, Richard, and Michael Watts. 1996. *Liberation Ecologies: Environment, Development, Social Movements*. London and New York: Routledge.

Pellow, D.N. 2002. *Garbage Wars: The Struggle for Environmental Justice in Chicago*. Cambridge, MA: MIT Press.

Peluso, N.L. 1992. *Rich Forests, Poor People: Resource Control and Resistance in Java*. Berkeley, CA: University of California Press.

Peluso, N.L., and M. Watts. 2001. *Violent Environments*. Ithaca, NY: Cornell University Press.

Pepper, David. 1993. *Eco-Socialism: From Deep Ecology to Social Justice*. London and New York: Routledge.

Putnam, Robert D. 2000. *Bowling Alone: The Collapse and Revival of American Community*. New York: Touchstone.

Register, Richard. 1996. An Encounter with Tomorrow's Auto-crats: Ecological Cities

"Yes"; Electric Cars "No." In: *Culture Change*. www.culturechange.org/issue9/electric carsno.html: Auto-Free Times.

Ross, Andrew. 1999. *The Celebration Chronicles: Life, Liberty, and the Pursuit of Property Value in Disney's New Town*. New York: Ballantine Books.

Sanjek, R. 1990. *Fieldnotes: The Makings of Anthropology*. Ithaca, NY: Cornell University Press.

Sarkar, Saral. 1999. *Eco-Socialism or Eco-Capitalism? A Critical Analysis of Humanity's Fundamental Choices*. New York: Zed Books.

Shiva, Vandana. 1993. *Staying Alive: Women, Ecology, and Development*. London: Zed Books.

Shove, Elizabeth. 2003. *Comfort, Cleanliness and Convenience: The Social Organization of Normality*. Oxford and New York: Berg.

Smith, Neil. 1998a. Nature at the Millennium: Production and Re-Enchantment. In: *Remaking Reality: Nature at the Millennium*. B. Castree, ed. pp. 271–286. London and New York: Routledge.

Smith, Toby M. 1998b. *The Myth of Green Marketing: Tending Our Goats at the Edge of Apocalypse*. Toronto, Buffalo, London: University of Toronto Press, Inc.

Smith, R. 2013. Capitalism and the Destruction of Life on Earth: Six Theses on Saving the Humans. *Real-World Economics Review*, 64, 125–150.

Soper, Kate. 1996. Nature/'nature'. In: *FutureNatural: Nature, Science, Culture*. G. Robertson, et al., eds. London and New York: Routledge.

Sorkin, Michael, ed. 1992. *Variations on a Theme Park: The New American City and the End of Public Space*. New York: Hill and Wang.

Sponsel, Leslie E. 1997. The Master Thief: Gold Mining and Mercury Contamination in the Amazon. In: *Life and Death Matters: Human Rights and the Environment at the End of the Millennium*. B.R. Johnston, ed. pp. 99–127. Walnut Creek: AltaMira Press.

Szasz, A. 2007. *Shopping Our Way to Safety: How We Changed from Protecting the Environment to Protecting Ourselves*. Minneapolis: University of Minnesota Press.

Taylor, D.E. 2009. *The Environment and the People in American Cities, 1600s–1900s: Disorder, Inequality, and Social Change*. Durham, NC: Duke University Press.

Trainer, Ted. 1997. The Global Sustainability Crisis: Implications for Community. *International Journal of Social Economics*, 24(11), 1219–1240.

Tsing, Anna Lowenhaupt. 2001. Nature in the Making. In: *New Directions in Anthropology and Environment: Intersections*. C.L. Crumley, ed. pp. 3–23. Walnut Creek: Altamira.

Walker, Liz. 2005. *EcoVillage at Ithaca: Pioneering a Sustainable Culture*. Gabriola Island, BC: New Society Publishers.

Walker, L. 2012. *EcoVillage at Ithaca; Principles, Best Practices and Lessons Learned*. A Report to the EPA Climate Showcase Communities Grant.

Wolf, Eric. 1972. Ownership and Political Ecology. *Anthropology Quarterly*, 45, 201–205.

Zehner, O. 2012. *Green Illusions: The Dirty Secrets of Clean Energy and the Future of Environmentalism*. Lincoln: University of Nebraska Press.

4   Making community green

It is extremely important for me and my family not to feel isolated up here in this little weird enclave. The towns that surround us are pretty low-income for the most part. We have a lot of rural neighbors that are farmers and house trailer park folks; it can be easy to not have your family mix with people like that.

(Sandra)

[I appreciate] the fact that the kids could just run out and play. We lived in Manhattan so I knew people who could not go out to play by themselves until they were teenagers practically because it just wasn't a safe environment to send kids out unsupervised.

(Kevin)

Communities are spaces that can embody our expressions of social relationships. They are places where we feel comfortable—"at home"—or spaces we go back to or are exiled from. In that sense, community embodies the spaces, imagined through socially constructed or physical boundaries that represent how our lives are enmeshed within larger social processes. These complex and contested community spaces have been the focus of debates within the social sciences and continue to be the site of social and political struggle (Gregory 1998; Low 2000; Redfield 1962). Although the concept of community has been pervasive, new forms of community are raising old questions as well as new ones. As local and global expansion continues to produce new challenges that affect where we live and how we gain access to resources, spaces that once formed the framework for political action and social interaction are being reconfigured, recognized as problematic, and, in the case of ecological cohousing communities, re-envisioned as ideal locations to address larger questions of social cohesion and environmental sustainability.

The late twentieth century has produced a plethora of discussion about community and environmental sustainability in the United States. Various social transformations have resulted in a resurgence of a search for "community" (Brown 2001) and have produced a multiplicity of new forms of rural and urban planning and architecture. These social and ecological transformations of the importance of place have, in part, grown out of the changing landscape of the political atmosphere in the United States. More specifically, as the cultural revolution of the 1960s and 1970s produced a heightened awareness, and suspicion of government and its role in protecting people from social and environmental injustice, the resultant civil rights, environmental, and feminist movements gave rise to conscientious leaders who worked to change the way the conservative government functioned. This process, according to Low, produced new meaning for spaces of public protest (Low 2000), new communities, new neighborhoods, new federal laws and regulations, and illuminated the reality of diminishing natural resources. It is within this context that today's ecovillages are emerging in large numbers across the United States. These communities are searching for a kind of modern utopia that is envisioned as a harmonious place for people and nature. Its reality as played out in the everyday lives of residents reveals some of the same tensions and contradictions of earlier communal experiments (Brown 2001). The success of EcoVillage at Ithaca (EVI) makes evident that many people in the United States are still looking for a way to create what Howard and Mumford envisioned as meaningful social relations while being conscientious about the environment.

The history of studying communities in anthropology embodies the rhetoric that many residents of EVI utilized in their daily interactions: "the tribe," "kinship," and Margaret Mead's "it takes a village" all represent efforts to recreate an imagined community that is idealized as living in harmony with the environment. Unique to these ideas is the reliance on "primitive society" as representing idealized social harmony, sustainability, and being close to nature, if not being nature itself, or a nostalgia for utopia. Elena, one of the founding participants, remarked: "What we are doing is reinventing the tribe." EVI is well suited for an anthropological study because it connects the ideas of early ethnography of indigenous societies with Western reactions to the problems of modernity, producing a kind of social, political, and ecological transformation that attempts to redesign the way we represent our interaction with each other and with nature.

EcoVillage at Ithaca, just west of the city of Ithaca, seems at first glance to be an ideal location to practice social and ecological sustainability. In addition to the abundance of land that is allowed to grow fallow, the care residents have taken to minimize the distance between their built environment and nature is revealed in the details of the everyday life of residents. Residents appreciate the location of the community because it is placed within what Soper (1996) describes as a culturally constructed nature that represents an imagined nature without human intervention or domestication. The open fields that are dotted with daisies, the hiking or cross-country skiing trails that cross through young forest, the organic farm with edible and ornamental sunflowers and organic raspberries, and the panoramic views that stretch across the glacial valley, all help to create the sense that residents are living within nature. Yet, residents revealed contradictory sentiment about the importance of conserving and preserving the environment, creating a sense of community amongst neighbors, and the importance of the place where EVI is located.

Table 4.1 Activities that express commitment to social and ecological causes

Activity	No. of responses
Moving to EVI, living at EVI	24
Avoid unnecessary consumption	15
Donate or volunteer with environmental organizations	35
Choose to limit number of children (0–2)	4
Join CSA, eat locally, grow own food	9
Use alternative transport, avoid flying	4
Vegan diet	2
Adopt green technology	5
Friendship with diverse people	1
Mindfulness meditation, yoga	3
Political action, vote	1
Education, teach others, inform self, homeschool	16
Share resources	1
Don't do enough	1

Source: Author.

There is no consensus among residents on what it means to connect to the environment, but residents generally respond by describing their collective efforts to reduce their use of non-renewable energy sources such as fossil fuels for heating and driving and to support charitable organizations, as well as their ability to preserve the majority of the EVI land from development. Table 4.1 shows that for many residents, simply moving to EVI is an expression of their commitment to social and ecological causes. There is no agreement on the relevance of "place" to the EcoVillage project; instead, residents who participated construct personal narratives to explain their relationship to the land. In addition, upon close examination, important rituals such as the use of consensus and, more recently, dynamic governance, reveal a deep complexity that expresses internal class and power struggles even as a sense of community is sought.

This chapter explores how EVI merges the goals of creating a sense of community and environmentalism through the choice, design, and designation of particular places and spaces for specific community or environmental functions. It discusses how EVI attempts to create intentional spaces and places that foster community and that protect the environment through the consumption of green commodities, but also by the consumption of "place," imbued with meaning specifically through the necessity to purchase specially designed homes that provide access to nature and construct a sense of community. The chapter questions whether the centrality of consumption of place is necessary for the possibility of being a model of sustainable living. Although multiple agents (the board of directors of the nonprofit and residents of the neighborhoods) view sustainability differently, it is non-trivial that purchasing a home in EVI is expressed as the entry point of building a sustainable community.

The place for nature and the nature of place

Buying a house in EVI is more than simply purchasing a few shares (the actual exchanged good in the cooperative); rather it includes the acquisition, although temporary and not necessarily wholly, of a place in nature. This place in nature is constructed as a space to be left alone to grow fallow and, at the same time, manicured with wildflower mixes and protected from invasive species that threaten to take over from plants that are thought to "belong" to the region. Further, nature is enhanced with amenities that meet human needs and desires such as ponds and vegetable gardens. The effort of residents to balance the "natural" and "built" environment has created contradictory ideas and practices within the community.

Constructing and defining nature as outside of human manipulation is arguably a contradiction; humans have interacted with their environment for millennia, thus to imagine a nature without humans, a wilderness, is a cultural construction that has political and economic motivations (Escobar 1996; Soper 1996). Nature in EVI is at once imaged as wilderness, through the new growth forests and the occasional uncultivated front yard, and "manufactured" through the carefully manicured flower gardens or a "natural" dirt road.

The intentional physical design of the community includes closely clustered houses, inwardly facing windows to see neighbors (but also outwardly facing ones to see nature), and landscaped gardens, and these features drew families to join the community. One adult resident who moved with his family from the West Coast explained the significance of the location:

> If [EVI] was in the middle of town, I would feel it was more politically correct, but it would have appealed to me less, because I like the open space. I like the fact that it is pretty substantially interconnected to the region, and to the city, but that it has the open space.
>
> (Christopher)

Residents on one hand want to preserve the open "imagined" wilderness and, at the same time, occupy houses in a central location in that wilderness as a way of demonstrating sustainable co-existence with nature. Despite the central premise that EVI is an alternative to sprawl and the claim by some residents that it is not itself sprawl, but instead represents a model of "anti-sprawl," other participants felt a contradiction in the cutting down of trees and developing new houses in open space on the outskirts of the city. A significant reminder of this contradiction was described by one of the early participants of the project. Andreas, a self-employed resident of Ithaca in his late forties, dropped out of the EVI project when it became clear to him that the goals of the leaders were contrary to modeling sustainable housing. He explained that the high cost of building the FROG (and later, SONG and TREE) was primarily due to the refusal of the city of Ithaca to provide city infrastructure—water, sewer, and gas lines. The city of Ithaca was committed to reducing sprawl and therefore required developers outside the city limits to pay for their own city water and sewer infrastructure. Because EVI is located outside the city limits, it was required to add infrastructure to the cost of the homes, thereby making the houses expensive.

The founders of EVI recognized the beauty of green communities and designing neighborhoods that are accessible to local businesses and other amenities. EVI successfully creates garden cities by placing the houses together and surrounding them with open land. While some US ecovillages are urban, such as the Los Angeles Ecovillage (Fosket and Mamo 2009), others are created as new suburban developments. EVI can be understood as a new kind of place, similar to Ebenezer Howard's garden city, but a themed space (Ross 1999; Sorkin 1992).

Green sprawl

The nonprofit EcoVillage at Ithaca, Incorporated (EVI, Inc.), based out of Cornell University's Center for Religion, Ethics, and Social Policy (CRESP) in 1991, now the Center for Transformative Action, enabled a group of donors to purchase 176 acres. Concurrently, in 1992, a small group of households began to meet to discuss the EVI project. The households would represent the nonprofit's model of a sustainable lifestyle and the nonprofit would own the land that surrounded the residents. Soon after the First Resident Group[1] (FROG) was large enough to begin building homes; the board of directors of the EVI nonprofit sold the group a three and a half acre plot of land as well as the necessary acres of the road and community gardens. This purchase legally separated EVI, Inc. from the resident groups. The mission of the FROG to build energy-efficient homes as part of a demonstration community fit appropriately within the mission of the nonprofit. In fact, they were very similar since many residents were active in creating the nonprofit umbrella group. Control over the remaining land would stay in the nonprofit, but residents would have some control in how the nonprofit land was used, for example, in the decision to lease land to the organic farmers. Through an easement and cooperation between the resident group and the nonprofit, most of the land is designated for agricultural use, including the organic community-supported agriculture farm and a U-pick berry farm. The nonprofit board of directors, which includes members of FROG, works closely with the resident group. Thus the residents agree to carry out the mission of the nonprofit by supporting its education mission to model sustainable living. The point is that the nonprofit resources make the community project possible. This is an important consideration if EVI is to be a replicable model of sustainable community.

The place selected for EVI was purchased outside the city, because EVI was imagined and sold as a place in nature. Lukas, who had tried to create an ecovillage in his former community, explained that the place where EVI was located was an important factor in his deciding to buy a home in the project.

> A small group of us wanted to make cohousing work in [a Southern California city] … but what we couldn't really do there was buy any quantity of

land because land was so scarce ... for building on. We were talking about putting 15 units on one acre or one-and-a-half acres ... [but] there was no land around us and it did not feel like the kind of spaciousness that I thought a community should have access to.

(Lukas)

Despite being offered free land ten miles outside of Ithaca, the founders chose to buy the EVI land to fulfill two primary goals. First, according to one of the founders, the project was conceived out of a concern for how open space was developed; the land would serve as a model for future developers and therefore starting from scratch was essential to demonstrate that new suburban development can be done in a way that does not require much sacrifice, and can be very attractive and comfortable. Second, the proximity to nature and the city would encourage residents to minimize carbon emissions. The two-mile distance to the center of Ithaca was imagined as an easy bike ride, long walk, or accessible by public transportation. At the same time, being surrounded by hiking trails, water, and woods provided space for residents to demonstrate the benefits of preserving nature. The residents in FROG, SONG, and TREE fulfill this mission by demonstrating green design, sharing, and social cohesiveness.

Except for the few residents who moved into EVI to be close to their family, most residents I spoke with value the place where EcoVillage is located and moved there because they were attracted to the land. The house windows face outwards, towards beautiful meadows and rolling hillsides; easements that prevent future developers from blocking the view[2] ensure access to this land will be preserved. The views make up for the small houses. Residents are proud that their house is smaller than the one they used to live in, or at least smaller than one they could afford to buy (see Figure 4.1). In addition, they know their neighbors and enjoy feeling connected to their small community.

One of the founders of the EVI project explained the process that the initial resident group went through when deciding which land to buy.

In September of 1991 we held our first village meeting and we ... looked at various pieces of land.... There was land that was offered for free out in Brooktondale by somebody ... we also looked at the possibility of buying an old factory. One reason we did not [want this] is because we were worried about toxins, even though they had not uncovered anything ... we thought, an old gun factory was not a real great environment for kids.... People grouped themselves where they would most prefer to live ... virtually everybody was right around two–three miles outside of the city. I think one person was downtown and one person was rural.

(Gina 2001)

Why had only one person imagined a downtown setting to be ecological, especially considering the proximity to work, grocery stores, and easy access to an already well-established public transportation system? Some residents are proud

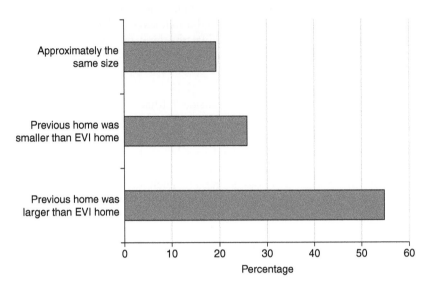

Figure 4.1 Size of homes in EVI compared with previous residence.

Source: Author.

that the community is not contributing to sprawl because it has been built only two miles from the city. Other residents felt that the location of EVI was a great improvement to where they had previously lived, specifically the access to open space, nature, and close proximity to the city. This comparison of EVI with former neighborhoods or arguing that their family could have afforded to build a bigger house, but chose not to, provided a safety net from criticism that EVI was some variation of sprawl, and that it expands the boundaries of the city even further out into open space. A car is necessary on almost a daily basis to go to work or school, visit a library, or shop for groceries, the same challenges presented by other forms of suburban sprawl.

Garden cities, techno cities, edge city

> My parents' decision was influenced by a desire to be living in a community. They wanted to be in deeper connection with the Earth. They wanted to share this life with other incredible and warm people in an extended family type way. They wanted a large amount of land and a safe place for their children to grow up in.
>
> (EVI survey 2015)

The EVI housing model bears a strong resemblance to Ebenezer Howard's "garden cities"; as such, EVI is also open to the same criticism of Howard's city. The garden cities were based on the premise that people functioned best when they are surrounded by nature, have access to fertile agriculture, and are able to develop meaningful social relations (Howard 1902). Howard, like other liberal city planners at the time, felt that the city was growing out of control and represented a destructive force for people and the environment. In response, the garden cities would be small and sustainable communities surrounded by nature, and a short distance from other such garden cities. The burgeoning cities would be replaced with smaller versions that enable people to easily move between town and country as well as create distinctions between home and work. Lloyd Rodwin (1945) emerged as a major critic of Howard, arguing that the garden cities "overlooked some of the essential tasks of the metropolis and the necessary functional and administrative interrelationships" (Rodwin 1945: 270). He argued that the garden cities failed to consider "the problems confronting existing communities" (270). Like EVI, the garden cities would be built as new developments outside of the city, and did not consider the impact abandoning city centers would have on the environment. Mumford, in Howard's defense, argued that the garden cities would simply be improved post-war suburbs compared with the ones that were already being created. That is, planners were already building on virgin soil, and thus the garden city, like ecovillages, would demonstrate a more sustainable model of development (Mumford 1946). Both planners were concerned with the rapid development of land outside of the city.

Since the turn of the nineteenth century, city planners and environmental groups have been concerned with the rapid development of suburbia. The post-World War II decades ushered in a period of urban decentralization, what Fishman (1987) calls the age of the great suburb; new single-family track homes were built outside of cities. Unlike the "little" boxes on the hillside, today's suburban developments are dotted with large custom houses. These communities could be described as the first exodus from the city (Davis 1992). In an analysis of Los Angeles, Davis (1992) demonstrates how the construction of the "fortress city" results in the creation of exclusionary public spaces, which prevent minorities (or other excluded populations) from participating in the political process (Davis 1992; Low 1996). The suburbs of the 1950s were neighborhoods that were intimately connected to the city through regional railroad lines and other forms of mass transit that brought commuters to and from work or shopping centers—an "expanded metropolis" (Fishman 1987: 183). The second exodus in the 1960s and 1970s saw further emigration from the city and white flight (Gregory 1998), which left urban communities with a void. Soon after people moved out, businesses followed. The 1980s saw a new kind of sprawl, what Garreau (1991) calls "edge cities" and Fishman (1987) refers to as "techno(logy) cities." These edge cities are small, established commercial spaces outside the city centers which include shopping malls and office buildings (Garreau 1991). These spaces differ from earlier suburbs because they tend to offer housing, industry, and office jobs and are thus no longer dependent on the urban center, "a decentralized environment that nevertheless possesses all the economic and technological dynamism we associate with the city" (Fishman 1987: 184). Residents in EcoVillage spoke of their disappointment in the continuous development of the US landscape into suburbs that drains life out of the city and forms generic shopping strips with the usual chain fast-food restaurants and hotels that have begun to define US highways and cities, what Ritzer (1993) calls McDonaldization.

EcoVillage has a mission to model a sustainable community—a garden city— with clustered homes and surrounded by nature. The similarities between Eco-Village at Ithaca and an edge city are not immediately obvious or intentional, but nonetheless akin. The original plan for the five neighborhoods was to establish an education center—part of the basis for creating the nonprofit—a village center, and small businesses.³ Such amenities would allow families to live close to work and thus require less automobile use—a significant factor that one resident said would be more ecological.

ELENA: I drive my car a lot and I wish I did not drive it, but I am a commuter and that is how I get to work.

When asked about carpooling, a new tension emerged:

ELENA: I suppose I could carpool, but then I would have to be subject to someone else's schedule. I think that to be really a true friend of the environment you have to give up a lot of your individualism, and I have not been willing to do that … it is so much easier to just get inside my car and go when I feel like.

The early planners of the community envisioned employment opportunities for residents in the education or village center, which would avoid not only the need to commute long distances to work, but also sacrificing individual need for flexibility in mobility. This community would take the good aspects of suburbia—individualism and access to the city, but not its pollution and open space—and merge it with good ecological practices such as driving less. For several residents this works very well. Although working at EVI is a positive ecological option for residents who save energy by not driving, it requires anyone serviced by EVI or clients of residents to drive into the community. While working at EVI reduces the environmental impact from residents, it does not solve the problem; rather it simply deflects the resource use from residents to their clients. This paradox also reflects the inwardly focused nature of the project: the environment that needs to be preserved is the one in EcoVillage; the community that needs to be connected is also within the boundaries of the EVI project.

I wanted my own space—a small home of my own. I preferred to live more in the country, but did not want to be isolated. I liked the idea of building a community and making it work by doing the work and connecting with neighbors. Also, EcoVillage was affordable and offered many plusses: trails, a pond, woods, a farm, a berry farm, etc.

(Manuel)

What residents also object to in suburban sprawl is the isolation it caused to those who lived there, and the wasteful nature of dividing land into small plots instead of clustering homes, then preserving open space for its own sake and for recreation. A commonly held belief amongst participants was that a former purchaser of the land was a developer who had planned to build 150 homes on one-acre lots across the 176-acre former farmland, but apparently went bankrupt. During public presentations, community meetings, and in interviews, it was often stated that this developer would have created the typical suburban community like those that blanket the US landscape; therefore it was essential that EVI buy the land and save it from this unsustainable development plan. I was never able to verify that these plans were a real possibility. A non-resident participant (Bernadette) insisted that the 150-houses-on-one-acre-lots was a rumor and that the city of Ithaca had rejected the idea. Further, Bernadette commented that the developer changed his mind when it became clear that to discourage development outside the city limits, the city would not provide any infrastructure. According to Bernadette, a former member of the EVI board, the effect of the city's tough development requirements encouraged the original developer to drop the project. Frustrated by what she felt was misinformation about the efforts of the city to slow the growth of sprawl, Bernadette commented that she found

> it very offensive that for many years [the founders and organizers of EVI] would show these designs and say, "see, if he built, this is what we would have and we are so much greater." [These] designs never made it to the city planning process … the town immediately said "you can't do this."
>
> (Bernadette)

It was based on this belief that early planners decided to demonstrate the ability to construct the same number of houses on significantly less land. Clearly the EVI model, with five clustered neighborhoods, would be an impressive alternative to the one-acre-per-household design. The model of community would be self-supporting with a small farm and recycled waste, and have employment opportunities of various kinds. Although this vision has not yet been realized, it had not been entirely abandoned in 2002. During some interviews, residents expressed reservations to fulfilling the original vision because they felt more than two neighborhoods would be overwhelming. Two FROG households felt the second neighborhood was already too many people to be able to enjoy the land and create a strong sense of community. On the other hand, one household feared that creating a large village in EVI would widen the social distance between the larger community and EcoVillage. By 2014 residents in TREE had begun to move into the community.

Some residents questioned whether EcoVillage was not itself a variation of sprawl—green sprawl. A participant was concerned that local Ithaca residents referred to EVI as a green-gated community, while other members of the EVI project publicly raised the concern that the larger community refers to EVI as "yuppie-ville." The way EVI was perceived outside of the neighborhood

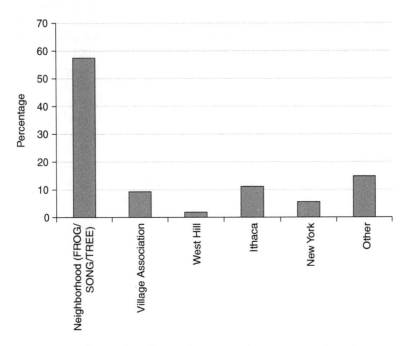

Figure 4.2 Highest rank of what residents see as their community boundary.
Source: Author.

boundaries was of concern for one resident who frequently interacted with the Ithaca community, because it demonstrated a failure of EVI to be integrated into the city of Ithaca, and instead was perceived as a group of outsiders trying to show the local Ithaca residents how to build neighborhoods. Individual EVI households were so busy building and paying for their homes and creating the new model village that little time was spent working to integrate EVI into the city of Ithaca. A couple from Ithaca pointed out that many of the participants in EVI were not familiar with the Ithaca community and had an arrogant way of describing their project.

> A lot of people moved here from very far away and don't know Ithaca … [a man who later moved out of FROG] gave this talk about what "a good gift [EVI] was giving to Ithaca." No knowledge that Ithaca planning … has been a major issue for as long as I've been here. And people who are just not grounded in the history … a lot of people considered them fairly outra-geous statements about, "we've arrived, we're gonna show you how it's done" … people would come and say, "this is the greatest thing, I moved here from California to be part of it." [EcoVillagers] really see their neigh-borhood as an island and not as a continuous piece of this place [Ithaca].
>
> (Jessie)

The lack of integration with the larger city of Ithaca meant that some of EVI's neighbors were unsupportive of the project. The building of SONG was advertised as demonstrating affordable housing, but when completed, the houses cost more than the average home in Ithaca. Some residents expressed that building a second neighborhood further in the middle of the open land obstructed their views of nature. At a town hall meeting, a FROG neighbor argued that building in the middle of the field (her viewshed) seemed counter to preserving open land. This contradiction exposed one of the tensions of the EVI project: that the emphasis on conserving land and preserving open space has more to do with creating a specific green-themed space than building in a way that decreases environmental degradation. EcoVillage encompasses some of the features of Sorkin's (1992) themed spaces; EVI's idea of sustainable living in nature helps to create a green-themed community.

Creating a community for environmental conservation

> One of the nice things [about living up here] is to wake up and not having any traffic noises, you have a beautiful view so we see the sun coming up, we see the wide variety of wildlife just out of your bedroom window. And if it's snowing you can go from your front doorstep cross-country skiing into the woods and back. If you want to go running, you run out of your house. If you want to go on a bike ride, you ride right in front of your house to wherever you want to go. So ... you can be here for days at a time without feeling the need to go anywhere else. It's like a retreat. I have lots of friends visiting me here, and they take it sort of as a retreat, being away from it all, and having all these wonderful nature resources.
>
> (Dean)

Understanding the context in which EVI is designed, and the needs it is responding to, is a useful tool to explore how our communities can become more sustainable places to live, both for humans and non-humans. The planners and future residents of EVI embarked on a project to "redefine the human habitat" by creating a themed space for the land that would be preserved (nurtured and cared for) by the residents, while the land would in turn provide resources for the community. The idea of a sustainability theme was a natural choice and would be one that anyone could agree on (who could be against sustainability?). This model would include intentionally designed spaces set apart from the larger community, providing places that would be protected from strangers, crime, and other ills of the city. At the same time, the land and the inhabitants would bring families closer together socially through the medium of the surrounding land. These characteristics help to identify the community as an ecovillage, but also contain many of the features that relate to a growing trend of creating themed spaces (Gottdiener 2001; Sorkin 1992). EVI is not unique in its effort to create a community that emphasizes a particular social need. Other communities, such as Celebration, Florida, are designed to invoke a nostalgia for an imagined and idealized bygone era of neighborhoods and a regained "sense of community" amongst neighbors, within a particularly defined space (Putnam 2000; Ross 1999; Sorkin 1992).

Three distinct characteristics imbedded in EVI create a themed community. First, according to Sorkin, an ageographic place is one that is not attached to any particular city and can be "inserted equally in an open field or in the heart of the town" (xiii). Second, the use of both technological and physical surveillance as a way of maintaining distinction of its green lifestyle; and third, the creation of themed spaces through architecture. Sorkin argues that this "elaborate apparatus is at pains to assert its ties to the kind of city life it is in the process of obliterating" (xiv). The tension of creating an ecovillage that is at once separating itself from the larger community through building in open space, and as a way to recreate a sense of community that preserves open space, is one of the challenges residents of EcoVillage at Ithaca confront.

EcoVillage meets Sorkin's definition of a themed community by creating three parallel characteristics that are at once essential to the EVI project and at the same time contradictory. I explore how theming in EcoVillage is both resisted and employed by residents as a way to create a sense of community and sustainability within the context of theming efforts in the United States (Gottdiener 2001).

Ageography

Residents moved from around the country to live on the land and in the community that was being envisioned (see Table 4.2). Many families moved from cities on the West Coast, such as Los Angeles, Santa Cruz, San Francisco, and Berkeley, which were becoming increasingly expensive. According to one of the planners, the choice of Ithaca as the location for the model sustainable community grew out of the Global Walk for a Livable Planet (see Chapter 3). The year-long walk across the United States led up to the search for a place to create the "livable" community. According to documents from early planning meetings, EVI would serve to demonstrate how communities can be self-supporting by reusing resources through recycling and limiting the amount of energy required to live comfortably. This community would be replicable and, according to the founder, its location in Ithaca was more a coincidence than a requirement. This flexibility in location is what Sorkin (1992) refers to as ageographic.

Table 4.2 Where residents moved from

Northeast	48
Southeast	3
Northwest	1
Southwest	5
International	2

Source: Author.

The community could be anywhere, as its locality has little to do with the surrounding community; the ageographic place is, as EcoVillage, a place of its own.

According to Lisa, a retired resident, "the location of EcoVillage is like being on a giant estate without the servants." Other residents value a connection to the land by walking barefoot or working in one of the many flower or vegetable gardens that surround the homes. The abundance of nature—gardens, wildflowers, and young forest—is important to the community, in part because of the beauty and the access to open land, the animals that live within it, and the sense of living within nature. Appendix C demonstrates that the EVI landscape was the second listed reason why households chose to move to EVI. In random conversations, residents would describe imagined and nostalgic ideas of communities in regions beyond the United States, specifically in European cities or third-world countries (often, though rarely said explicitly, they were referring to rural areas of third-world countries and not the rapidly expanding urban ones). These idealized "African villages" or "European hamlets" were imagined as being more in harmony with nature by having fewer resources, that is, "living simply." In the case of a generic African village, Paul, a new father, somewhat jokingly explained: "I would live in a grass hut if it was just me ... all of the baby supplies and equipment would take up two huts!" and in the case of Europe, Paul admired the pedestrian-friendly downtown spaces called Fussgängerzone.

EcoVillage creates its own community. Figure 4.2 shows that 57.4 percent of survey takers define community boundary to be the resident neighborhoods, showing a preference to create human connections outside the city and within the boundaries of its own privatized space (Sorkin 1992). But some residents have mixed feelings about where the community is located and, specifically, that it is not attached to the city:

> In a sort of abstract way, I think it is nice to have all this land ... to experiment on ... but on the other hand it makes it really hard to live lightly ... maybe when the SONG is here we can have shared vans or cooperative taxi vans ... all these environmentally conscious people and not biking, [biking] is never going to be a number one solution here, it seems like a drag.
>
> (Paul)

The irony of living lightly on the earth in FROG but requiring a car to access the city made some residents uncomfortable. It is clear to some participants that such contradictions meant that the main thrust of the project was not always to create ecological and social sustainability. "There was a sense that [the planners] need to place [the homes] in a place that's going to make [the lenders] think that their investment was worthwhile, that it has a very beautiful view" (Sam).

Surveillance

> Susi loves the location of her home. It is right in front of the main path
> from the visitors' parking lot and the resident carports. More important,
> however, it is very close to the Common House; she enjoys being close to
> where the action is, front row seats to the heart of the community. From
> her kitchen window she can see who is coming and going—visitors, family
> members of neighbors, and people going for a walk. She can predict when
> to do her laundry as she counts the number of laundry-basket-carrying resi-
> dents making their way to the common laundry room. She definitely feels
> more connected to her neighbors, just because she sees them on a regular
> basis. Although some residents hire a gardener to plant and maintain their
> small front yards, Susi enjoys the work herself. Most passersby stop to ask
> about her day when they see her planting and weeding. They often compli-
> ment her on the beautiful perennial flower garden that envelops her front
> door. It is especially rewarding to her when neighbors ask for horticultural
> advice. She knows her neighbors and they know her, they take care of each
> other; this, she tells me, is what creates community, this is why she moved
> to EcoVillage.

The FROG, SONG, and TREE neighborhoods create their own sense of community by physically designing the houses to produce opportunities for families to
congregate and engage in spontaneous social interaction, and support the reliance
on shared resources as a way to reduce their consumption. The community is fash-
ioned by the use of specially designed features that allow residents to be in physical and virtual contact with each other. This enables neighbors to see who is
home, and thus increases the opportunity to engage in conversations and visits.
The closeness of the homes also serves as a surveillance mechanism that allows
residents to keep an eye on neighbors' homes when they go on vacation.

While surveillance, according to Sorkin (1992), is a tool used to control
security and enforce distinction in theme parks for the middle class, in EVI's
first neighborhood, surveillance is one way residents feel connected to each
other and create a sense of community. Indirectly and inconspicuously, surveillance by neighbors is also used to ensure security within the community. Neighbors surveyed the community by questioning (in a friendly inquisitive manner)
unfamiliar persons walking on the land as well as by asking each other about
unfamiliar cars that are parked in the various parking lots. At the same time,
residents announce to the community when they will bring an unfamiliar person
to the village, for example, when a group of students from one of the local campuses comes to a workshop, or when a household has a relative or friend visit
them. Many residents make an effort to let the community know who is staying
in their home and ask that neighbors make their guests feel welcome. Not
everyone who visits feels welcome. Surveillance, conscious or unconscious, is
such an integral part of the community that one household described feeling the
need to protect their privacy by controlling who had visual access to the inside

of their house—they kept their window blinds closed and invited neighbors for dinner infrequently. In this case, the built-in surveillance of their home became a restrictive feature, making them feel constantly exposed to their neighbors' inquisitive gaze. The emphasis on creating opportunities to get to know their neighbors resulted in their need to prevent their neighbors from encroaching on their personal space. Other residents echoed this concern when they invited me to dinner and asked me not to tell anyone or a specific neighbor. This occurred not because my dinner host disliked any resident, or wanted to gossip about them; my host simply did not want to include other people in the dinner she was preparing for her family.

Almost all residents I interviewed felt a sense of community in EVI simply because they ran into neighbors on a regular basis. Meeting neighbors in the many private-public[4] spaces, such as in front of their houses, on one of the many trails, or sitting by the pond, makes most residents feel less isolated and lonely. Not being isolated but instead surrounded by neighbors gave residents a sense of security. One resident told me that she felt safe[5] because her neighbors were attentive to suspicious behavior in the community. Surveillance to her was an attractive feature of EVI; she felt it was an integral part of sharing her life with her neighbors, and one of the reasons she moved there. She wanted people to check in on her by visiting her frequently and spontaneously, and be concerned about her well-being. From observations, parents also felt that having other adults who would passively monitor their children or someone whom their child could trust was especially helpful when they needed to do small tasks like collect their laundry from the Common House or make an important phone call.

The physical design of the neighborhoods makes being a newcomer or visitor to the community obvious. Despite most of the land belonging to the EVI, Inc. nonprofit, there are no spaces that are explicitly open to the general public in EVI, although neighbors living on West Hill often walked freely on the wooded paths that criss-crossed the EVI, Inc. land. People who came to EVI during my stay fell into two general categories: they were either would-be residents or visitors who were usually meeting with a specific family, or visitors accompanied by a representative from the EVI board of directors or office staff. Unlike public parks in the greater Ithaca community, people unknown to anyone in the community were rarely seen visiting the pond or hiking on trails. At a community meeting where public transportation was being considered, a resident objected to bringing the local bus closer to the center of the community for fear that it would enable strangers to be dropped in the middle of the community. Parents of young children who appreciated being able to allow their children to play outside without fear echoed this concern. The structure of the nonprofit and neighborhoods gives residents the sense that the nonprofit land (the acres that are not owned by either the FROG or SONG) is also accessible to residents, thus the residents steward the land as if it were their own backyard, careful to make sure no one is abusive to it, such as by driving recklessly on the dirt road. Because the physical design of the community is densely clustered, residents who are sitting in their homes or working in their gardens are often displayed as community personified. Stephanie, a resident who works at home raising her family, complained about unannounced tours that would catch her weeding her garden in clothes she would rather not be seen wearing by tourists and visitors to the neighborhood. Being in the neighborhood added a level of pressure she felt would not exist in a suburb:

> There are things that I feel like I'd better do today, because it impacts the community or what people will think of the community ... silly things like ... I'd better pick up all the toys in the front walkway, cause visitors will think we're slobs! Sometimes I feel like there's a list of "should" that I need to do just because I live here and we're on display.
>
> (Stephanie)

The many tours that the community conducts make Stephanie constantly vigilant of how her home is presented and what it says about the community. Often residents will be asked (with advanced notice) if a tour group could walk through their home; this made Susi, a part-time employee in Ithaca, proud to be able to show off the features of her home she so much appreciated: the large windows, the open space that connected the downstairs, and the small footprint it occupied. At the same time, she was certain to make sure her house was always clean and presentable. This implicit self-surveillance by being on display contributes to a degree of artificialness in the construction of community.

Residents I interviewed appreciated knowing that their neighbors would keep an eye on their home while they were away. Neighbors often announced that they would be away on the community LISTSERV and generously offered their unoccupied house to potential visitors or to couples who needed space. EVI residents exhibited incredible generosity throughout my stay in the village.

Residents use email both to stay updated on the events in the neighborhood and to inform each other of their whereabouts. Often a family will post their vacation schedule with flight details and emergency phone numbers, should one of their neighbors need to contact them. Or they announce special houseguests in emails: "Hope everyone who knows [my sister] ... will welcome her along the path and at Common House meals when you see her." Personal information is also announced on the community LISTSERV such as when Gina wanted to share her recently diagnosed illness with the community: "I am writing this email to let everyone know what is going on with me." Such personal and somewhat private conversations allow residents to be sympathetic; calls for best wishes, love, virtual hugs, and offers to do errands are the typical response. Some residents found email irritating and disliked the posting of personal information; they purposefully avoided checking their email. One resident admitted that she felt more peaceful when she avoids reading email every day because there is "always some controversial thing" that makes her apprehensive. The geek team, one of the five recognized work teams that each adult member of FROG is required to participate in, set up several different LISTSERVs in response to residents who were irritated by the massive amount of email that the community generated.

Another element of surveillance that is appreciated by residents is the physical and practical design of the homes that allows neighbors to see who is coming and going. After a few years, some residents decided to put up curtains. "When we first moved in here, nobody had curtains on the windows. Now almost everybody has curtains on the windows just because it feels more comfortable that way" (Lukas). The architecture of the houses, another characteristic of themed spaces, was designed to allow frequent contact with neighbors, including large inward-facing windows which serve as a way for the community to conduct surveillance of the inside of others' homes, but also a gateway into the community.

Architecture

The architecture of EVI neighborhoods is designed to create a sense of community. Approaching the community from Mecklenburg Road, one is immediately connected to nature through sights and sounds. The long dirt road serves as a meditative entryway, away from the rest of world, and into a peaceful, natural place. The traffic slows down (usually only one other car is making its way in or out of the community, depending on the time of day) and a calmness takes over. The road has been intentionally left unpaved, despite complaints about dust and its respiratory effects on the pedestrians walking nearby, or the TREE families whose Passivhaus homes fill with dust when the windows are open. Residents liked the "look" of the dirt road as a way to introduce EVI to visitors. In 2001–2002 I attended many community meetings dedicated to finding a solution to the dust along the half-mile stretch of unpaved road.

Upon arriving at the neighborhoods, a sea of parked cars is the first to greet you. The parking spaces for residents and visitors are set aside from the community. One resident complained that "there are a lot of things … in the city, even a small city like Ithaca, that seem too out of control … [like] the predominance of cars …" (Eric). Eric appreciated the lack of cars directly in the neighborhood; other residents felt it was easy for children to run between homes and visit friends without negotiating fast cars.

The houses that make up the FROG neighborhood are variations of four architectural designs of differing sizes. The community is made up of two rows of houses which focus inward, into the pedestrian path. The first floor of each FROG home consists of one large room that locates the kitchen towards the neighborhood; only a few small steps divide the dining area and living space. This open design of the home allows the cook to stay connected to family and friends sitting in the living area and look out into the neighborhood—another opportunity to feel connected to the community. One can leave the house either into the vast meadow of goldenrod and wild berries, the pond, or in the case of the north-facing homes, a small backyard that abuts the carports. It is very easy to spontaneously meet a neighbor as one walks from the house to the carports, or walking to a neighbor's house, or to the Common House.

The Common House, comparable with a town hall, represents the heart of the community, where important decisions are made in neighborhood, village, and board meetings. Each neighborhood has its own Common House. The Common Houses in FROG and TREE are architecturally designed to be at the top of the community, looking down the pedestrian pathway at the homes standing on the sidelines. SONG located its Common House in the middle of the community. Each SONG house was designed to give its occupants the ability to see what was going on at the Common House, and therefore be able to participate in whatever community event was taking place there. Inside the Common House, families can gather in the large dining room, which opens to the community kitchen where meals are prepared three nights a week for anyone in the neighborhood to partake. One resident enjoyed just being present at the meals and observing the community sitting together to eat: "I like going to Common House meals. Somehow just the ambience of people being together kind of makes me happy" (Derrick).

Not all residents believe that the Common House is essential to creating a sense of community, nor did all residents find the common meals enjoyable. The partner of Derrick felt just the opposite: the Common House meals were noisy, and sometimes crowded and disorganized. She felt she was too busy focusing on her children and found it impossible to talk to neighbors over the noise of clanking plates, children's cries, and other people's conversations. Another resident, a woman who moved to EcoVillage because she felt a strong desire to live close to nature and experiment with developing deep relationships with people, was concerned that "people get caught up in the architecture of cohousing [because they think that] the problems of their lives are going to be solved if they get their windows in the right place" (Carolyn).

Other constructed features of the project such as the pond were imagined to create a sense of community and harmony with nature. Lenny, who has a passion for nature both professionally (biology) and personally, imagined teaching the young children in the community how to fish, like he experienced growing up. Lenny unwittingly added young fish to the pond, thinking it would be a lovely surprise for the kids. One of the vegan residents was furious when she found out about the plan to catch and eat the fish. This disappointment was exacerbated by the fact that Lenny had not sought the community's consensus before stocking the pond. The pond is primarily used for swimming and boating, its aesthetic beauty, and as a habitat for desirable wildlife. At the end of 2002, fishing was not encouraged except during a supervised Harvest Festival when the community created a ritual to acknowledge the multiple uses of the pond and appreciate the fish for the nourishment they provide for the body of those who eat them.[6]

The use of architecture to create a sense of community is a characteristic of other themed spaces (Di Chiro 1996; Hannigan 1998; Sorkin 1992) that is easy to observe in EcoVillage. The placement of the farm and lightly mowed trails that border the land brings residents who walk on the land in close contact with the wildflowers, forest, streams, the organic farm, and blackberries, all, as one resident described, symbols of a community that integrates nature with people. Residents expressed that it was easy to connect with neighbors because the houses helped to facilitate spontaneous interactions. Because the homes were built in the middle of the land, residents are automatically surrounded—and thus reminded—of their connection to nature. The architecture of the community creates effortless opportunities to socialize.

In this sense, EVI represents a growing trend in the United States of what Gottdiener calls the theming of America and, specifically, themed environments that are designed to be spaces for commoditized human experiences (Gottdiener 2001). These themed environments are creating intentional spaces that at once include some people, but also exclude others. From shopping malls to museums to corporate-sponsored towns like Celebration, Florida, these new communities offer residents, through carefully designed architecture, a commodity to be consumed: a safari experience, a cultural dining experience, nostalgic community. Celebration, Florida, a Disney-sponsored community, advertises itself as an ideal community that recreates neighborhoods of yesteryears complete with porches, sidewalks, and shared community resources in the community center. It is also marketed as an ideal, idyllic, safe neighborhood within easy commute to the Disney World theme parks (Ross 1999). Itself a kind of theme park, Celebration's guidelines include the permissible height of grass and the allowable color of curtains. Increasingly, developers and home associations are assuming the role of city planners and municipal facilities, planning once-public facilities on private land. Sorkin cautions that these new communities, built to exclude public spaces which historically have had an essential function to be locations for social and political activism (such as sidewalks, plazas, etc.), change the nature of communities (Low 2000; Sorkin 1992).

Residents of EVI produce and consume a sense of community privately, public only for the residents who live there. These new private-public spaces, such as the Common House, give the impression of a public space; however, because they explicitly limit that public to those who can afford to live in the community, or visitors of household members, they create a class-specific public space. Some residents at EcoVillage are keenly aware of this segregation and struggle to ignore, excuse, justify, or come to accept this uncomfortable reality. One resident lamented that she felt it is selfish to have all of this space and community to themselves, but doesn't know how to deal with it, and felt alone in her concern (Sandra).

The landscape architectural features that make EVI desirable, including the pond and the open land with hiking trails, are not easily accessible nor is there a strong desire to make them publicly accessible to non-EcoVillage residents, despite much of the land belonging to the nonprofit. Like other theme parks, EcoVillage attracts captive participants by marketing to specific audiences: those who long for a connection to fellow neighbors, but want to do so in a somewhat controlled and intentional way. EcoVillage also attracts those searching to reconcile their consumption-driven lifestyle with the environment.

And like most theme parks and themed communities, EVI attracts upper-middle-class educated whites (Sandra).

The theme of being green, which functions as one of the central unifying ideas in EVI, is not unlike the use of themes to create parks and shopping malls. Disney's founder, Walt Disney, created his theme park in response to his disappointment with the post–World War II urban sprawl that was taking over California. The theme park that is today Disney World would recapture a bygone day of friendly, safe streets void of the urban ills, and present the nostalgia of the happy family (Ross 1999). These themed spaces thus incorporated deliberate planning and design to foster a specific experience. Ironically, the popularity of the park attracted an edge city of hotels and fast-food restaurant development in the surrounding communities.

Certain features of the EVI project, like those in Celebration, create exclusionary spaces through the lack of paved surfaces that would allow someone in a wheelchair easy access to the community. According to a former resident, when it was revealed that the Common House would have to be handicap-accessible because it was considered a "public" building for the community, many residents resisted the requirement to install elevators. But perhaps more revealing of the exclusion of persons with disabilities from EVI is the vertical design of the first resident group homes with five sets of stairs that are impossible for someone in a wheelchair or an elderly participant to climb. The vertical duplexes were designed to minimize the footprint and provide views of the surrounding nature. The two houses in the FROG neighborhood that are considered by most residents to be handicap-accessible merely allow the occupant to live on the first floor (leaving the question of what use the second floor would have).

My role as an anthropologist also contributed to reinforce the theme of EcoVillage as a village—after all, anthropologists study villages, and social relationships within villages. The fact that I am a Zimbabwean and an anthropologist studying a Western "village" contributed to crystallize some residents' definition of a village. A resident pointed out that it was exotic to have an African anthropologist studying a Western village, and that this reversal of roles was a positive product of modernity. The anthropologist also contributes to the architecture of the community as it is imagined in non-Western villages. I was often affectionately introduced as the village anthropologist.

The theme of green living

> "Coming home almost feels like a vacation."
>
> (Ronald)

According to White, "nature may turn out to look a lot like an organic Disneyland, except it will be harder to park" (1996: 185). Indeed, living in EVI is like being on vacation. Similar to other vacation destinations, EVI provides the family an opportunity to experience the mission of the community. That is, the attractions of the community that include running into friendly[7] neighbors and having access to beautiful land are what residents appreciated about their unique community. As a green-themed community, what is the significance of the green theme that EVI is formulating? Will ecovillages signify new exclusionary communities that protect the middle class from confronting social and ecological degradation in the larger community they are connected to? How will ecovillages improve our environments or model sustainable living if they exclude such cultural realities as poverty, inequality, and racism, especially because these realities are often related? Or does the ecovillage effort have the potential to build an inclusive sustainable community movement?

In some ways ecovillages in general, and EVI in particular, embody similar methods and techniques to attract families to themed spaces, such as the opportunity to escape from the perplexing intricacies of everyday life through creatively constructing an idealized place. A resident felt attracted to EcoVillage because "it's sort of a replication of old-fashion neighborhood where people knew each other…. We don't have that in suburbs anymore, not even on cul-de-sacs or subdivisions and small towns, people don't interact with each other" (Stephanie).

Tensions and negotiations

Inherent to the EVI project is a tension between the idea of creating a model of sustainable living and the reality that EcoVillage is inaccessible to many people, physically and financially, and that not everyone living in EVI adheres to its ecological and social guiding principles. From extensive observations and in interviews with former participants, ideas about exclusion and idealism demonstrate a tension that is seldom addressed publicly, but nonetheless contemplated privately. A former participant of SONG attempted to explain this tension.

> We lived in a suburb in [a medium-sized Midwest city]. And so we were living in probably the most standard [US] American dream-type situation … we had a typical house in the suburbs, right by the elementary school, typical—it was just a two-story house and everybody drove their cars into their garages, nobody talked to each other…. We were looking for some other way of raising our family, some other way of living, than what is normally expected on the [road] society sort of takes you down…. We got married and we just sort of [thought] "I guess we're supposed to buy a house out in the suburbs." … But we sort of stopped and opened our minds a little bit and said we don't really have to do it this way. That's what drew us to cohousing. And I think … a big part of it was that in cohousing, you're meeting people that are sort of like-minded. I think that was the nice part about EcoVillage is that the people who are drawn to it have similar interests and beliefs about the environment and so, you have a lot more … control about who your neighbors are. Rather than sort of tolerating the neighbors … the idea was that you'd be making good friends with people that thought like you did.
>
> (Tamara)

Tamara was supportive of living in an ethnically and socially diverse community, but she also felt that EVI was too isolated from the larger society and often failed to integrate itself into the wider community.

TAMARA: It's beautiful up there, but part of what happens when I go up there is I feel sort of like … it's elitist or something. I just feel as though it's more elitist here [but] I am sort of wanting to be part of the movement to make … little sacrifices so we're not living in these huge houses and feeling like, as [US] Americans that we need so much and so big, and so much of everything. And yet, when I go to move to EcoVillage, this is part of my feeling. I go up there and it is like … we're on this beautiful piece of land, and people are talking about the views, and how important, how beautiful they want everything to be, which I can see, but on the other hand … I think it's … it's so hard for me sometimes, because I can see why people want to live up here, but I think the wiser decision would have been to build it closer to the road, or to try to find a site that was closer in town so people could walk. All those things are part of the disappointments … and I also … know learning about people in the greater Ithaca community I think … a lot of people have a sense of all those houses are really expensive up there … I heard somebody—this was a couple of years ago—I heard the term "egovillage."
TENDAI: Can you name one [of the things you found troubling]?
TAMARA: You come, you go into this nice little [neighborhood], up at EcoVillage, and you're with all these great people and then you go home. And you don't get any other view about what other people think about it, or what were some of the mistakes that were made, or what people think are mistakes.

Tamara's conflicted feelings about the EVI project reflect the tensions and negotiations of being isolated and physically separated from the larger society. Other residents felt embarrassed that on one hand the community was trying to demonstrate ways to model sustainable community living, but in reality EVI was only affordable to middle- and upper-middle-class households. One of the tensions that became apparent was in the relationship to work. Through both observation and by talking with various residents in both FROG and SONG, it is evident that to participate in EVI, households need a lot of flexible "free" time such as on weekends, evenings, and occasionally during the day. Several important meetings during the design and construction phrase of the SONG took place in the middle of the morning or afternoon. Anyone holding a full-time job (and possibly part-time) would need to take time off in order to participate. One family was disappointed that fewer adults in SONG worked full-time. Jill felt it made her husband, a hard worker who did not make a lot of money, appear uninterested in the community. Most of the members who can afford to participate in community meetings and perform volunteer activities are retired, work at home, run their own businesses that allow them to plan their own work hours, are hired by the community so their meeting hours are part of their paid employment,[8] or are wealthy enough to take significant time off.

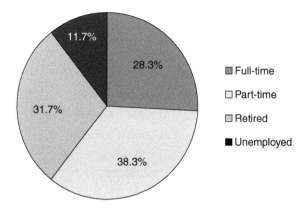

Figure 4.3 Employment status.
Source: Author.

White (1996) raises the contradictions of work and environmentalism, arguing that productive work in nature such as logging is often equated with the destruction of the environment. According to White, "environmentalists so often seem self-righteous, privileged, and arrogant because they so readily consent to identifying nature with play and making it by definition a place where leisured humans come only to visit and not to work, stay or live" (1996: 173). EVI has successfully enabled its residents to live in nature, while many residents have also been successfully hired by the project or bring their work to the community, like the farmers, thus connecting nature with their work.

Being able to transfer one's occupation to EVI requires access to specific social and economic privilege, such as having an advanced degree, having resources to start a business, or having access to inherited wealth. I was often surprised that this reality was sometimes overlooked. On one hand when the farmer needed to shoot the deer and build a fence to keep them out, the community supported them with a fundraiser to cover their unexpected costs. On the other hand, after explaining to a prominent community member that my household could not afford to buy a home, let alone pay the monthly community fees, I asked how she was able to buy a house and live in the community. She was a lifelong political and community activist and often told me that she was short of money. She responded that it was possible for me to live in EcoVillage despite my lack of financial resources; after all, she considered herself to be low-income and based on the salary she brought into her household, it was true that she literally earned a low income. Yet she had bought a house, paid monthly dues to the cooperative, owned a car, and took international vacations. I asked again, how was she able to buy a home when her income was unpredictable and sometimes non-existent? She finally confessed, as if I had compelled her to reveal a secret; her uncle had passed away and left her a large inheritance that she used for the down payment. The thread of our conversation ended

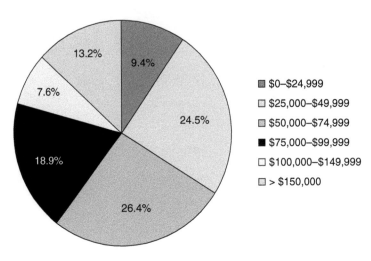

Figure 4.4 Income range.
Source: Author.

when I told her that I did not have such an uncle. During a separate conversation, another participant said that he was waiting for "a major inheritance before [his family] could build a home" (Christopher).

Access to wealth or income is essential for living in EVI, although few people would readily admit to having significant financial resources. Most participants were unwilling to reveal to the community how much money their household made, thus data from Figure 4.4 provides much-needed insight into the neighborhood resources. From conversations, it appeared that residents were reluctant to identify the community as exclusive to wealthy families. Despite needing significant financial resources to live in EVI, few residents actively discussed the class distinction and how to change the community to make it more open and affordable.

Examining the challenge of confronting the reality of what the privileged upper-middle-class lifestyle in the US affords, while at the same time seeking a lifestyle that is socially and environmentally sustainable, helps to understand how the redirection of energy and resources towards purchasing personal green commodities is possible. This juxtaposition is intertwined with the impossibility of negotiating capitalism and environmentalism. Class distinction is what makes it possible to live in EcoVillage, and while some residents told me they wanted to make the community more affordable, a stay-at-home mother explained her frustration with the suggestion that low-income families could live in EVI:

Rich people can afford organic food and hybrid electric cars and there are certain things about the neighborhoods that cost money, like stone patios. There would just be a lot of challenges around commonly owned things and food, and anything that we held in common [if a low-income family moved in]. There always would have to be. That would always be the main focus: can everybody afford it? And that [would] put those kinds of people that really were in a tight spot, on the spot, all the time. Which would always set those people apart. It is challenging enough to live in a community where you are kind of all the same, or are really close to being the same [social class?] but with that [lower class?] added factor I think it would be really hard.

(Natasha)

The concern that low-income families would be a challenge to living in Eco-Village related to deeper assumptions about class and exposed a central conflict in the general project. As mentioned earlier, EcoVillage was never designed to be a low-income or an affordable housing community. Its mission to be a model for upper-middle-class households was the result of a conflict between early planners who wanted to model social and ecological justice and affordable housing and those who desired an alternative for the middle classes (Walker 2005: 56–57). The tension regarding affordability can be attributed to a lack of understanding of the history and mission of the community on the part of some participants; but it also reflects the desires of some participants to change the fundamental ways our society creates separate housing models for different social classes. According to some participants, little effort was made to openly discuss the history, mission, and goals of the community, especially as disgruntled families leave and new members join. According to an active community member, this kind of conversation would provide the desired openness about affordability.

Table 4.3 Highest level of schooling (%)

12th grade or less (no diploma)	0.0
High school diploma/GED	0.0
Some college (no degree)	8.3
Associate's degree	5.0
Bachelor's degree	20.0
Graduate degree	66.7

Source: Author.

Table 4.4 Religious practice (%)

None	51.7
Buddhist	10.3
Christian	15.5
Hindu	1.7
Islam	0.0
Judaism	10.3
I am active	22.4
I am not active	13.8
Other	32.8

Source: Author.

Table 4.5 Political affiliation/party (%)

Anarchist	3.5
Communist	0.0
Democrat	66.7
Green	38.6
Libertarian	12.3
Independent	26.3
Republican	0.0
Socialist	15.8
Tea Party	0.0
Undecided	0.0
Engage in political activities (vote, campaign, rally, etc.)	42.1
Do not engage in political activities	8.8
Other	14.0

Source: Author.

An effort was made to create an affordable second neighborhood through offering subsidy units in SONG.[9] A successful grant application resulted in several units offered for low-income households; in reality, $20,000 was offered off the price of the home. Other residents and former residents mentioned that this was not enough to offset the $180,000 cost of a home in SONG, and that subsidies would not necessarily make the community affordable. Sandra was further concerned that those who advocated for subsidies did not think of the complexity it would involve:

> I am worried about the subsidy units, because I feel like while affordability was prime in the minds of [participants in the] previous incarnation of the SONG group, and maybe in EcoVillage as whole, people really aren't thinking about what those implications are, especially for the people that need affordable housing. They [low-income families] are already set apart by society. I am not saying that all the people that need money are involved in, you know, government programs or anything like that, but take for example [a single mother who was interested in living in FROG]. She is on section 8 housing, and I don't know if she has food stamps, but she's made several references to depending on a food pantry for their food. I mean that's just not the type of person that lives here.

At the same time, Sandra acknowledges that a community like EVI can enable someone to gain the support necessary to get out of poverty. Because residents at EcoVillage are busy creating the complex project, little time is allocated to work on addressing concerns like these that many other residents had regarding affordability and accessibility.

> It seems to me that when [low-income] people want to make a change what they don't have is a support system to help them make [that] change. The

future of this planet and maybe this society ... depends on—not periodic programs that run out of money ... like government programs [that] maybe last for three years. That is not long enough for somebody to change their life that they might have been living for 40 years. It is not enough to change the direction of poverty.

Sandra doesn't know the solution, but is frustrated that other residents don't seem to want to talk about larger issues of affordable housing.

Residents of EVI are religiously, professionally, and politically diverse; there are lesbian and gay households. However, Lucia, who moved from a large city, felt awkward living in a privileged community because it lacked racial and ethnic diversity.

[The neighborhood] is not diverse enough; there are virtually no minorities here, except people's adopted children. You have to be pretty well off to move in and everyone here would agree that they would like it to be more diverse, and they would like to be more equitable but nothing ever happens to make it possible for anybody to live here: the handicapped person or a poor person or you know, let alone a welfare mother.

(Lucia)

She lamented that she left an ethnically diverse neighborhood and community to join a predominantly white community. Jimmy, who actively built relationships with people in the Ithaca community, expressed his aspirations for EVI to be more inclusive after describing the experience of a young black Jamaican who was growing food on the EVI, Inc., land and was stopped by some residents biking home: "... they stopped him and had some interaction, where they told him he couldn't be driving up that road. And he perceived it as being a racial attack." Jimmy continued:

... while I think it was fine that we tried to deal with that issue and figure out what happened and what we could be doing differently—I wish we were doing other things, such as, working with [GIAC][10] so we can get some kids from downtown up here on a regular basis to do some gardening. Or some, I think once a year, there's some kids from [GIAC] come and they swim in the pond. And I think [one of residents] sponsors that group. But some more ongoing relationships with people in the greater community and deal with developing relationships with the African-American community in town and the Asian-American communities that we have, that go beyond just responding to a crisis or going down to a march when there's police abuse.

(Jimmy)

Some residents in EVI have felt overwhelmed trying to process larger issues of social justice and have retreated inwards. Hans feels that he is "... just taking care of this corner of the world." They are making an effort within their social and economic means, even if it means owning 1/6 of the neighborhood washing machine instead of the very real option of owning their own machine privately. When I asked a resident who used paper plates and plastic cutlery if there was a contradiction, she responded that she does not like to do dishes and after all she had not moved to the neighborhood because of a strong concern for the environment (see Appendix C).

One resident felt confident that his participating in EVI was a positive model of sustainable living and was happy with the way the community modeled sustainable living: "one of the things which makes me feel really good about living here is telling other people about it, and enlighten them" (Sean). Some residents are uncomfortable with the tension between being a model, being a prototype of environmentalism, and the reality of class stratification. Some residents justified their place in EcoVillage by pointing to their ability to purchase green commodities, which will lead to an increase in demand, thus an increase in production and potentially affordable prices of green commodities for the poor. Another resident questioned whether EcoVillage is just a privileged community located up on a hill, with great views and access to organic food.

> … I know people who are living in [Ithaca and] who have a great deal of community, who are living ecologically, who are doing a lot of the same things that EcoVillage now says they are doing. One friend of mine was kind of joking about EcoVillage and she said, "yeah right, they say we are creating a neighborhood, but well, hey guys, look around you, there are neighborhoods everywhere, you did not invent this you know." There is this attitude that maybe it is a bunch of people who are really full of themselves and think they're doing something so brilliant and they are sort of [saying] sure you can do that if you have got $100,000 and $150,000 to spend on a nice house in a nice field up on the hill.
>
> (Anne)

Other neighbors see no contradictions between living in an expensive, exclusive, eco-themed community and the values they hold of social and ecological justice. Rather, these residents point out that the choice was between living in a typical suburb where everyone keeps to themselves and living in a cohousing community that had energy-efficient homes that automatically make their lifestyle more eco-friendly. Some residents mentioned that they could have easily afforded a much larger home, with more private space. They were being good stewards to the land by demonstrating to other wealthy families that it is possible to live a comfortable lifestyle, without sacrificing a lot, and at the same time, do good things for the environment. This, I argue, is the attraction of the theme community: EVI has a compost team to make composting easier for neighbors, and a cook team to make socializing with neighbors over dinner ordinary. Thus it is the deliberate ways to experience living in the EcoVillage.

Another significant factor related to affordability is access to spare time. The energy and resources required to create a community in harmony with the environment requires vast amounts of time for meetings, work team duties, informal gatherings, and family. Households where two adults worked outside of the home often mentioned that community activities, especially the meetings, were stressful because they were lengthy and during times when participants could otherwise spend time with their families. Two women on separate occasions voiced the concern that their families were torn between being with the community and being with their family. For Stephanie, it was hard to "carve out a day or two or a whole weekend when you're not doing something for the community." Time is essential because making decisions by consensus requires residents to be physically present at meetings for discussions and decision-making. Some families with small children and two full-time jobs found this commitment burdensome. During one particular month there were many meetings that lasted an average of three hours each. Some families with more than one adult were able to divide the attendance at meetings, while it was not uncommon to send someone from the meeting (usually I volunteered) to walk door-to-door looking for neighbors to establish the two-thirds of households required for quorum. At times, these quorum residents would only stay until their usefulness in consensus was over and then return to their homes, making the goals of consensus appear more procedural than authentic. The time costs to families and the financial expenditure of initially purchasing a home, but also paying monthly community fees, make the community challenging to most families where both adults need to work. When both adults were working full-time outside of the home, they were too tired to participate in lengthy meetings; yet, participation in meetings is essential for the community to function effectively, which posed a dilemma to households that needed full-time employment.

While participants I spoke with expressed satisfaction with the community, others were concerned about contradictions they experienced in their daily life. Specifically, one resident felt trapped in a larger social structure that, despite his best efforts to live simply, he was unable to find a way out of what he recognized as a consumer culture. "I think I am a victim of our own cultural norms and expectations" (Jordan).

Constructing place through rituals and celebrations

There is no single unifying concept of community or environmentalism that this research found to exist in EVI. Most of the residents had a unique way of framing their attraction to the EcoVillage project and their level of commitment to either the community or the environment. For the most part, it was the construction of the place of EcoVillage that ultimately brought households into the neighborhoods. One significant way neighbors felt connected was through the construction of social rituals that brought neighbors together in shared new traditions. Guys Baking Pies and Women Goin' Swimmin' are the kinds of event that epitomize the opportunity EVI gives residents to be close to nature and become close to each other through rituals. The story below is an example of two rituals in EcoVillage:

> Early one afternoon, the men went hunting. They roamed through the open fields of the hills overlooking the city below. The tall grass hid most of the hunters but their bright hats and sunglasses were visible to the women and children left behind in the village. By afternoon they had gathered more than 10 pounds of berries to be baked into pies. The single woman allowed in this annual ritual was Claire. She was known in the village as one of the best cooks, and she would assist the men in their "Guys Baking Pies" ritual.
>
> The men gathered in the community kitchen hovering over the large island as Claire instructed them on how to gently mix the chilled butter into the flour. An hour later, the young boys and their male mentors were forming pie shapes and filling them with juicy berries, licking the spoons and their fingers as they worked. Shirtless, some of the men posed for pictures, proud to show their artwork that would be shared with the women.
>
> The community bell rang and the women who had stayed home poured into the Common House laughing and joking about this ritual and light-heartedly irritated by the gendered nature of the event. A Marxist in the group complained but no one listened; she always complains and it is just for fun anyway, what does it matter? The ceremony was elaborate. The men had cleaned the kitchen island and decorated it with their various pies, ice cream, and whipped cream. Before being served we, the women, listened to poems, songs, and stories about the bounty of the earth on this beautiful land, the sweetness of the berries, the community, and the efforts of the young boys who worked hard. The sole woman on the team was recognized and thanked for her supervision. As the men passed out pies, and neighbors chatted about the day's events and politics, an announcement of the women's event was made. "Women Goin' Swimmin' will take place at the fire pit at 9:00 p.m."
>
> Few women participated in the Women Goin' Swimmin' event and I find out why as we gathered around the fire pit. It was a nude event and, as a good anthropologist, I stripped down. Naked and desperate to warm ourselves by the fire, we huddled close together. The leader described the history of the event. It was a way to counter the Guys Baking Pies. One thing that had troubled the leader as a young adult was the negative self-image she had of her body; others nodded in agreement. Although we were distracted thinking of the men who might be sitting nearby listening to us, we took turns talking about our experience growing up with negative feelings about our bodies and shared how we tried to overcome them. Unhappiness with weight, buttocks, breast size, and sex gave way to loving support and supportive laughter. We were connecting with each other as women and, to what many of the women felt is the essence of nature, our nakedness.

After our gathering we jumped into the pond, a symbolic rebirthing, and enjoyed an evening of skinny-dipping, staring at falling stars, and good conversation.

Those who celebrate rituals at EVI treasure the opportunity to connect with each other and with nature. It is often through these interactive rituals that residents meet friends and members of the larger Ithaca community. What makes these rituals possible is the time and resources members of EVI put into creating ways to directly interact with nature through gathering fruit or enjoying the pond. White's (1996) analysis of nature as a leisure resource helps to explain the tension between working with nature and playing in nature. Through the purchase of the land, EVI is able to construct a community that merges working in nature (the farm) and playing in and celebrating nature (rituals). At the same time that residents are celebrating the land and the bounty it provides, consumerism is rampant in US culture (Lury 1996) and green consumerism is quickly becoming a fast growing industry. As franchises like The Nature Company defined what it meant to protect and support nature (Price 1996; Smith 1996), natural/green/eco-capitalism gains widespread support among people committed to environmental and social change (Hawken et al. 1999). In the process of constructing the community, individuals are careful to find a compromise between radical environmentalism and acceptable middle-class living standards. Residents overwhelmingly feel that the community is dramatically different than their previous home; it is like living in a park, living on an estate, and like being on a vacation, except it is home. EVI contains features of what Goldberger (1996) calls "urbanoid environments." These places are "private environments purporting to be public spaces" (Goldberger 1996; Hannigan 1998). At the same time, in its efforts to create a village, EVI relies on images of non-Western communities and creates a space where the disorganized fruition of authentic neighborhoods and communities is replaced with deliberately constructed spaces and places. These constructed spaces are designed to give all the beauty, diversity, and cultural opportunity of a village or city, without the adverse reality of poverty and inequality that plague the authentic community. Hannigan (1998) argues that the Fantasy City, like ecovillages, is a way that middle- and upper-middle-class US-Americans try to negotiate the tension between wanting to experience the imagined simple lifestyle, and not wanting to endure the risks that help create such a lifestyle. This tension is expressed, for example, through some neighbors' actively resisting vegetarianism. In one instance, early in my stay, a resident asked me if I was a vegetarian. I truthfully, though somewhat embarrassingly, said I was not, but that I was really trying. She quickly invited me to join her and a couple of other neighbors for steaks after the vegetarian community meal. During a separate incident a resident told me she felt that meat eaters were discriminated against because there was rarely a special meat option at the Common House meal like there was for vegans. Few residents I interviewed were pure vegetarians; some, for example, ate meat when they went to restaurants. At Thanksgiving, few residents ate any of the tofurky (tofu turkey) that was served. Residents are able to negotiate the conflicts between their own consumption and practice of environmentalism and community through ritual constructions and celebrations. Residents in EVI are creating a green lifestyle, one that enables the green sustainable theme park to become a desirable everyday life.

Notes

1 The First Resident Group is officially recorded as the EcoVillage Cooperative Corporation, although it is commonly referred to as the FROG.
2 During a discussion of alternative energy, it was found that the best location for windmills is in the open field, which would ostensibly change the view for residents with south-facing views. Objectors made reference to the easements and that the value of their homes would be negatively affected. Such were some of the contradictions residents and former residents expressed about the project.
3 There are currently 37 different small businesses at EVI. See Appendix A for a complete list.
4 I use *private-public* space to describe spaces that belong to the community or non-profit, but are not accessible to the larger public in Ithaca. These spaces are outside of one's home, but inside the borders of the EVI, Inc. land (route 79, Coy Glen, etc.). These spaces include the pond and hiking trails.
5 The meaning of safety was broadly and fluidly used by residents to describe a wide variety of feelings and experiences. Some residents felt safe from crime or physical harm, others felt emotionally safe to talk with someone if they had a problem, or safe from feeling isolated and uncared for.
6 By 2014, Lenny had moved out, as did the neighbor who initially objected to catching and eating the fish. The Harvest celebration was a chance for the vegans and omnivores to share their perspectives.
7 On only one occasion during my fieldwork did I meet a neighbor who was visibly upset and angry. In general, although residents often disagree and become upset with each other, very little was expressed in public, or in my presence. I observed the community to be a respectful, positive, nurturing, and caring place. I was told of residents who would yell and become angry during community meetings, but these residents had apparently moved out by the time I arrived.
8 This observation came after a short conversation I had with a paid resident who commented that he was fortunate to be paid for what he already enjoyed. Unfortunately, I did not collect specific data on who was paid, how much, and what part of their "participation" in the community was paid or volunteer.
9 At several orientation meetings I attended, including during my first visits to EcoVillage, the future resident-developers illustrated that homes in the SONG would be small and more affordable than in the FROG by allowing residents to design their own home and contribute significant sweat equity to their home. This prediction backfired when wealthier residents, attracted by the idea of designing their dream-green house, built larger homes than the FROG. This resulted in a 50–70 percent increase in costs of the original estimated.
10 The Greater Ithaca Activities Center (GIAC) "is a center for all ages, particularly youth and teens. It serves the immediate neighborhood and the greater Ithaca area by providing multicultural, educational, and recreational programs focused on social and individual development."

References

Brown, Susan Love, ed. 2001. *Intentional Community: An Anthropological Perspective.* New York: State. University of New York Press.

Davis, Mike. 1992. *City of Quartz: Excavating the Future in Los Angeles.* New York: Vintage Books.

Davis, Mike. 1998. *Ecology of Fear: Los Angeles and the Imagination of Disaster.* New York: Metropolitan Books.

Di Chiro, G. 1996. Nature as Community: The Convergence of Environment and Social Justice. In: *Uncommon Ground: Toward Reinventing Nature.* W. Cronon, ed. pp. 298–320. New York: W.W. Norton & Co.

Escobar, Arturo. 1996. Constructing Nature: Elements for a Post-structural Political Ecology. In: *Liberation Ecologies.* pp. 46–68. London: Routledge.

Fishman, Robert. 1987. *Bourgeois Utopias: The Rise and Fall of Suburbia.* New York: Basic Books, Inc.

Fosket, J., and L. Mamo. 2009. *Living Green: Communities that Sustain.* Gabriola Island, BC: New Society Publishers.

Garreau, Joel. 1991. *Edge City: Life on the New Frontier.* New York: Doubleday.

Goldberger, Paul. 1996. The Rise of the Private City. In: *Breaking Away: The Future of Cities.* J.V. Martin, ed. New York: The Twentieth Century Fund.

Gottdiener, Mark. 2001. *The Theming of America: American Dreams, Media Fantasies, and Themed Environments.* Boulder, CO: Westview Press.

Gregory, Steven. 1998. *Black Corona: Race and the Politics of Place in an Urban Community.* Princeton: Princeton University Press.

Hannigan, John. 1998. *Fantasy City: Pleasure and Profit in the Postmodern Metropolis.* London and New York: Routledge.

Hawken, Paul, Amory L. Lovins, and Hunter Lovins. 1999. *Natural Capitalism: Creating the Next Industrial Revolution.* Boston, New York, London: Little, Brown, and Co.

Howard, Ebenezer. 1902. *Garden Cities of Tomorrow.* London: S. Sonnenschein and Co., Ltd.

Low, Setha M. 1996. The Anthropology of Cities: Imagining and Theorizing the City. *Annual Review of Anthropology, 25,* 383–409.

Low, Setha M. 1999. *Theorizing the City: The New Urban Anthropology Reader.* New Brunswick, NJ: Rutgers University Press.

Low, Setha M. 2000. *On the Plaza: The Politics of Public Space and Culture.* Austin, Texas: University of Texas Press.

Low, Setha M. 2001. The Edge and the Center: Gated Communities and the Discourse of Urban Fear. American Anthropologist 103(1):45–58.

Lury, C. 1996. *Consumer Culture.* Cambridge: Polity.

Lynd, Robert Staughton. 1956. *Middletown; A Study in American Culture.* New York: Harcourt, Brace & World.

Mumford, Lewis. 1946. Garden Cities and the Metropolis: A Reply. *Journal of Land and Public Utility Economics, 22*(1), 66-69.

Price, Jennifer. 1996. Looking for Nature at the Mall: A Field Guide to the Nature Company. In: *Uncommon Ground: Towards Reinventing Nature.* W. Cronon, ed. pp. 186–203. New York: W.W. Norton.

Putnam, Robert D. 2000. *Bowling Alone: The Collapse and Revival of American Community.* New York: Touchstone.

Redfield, Robert. 1962. *The Little Community and Peasant Society and Culture.* Chicago: University of Chicago Press.

Reynolds, M., and E. Ball. 1963. *Little Boxes*. Essex Music of Australia Pty. Limited.

Ritzer, George. 1993. *The McDonaldization of Society*. Thousand Oaks, CA: Pine Forge Press.

Rodwin, Lloyd. 1945. Garden Cities and the Metropolis. *Journal of Land and Public Utility Economics, 21*(3), 268–281.

Ross, Andrew. 1999. *The Celebration Chronicles: Life, Liberty, and the Pursuit of Property Value in Disney's New Town*. New York: Ballantine Books.

Smith, Neil. 1996. The Production of Nature. In: *FutureNatural: Nature, Science, Culture*. J. Bird, et al., eds. London and New York: Routledge.

Soper, Kate. 1996. Nature/'nature'. In: *FutureNatural: Nature, Science, Culture*. G. Robertson, et al., eds. London and New York: Routledge.

Sorkin, Michael, ed. 1992. *Variations on a Theme Park: The New American City and the End of Public Space*. New York: Hill and Wang.

Walker, Liz. 2005. *EcoVillage at Ithaca: Pioneering a Sustainable Culture*. Gabriola Island, BC: New Society Publishers.

White, Richard. 1996. "Are You an Environmentalist or Do You Work for a Living?" Work and Nature. In: *Uncommon Ground: Toward Reinventing Nature*. W. Cronon, ed. pp. 171–185. New York: W.W. Norton & Co.

5 Emerging green lifestyles

Environmental justice scholarship has long argued that race and class need to be central, not merely an afterthought, to efforts of the environmental movement. According to Smith (1996), "only at the risk of jeopardizing a vital environmental movement do we forget that access to nature, and cultural constructions of nature, are centrally questions of class and race as well as gender and other dimensions of social difference" (43). While the environmental movement of the 1970s focused its lens outward on confronting problems affecting neighborhood health, endangered species, and national resource management, today's environmentalism mirrors what Szasz describes as an inverted quarantine, the individualized response to collective threat through shopping, the opposite of a social movement (Szasz 2007). The 1970s environmentalism resulted in the National Environmental Policy Act, the Environmental Protection Agency, and a series of policies governing our shared resources such as the Clean Air Act and the Clean Water Act. Further efforts produced 1994 Executive Order 12898, which explicitly addresses environmental justices in low-income and minority communities. Increasingly, however, green consumerism and consumption is producing personal green lifestyle choices that focus the lens inward, on an individual environmentalism.

This chapter explores how green lifestyles are formed when consumption is a means to express environmentalism. Through an attempt to model social and environmental sustainability, community residents struggle to avoid individual environmentalism in a culture driven by consumption, increasingly, through the promises of green consumerism. Creating a lifestyle that is comfortable and improves the environment runs the risk of focusing the environmental lens on individual efforts and personal benefits rather than finding solutions that could improve the social and physical environment of all people, and contribute to a just sustainability that recognizes the need for an inclusive environmental movement.

Constructing a green lifestyle

According to Kempton et al. (1996), "understanding culture is an essential part of understanding environmental problems because human cultures guide their members both when they accelerate environmental destruction and when they slow it down" (1). Living at EcoVillage is like living in a national park; hiking trails that wind in and out of young forest resemble paths in a well-funded and loved park. The open fields that accentuate views of rolling hills and prestigious universities are awesome; they are what attracted residents from around the country to the community. According to Ronald, a father and world traveler in his mid-thirties, EcoVillage is a place where city dwellers escape to on their vacations. It is quiet, peaceful, clean, and beautiful. The views from within and without EcoVillage are stunning. On any given day one can see children running barefoot, adults engaged in active conversation, and occasionally a deer prancing across the meadow, fearing only one of the neighborhood dogs defying community guidelines to be on leash at all times. EVI provides the opportunity for its residents to collectively experience community, family, leisure, and union with nature, a lifestyle that would otherwise be too expensive for any one family to afford.

Lifestyle changes, especially in the United States, are essential to reversing the current trend in social and environmental degradation; yet, creating models of what a new lifestyle might look like has been challenging. According to Myers (1997), populations in rich countries realize that changes in lifestyle and reducing consumption are essential if we are to overcome ecological and social problems. He likens this lifestyle shift to the 1980s when noticeable numbers of US-Americans began to quit smoking. Through public policy and education, US-Americans have come to accept smoking bans in most public places, including restaurants, bars, and increasingly in city parks and on college campuses.[1] Kempton et al. (1996) found that participants in their study of US environmentalists believed that "reducing our consumption can be done without reducing our 'standard of living' for the most part" (132). Participants in their study believed that, while lifestyle changes were necessary, drastic changes were unrealistic and unlikely to happen; instead, they argued for changes in technology as the solution to environmental problems (Kempton et al. 1996).

Similar to the views expressed by participants in Kempton's study, residents in EVI are confident that green technology and a green lifestyle will help to solve current environmental problems. Kempton et al. found evidence that some US-Americans "view environmentally conscious, lower-consumption lifestyles as being more satisfying" (Kempton et al. 1996); residents in EVI teeter on the balance between identifying consumption as a barrier to a satisfying lifestyle (expressed through emphasis on living simply) and the appeal of green technology as a fulfilling way to help the environment without sacrificing lifestyle choices.

I define a green lifestyle as the embodiment of five key lifestyle features that include focusing environmentalist concern on personal action, an increase in reliance on and consumption of green technology, a proactive effort to share resources, an easy access to nature, and a green identity. The case study of EVI illustrates the green lifestyle effort, presenting both the opportunities and challenges of creating a green lifestyle as we search for a better way to live with each other and the natural environment.

Personal environmentalism

The concept of a green lifestyle embodies specific tastes and a distinctive style of living with neighbors and nature (Katz-Gerro and Shavit 1998: 370). It also reflects what Szasz (2007) calls *inverted quarantine*, where instead of focusing outwards on societal solutions, participants quarantine themselves and focus environmentalist efforts inward on personal efforts and benefits. Like other ecovillage communities, the goal of EVI is to create a lifestyle that is good for the environment and the people who live in it. The lifestyle sought by many residents is to live in a way that is mutually beneficial: the environment is preserved and protected by residents, and residents benefit from the natural surroundings. Claire summarized this sentiment: "I do feel more connected to humanity than I did living on my own in New York City or in New Haven … in that you learn about all the different things that are happening to people, what they are experiencing." The humanity that Claire refers to includes her fellow neighbors, whom she has gotten to know very well through being on work teams and sharing laundry facilities.

The physical design of the community was not the only means of creating a green lifestyle. According to early planners, the EcoVillage "green" lifestyle was intended to impose minimal sacrifice of the comforts of suburban homes. For many residents, creating and living in an ecovillage was reminiscent of living in a college dorm.

> Cohousing is almost like living on a campus. I remember the first night we stayed here; it seemed a whole lot like living in the dorms again. There are a lot of very well-educated people and maybe we have selected this lifestyle because it is like when we were going to school.
>
> (Jeff)

Yet, according to Jeff, the project is also about defining the community as protectors of the environment in a way that feels right. A father of two, Jeff acknowledged that living a green lifestyle was challenging on many fronts: "You don't know if your lifestyle is really sustainable … or if there is any point in doing that when everybody else in the society around us is doing something else." Jeff's struggle to explain what other residents had tired of, or resigned to ignore, was the looming question of how to change cultural habits, such as consumption, that result in degraded environments and communities, while being immersed in that culture. We discussed US consumption and non-renewable energy sources:

TENDAI: You'd be short on a lot of gas if you boycotted all the oil companies that had disasters like the Exxon Valdez accident, because I think every major oil company is doing some horrible things around the world.

JEFF: Yeah. And Shell and BP are probably just as bad as everybody else, but they also talk about developing renewable energy in the future. So they are sort of greenwashing. So should you use Shell and BP in preference to the other ones? Or does it really matter at all? In here (EVI) we try to live more lightly on the land, but I think I feel like we are still using a lot more resources than people outside of the United States, even though we use less than the average [US] American … so are we really doing enough here, or is it just sort of a thing that is making us all feel more comfortable because we are better than other people in the United States?

Many features of the EVI project point towards the creation of a personal green lifestyle rather than establishing reaching practices that decrease environmental degradation. For example, while access to mass transit is one of the most ecological solutions to reducing automobile use and carbon emissions, the community's housing design in the middle of the property and away from the road, and resistance to paving the road, points to different priorities, specifically, better views and a rustic dirt road, which contribute to a satisfying lifestyle. Another example of the tension between green lifestyle choices and environmental efforts is the sauna project enthusiastically taken on by two residents, while the work needed to design a bus shelter to serve EVI residents was primarily pursued by students in a sustainable communities class (Walker 2005).

Only a limited number of buses run along the main road adjacent to the entrance of the EVI community. Requests by some residents to provide bus access closer to the neighborhood were rejected, because it would do a number of things some families wanted to avoid, such as give the city certain rights over the long dirt road, or result in the likelihood that the dirt road would have to be paved and maintained by the city, something some residents felt would be less "natural." Other neighbors expressed the concern that public buses would bring strangers into the community and make the neighborhoods less safe, especially for children. The community remained resistant to allowing city buses in the neighborhood despite the general agreement that more accessible public transportation would lead to reduced automobile use (Fishman 1987).

This rejection of public transportation aligns EVI with the processes that exclude the public from other constructed public/private spaces such as in shopping malls or theme parks, which have used public accessibility as a means of excluding certain visitors (Goss 1993). Free parking and limited public transportation at large private shopping malls and theme parks are designed into the plans to be exclusionary. No effort was made during my research to persuade the city of Ithaca to increase bus service to the community; instead residents focused on creating internal car-sharing. As mentioned earlier, the danger of these public/private spaces, like those of a shopping mall (which are now designed to resemble old-fashioned Main Street, with arboretums lined with trees, park benches, fountains, and ice cream stands), is their emphasis on enclosure, protection, and control (Jackson 1996). Like EVI, these spaces protect users from litter, the homeless and panhandlers, suspicious characters, and protestors. Despite the fact that many residents are politically active outside the community, the discomfort within is a persistent concern. These tensions and contradictions are only a few of the challenges that characterize the green lifestyle.

Green consumption/green technology

For only a handful of residents, a deep concern for the earth and a strong commitment to proactively improving the way new homes and communities are built were the principal justifications for creating an ecological cohousing community. For some residents "raising the green bar" and being a model of innovative technology were the driving forces behind moving to the community. This distinction between living harmoniously in nature and being a model of innovative green technology is well pronounced in the SONG, where many individual homes are impressively designed with straw bale insulation, solar panels, composting toilets, and in one home, several large structural solid wooden beams which were cut and erected manually without the use of electric drills. During an afternoon of sweat equity, a future resident of the SONG told me how important it was that her house be biodegradable when she no longer needs it. Some of the efforts to raise the green bar included importing builders from out of state to give workshops on innovative technology.

The consumption of products that were considered to be green was an important part of being environmentally conscious for some residents. They were asked in the 2015 census/survey: what activities, decisions, and choices do you make that express your commitment to addressing social and environmental problems? Residents' responses are shown in Table 5.1.

Christina, a woman in her mid-forties, felt that turning up her thermostat was not in harmony with nature, but preferred to chop wood. "Even though there is some pollution aspects to wood stoves, there is still something spiritually connected to me about that process" (2001). Gianina also felt that living in harmony was not about economics:

> I don't think it is economic. I think it has to do with courage, it has to do with … habits of ways of living, and so the courage to move beyond ways of living, things we think we need and don't need … I think that it is cheaper and simpler ultimately to live in harmony with the environment.

One resident said that she did not feel "great about my reliance on a car, but I live in the world as it exists at this point and so I'm not in a major guilt trip about it" (Constance). Constance also occasionally shopped at used clothing stores: "I tend to either shop at thrift stores or buy from really good catalogs that use organic cotton … so I have some expensive things." In some cases, green consumerism results in redirected consumerism that fails to consider the places where food and commodities originate, the living and working conditions of the people involved in their production, and the waste that is generated when those products are disregarded.

Table 5.1 Environmental goods (%)

	Already have	Want, but can't afford	Considering it	Don't want, can afford	Don't want, can't afford
Own a home in EVI	89.8	3.4	5.1	1.7	0.0
Home solar panels	50.0	14.8	22.2	9.3	3.7
Solar hot water	22.6	18.9	41.5	13.2	3.8
Hybrid/electric car	35.1	19.3	14.0	19.3	12.3
Holding on to my old vehicle with good gas mileage	87.8	0.0	2.4	9.8	0.0
Washing/drying machine in home	19.3	3.5	12.3	54.4	10.5
Dishwasher in home	43.1	1.7	3.5	44.8	6.9
West Haven Farm CSA share	48.2	3.6	14.3	33.9	0.0
Kestrel Perch Berry CSA	38.0	0.0	24.0	36.0	2.0
Consume locally grown food	98.3	1.7	0.0	0.0	0.0
Consume organic foods	98.3	1.7	0.0	0.0	0.0
Private vegetable beds in shared neighborhood garden	52.9	2.0	27.5	17.7	0.0
Private vegetable garden in front/back of home	62.0	2.0	18.0	16.0	2.0

Source: Author.

Sharing

Another effort to create a green lifestyle in EcoVillage is by engaging in a culture of resource sharing. Through sharing washing machines, lawn mowers, vacuum cleaners, and community meals, many residents try to simplify their life. The green lifestyle attempts to raise awareness of wasteful practices and encourages sharing, composting, consuming green products, and thereby becoming closer to nature. Families are able, in essence, to purchase a green lifestyle that automatically puts them physically closer to nature and engages them in an environment that fosters making good choices for the environment.

The sharing of resources through green lifestyle created by residents of Eco-Village means excluding families who cannot afford to buy a house in the community, live away from public transportation, and pay monthly dues to support the shared facilities such as the Common House and the common road. While there are no obvious physical gates and walls, the community restricts who is allowed in the village by rejecting public transportation and creating an economic barrier through high costs.

Car-sharing has been a driving force for Kenneth. He has continuously advocated for the EVI community to embark on creating a formal car-sharing program. Although some households share vehicles informally (I was always able to find someone to lend me their car when I lived there), as new neighborhoods joined, Kenneth was sure it would be possible for households to relinquish one of their cars in favor of sharing. With limited success organizing the

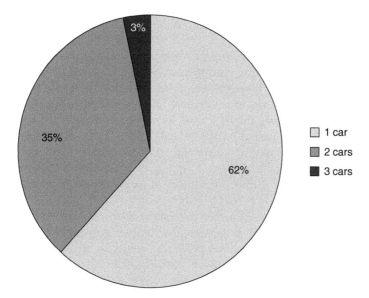

Figure 5.1 Number of cars per household.
Source: Author.

program in the neighborhood, Ithaca Carshare, a local nonprofit organization that provides easy short-term car-sharing across the greater Ithaca community, placed one of its cars in the EVI village. But less than a year after, the car was removed because it was not used often; when given the option, households at EVI still preferred to use their own cars. The 2015 survey revealed that only one person stated that they carpool with other EVI drivers and one other person answered that they rarely do. Three survey respondents said they regularly take the bus. Although saddened by the realization that limiting car use at EVI is a struggle, Kenneth is determined to keep trying.

Green access

"I never owned a car until I moved up here."

(Kevin)

While Veblen (1931) focuses on material goods to establish class and social distinction, Bourdieu places emphasis on symbolic features such as the ability for individuals to participate culturally in a distinct social class through what he calls cultural capital. EcoVillage embodies both symbolic (cultural capital) and material goods (organic products, open land) in creating a distinct green lifestyle. While material possessions, such as owning a home in one of the neighborhoods, are essential to being part of EcoVillage, being surrounded by open undeveloped land and having an opportunity to engage in the discourse of being green (the cultural capital of community and environment) are also important. Residents share a common appreciation for the beauty and luxury of connecting with nature, but would not consider themselves of a special "green class."[2] In EcoVillage, green needs, such as hybrid cars and organic shampoos, are marketed to a specific social class as social indicators of being concerned for the environment. For example, owning a composting toilet is one way one resident identified herself as belonging to a class of people who are concerned about protecting the environment. This fits into what Bourdieu describes as lifestyles in creating the "status of a symbolic system whose key organizing principle is distinction" (Applebaum 1998: 335). Bourdieu's concept of lifestyle is a useful tool to understand residents in EcoVillage who are trying to create a sustainable culture. The project is creating a lifestyle based on distinctive practices of the consumption of specific green commodities such as the EVI project.

Debates about consumption suggest that the emphasis on class distinction is being replaced by "consumption as a status and lifestyle generator" (Katz-Gerro and Shavit 1998: 370; Featherstone 1991). An emphasis on green consumption and lifestyle affects the residents at EcoVillage. Many residents are keenly aware of the class distinction that living in EcoVillage gives them. One resident downplayed her access to wealth by explaining that she and her partner had worked hard as young adults and thus earned their access to wealth. Some families try to be actively inclusive of other social classes, while others accept their privilege and try to make the best of it, often by being a model of how other middle- and upper-class families can spend their money in ways that are better for the community and the environment. Rikki felt sad that the neighborhood was not more financially diverse and described her effort to encourage subsidized housing. Another resident had just the opposite opinion; she insisted:

> I feel very strongly … that everyone should pay their own way … even though I'm one of the perhaps 30 percent who are very comfortable financially, I won't pay a buck for somebody else. Because I don't want to … I'm not going to subsidize you, even though you can't afford it and I can.
>
> (Samantha)

Although by 2014 Samantha had moved out of the community, I heard similar sentiment in 2014. There is a strong tension around class at EVI where some residents feel guilty and try to hide their class status, while others do not.

The narratives from residents about their access to live sustainably were often humorous, but sometimes sad and difficult. Residents were aware of the contradictions of their lifestyle and sometimes felt it was hard to admit that they lived in EcoVillage:

> … There is no reason why town house communities can't share a washing machine. In fact it happens all the time. We don't call it cohousing, we call it a Laundromat or coin-operated system, but they are doing it. People ask me all the time, what makes EVI different from a condo community and … well sometimes not much. And so I think we actually have a lot to learn from the outside world. Honestly … we're acting like it is so special and that it can only happen in this special way. I think it really hurts us and hurts our cause, if our cause is to help others live more sustainably, or help sustainable living become part of the [US] American norm. Other nations have bike-share programs, other cities I've heard in [the United States] even that have car-share programs … or are built more pedestrian friendly.
>
> (Wendy)

Wendy became frustrated by what she felt was an arrogant attitude:

> … it is sort of off-putting to people when I say I'm moving to EcoVillage within Ithaca and I really want to help kind of change that perception.

EcoVillage represents more complex issues than simply being a place to live with the environment and to get to know neighbors. It can be described as a commodity (Davis 1992), a themed space where one can escape from polluted, crowded, and lonely environments of the city and retreat into nature, fresh air, organic tomatoes, and friendly neighbors who stop in for tea. In the themed space of nature, residents are still isolated from a larger community, but they are isolated together. Residents are able to purchase a pre-packaged way of life that includes houses designed to encourage visual connections with neighbors and a pedestrian walkway to supply social interactions. With little effort but significant income, residents are able to purchase a sense of community and stewardship to the environment. Campbell (1995) suggests that consumer goods "commonly serve to communicate social distinctions or reinforce relationships of superiority and inferiority between individual groups" (111). In this case, EcoVillage is a commodity.

Another characteristic of a green lifestyle is the easy access to objects and places that are constructed as being green and part of "nature." Residents felt that they were protecting and preserving the environment by simply living in EVI. A young working mother—Eleanor—argued that EVI was doing a wonderful thing by preserving the land that otherwise would have been developed into a typical suburban development. Eleanor felt strongly about her responsibility to protect the land around her, despite the fact that the green space that was preserved only benefits a small group of families. Her argument for the privatization of nature as a way to preserve it reflects debates around the question of who speaks for nature and who benefits from privatizing nature (see, for example, Di Chiro 1996; Goldman 1998; Hardins 1968). Believing that by privatizing the land she was enabling it to be preserved was important because it allowed her to justify her privileged opportunity to live on beautiful land that is owned by the nonprofit she supports. Other residents believed that the EVI project was an imperative to prevent unsustainable growth of the land as sprawl. It did not, however, occur to Eleanor that perhaps EcoVillage was also contributing to sprawl. EcoVillage offers a model its residents believe can be used to build sustainable new suburban communities that are physically attractive and practically useful, and make positive impacts on the environment while accepting the reality that such kinds of communities will exclude certain populations. This is a tradeoff Eleanor said was for the greater good of saving the environment.

Green identity

EcoVillage allows its residents to choose their identity by the consumption of tangible and non-tangible commodities. Every year an announcement is made about the Angel Heart Sale, a pricey linen clothing boutique that has an annual significant discount sale in Ithaca, New York. Residents who are interested go shopping together. Campbell (1995) argues that material goods such as clothing are codes for social class. In EcoVillage, both material (organic food) and non-tangible items (views, open space, nature) place residents in a particular social class. The land debt meant that the community was forced to accept decisions that did not necessarily meet the environmental spirit of the mission statement, but instead provided financial stability to repay the loan. The need for the nonprofit to pay for the land through the lenders is what drove the hasty construction of the second neighborhood. A resident from SONG, Marian (2001), felt:

> in some ways SONGs are just dollar signs to a lot of FROGs … and a FROG member [said] "well the SONGs are coming, our lives should get cheaper here".… That exact quote has been said to me … the whole idea of people saying we want SONG to get built because that reduces the land debt.

This choice of land also meant that the group was selecting class distinction over other criteria like walkability and economic diversity. This decision has impacted the community in many ways, from creating a rift among early planners to portraying the community as elitist. A resident of the Ithaca community, Garth (2001), had the impression that EVI was "a group of wealthy individuals who had a lot of time, but were lonely and needy." The residents I spoke with felt saddened by this portrayal. A family moved out because they felt the priorities of the community moved away from being concerned with core values of environment and social sustainability to superficial concerns like geese droppings.

Class, taste, and lifestyle became more pronounced in SONG through the emphasis on viewshed. Some residents in the village strongly valued a natural viewshed[3] and installed large bay windows to bring their home and nature close together. A resident of FROG commented to me that windmills should not be put in the open field because they would block the viewshed of south-facing houses, obviously choosing lifestyle options over environmental needs. While participants told me of the importance of their viewshed, I had the impression that the view, house design, location, and community encompass characteristics of a green lifestyle that is in harmony with nature. However, microcosmic issues of class were still evident within the community. Another participant building on the south side of SONG half joked (with concern) that one corner of the neighborhood would be the "eco-ghetto" because it had very little viewshed, was to be designated for subsidy units, abutted a parking lot, and was next to the neighborhood trash cans. In fact, all residents of the SONG who moved from FROG had joined the FROG late in the project and were "stuck" with the north-side houses. Subsequently, three of the four families who moved out of the FROG and into the SONG left north-side homes and built larger homes with south-facing views. During a village-wide meeting a debate rose about views. A south-side SONG household (who used to live on the north side of FROG) argued, "view is not as important as keeping up with our mission." In response, a south-side FROG resident responded that she agreed with "ecology over views … [but] likes living on a hill with views."

The green lifestyle of EcoVillage allows residents to identify themselves as part of a larger effort to fight social and environmental degradation. It is this connection to doing the right social and ecological thing, or at least trying, that residents find attractive and successful in the EVI project.

> EcoVillage [brings me] closer to my idea of what I want to be, and EcoVillage is definitely getting me closer to that haven ... that is how it should be. Everybody should look at me and say, "this is how I want to live." ... I think what I do is better for the environment and the world, so if everybody would do it, it would be great.
>
> (Ronald)

Almost all the residents I interviewed were happy living at EcoVillage. They celebrated the warmth of their neighbors and abundance of open land around them. The common meals three nights a week, the opportunities to swim, and garden with neighbors were favorite reasons why residents were satisfied with the community and felt the project enriched their lives. But many residents also expressed how the community had helped them become more socially or ecologically aware of their lifestyle choices. Some composted more than they had in their previous home, while others felt that EVI made it easier for them to recycle and thus more likely that they would. The subtle reminders to reuse objects, the random discussions on how to save water, as well as the opportunities to engage in mediation when conflicts arose, were all encouraging mechanisms for creating a lifestyle that was rewarding, not only for them, but for nature and the environment in general.

Participants also felt proud that they were creating a lifestyle that was aspiring to be sustainable. Although residents often prefaced their comments with "it is not perfect," they also felt strongly that their EVI lifestyle was much better than the way they lived before. The project as a whole, and not necessarily any one piece of it, is what many residents felt was rewarding; they were part of a larger ecovillage community and often identified themselves as members of that community. In a small circle of women, a mother announced jokingly that her daughter's teacher reported the daughter telling her playmates, "you're not my real friends, my real friends live in EcoVillage." Laughing, but with some concern, the story reminded us of the sometimes contradictory nature of EVI: that there is a strong identity inside the community but one that is also exclusionary. The exclusionary nature of EVI on environmentalism and on sense of community segregates its residents in a boundary of trees and shrubs:

> I think there are members in the wider community who sort of thought, sustainability is another word for environmentalism that really was exclusionary and privileging. You know, sort of, bugs over people or nature over people.... It's something for me I've realized, I don't really know, I don't wear the ecovillage banner anymore.
>
> (Nikkola 2014)

Most discussions of US environmentalism aim to make a distinction between two worldviews: one that is considered environmentalism, and the other social justice (Harvey 1996). This distinction is useful to understand why some environmentalist circles seem to care little about social justice; it also helps to excuse the behavior of individuals who actively choose to overlook social justice. What was apparent in EVI is that people I spoke with were highly educated and well aware of the two forms of environmentalism: one that consisted of non-human nature, and another that emphasized social justice/environmental racism. Yet, as a means to respond to the overwhelming reality of choosing between fighting for social justice and pursuing personal desires, residents choose to protect their own interests. Consumption as a means to solve environmental problems contributes to the designing of exclusionary communities:

> In August 2014, two young African American children were biking home and followed by an off-duty police officer who suspected them of a crime. They were held at gunpoint by the police. A rally in front of Ithaca City Hall was called by concerned family, friends, and Ithaca community members. Less than a dozen EVI residents attended this local community gathering to demand accountability for racial profiling that resulted in handcuffing two elementary school children (Stein 2015).
>
> Around the same time, a massive climate change rally was being organized in New York City. The Peoples Climate March was planned for September 21, 2014. At least two buses from Ithaca were scheduled to depart early that morning and return early the next morning. It would be a 10-hour round-trip bus ride. There was a lot of excitement about joining carpools and sharing the experience. Some households bought extra tickets to subsidize those with limited incomes. When the second bus was ordered, the LISTSERV lit up. Fifty-one people from EVI attended the rally in New York City. I was among the small handful who attended the local climate march in downtown Ithaca. One resident reflected on the experience of going to New York City and shared her communication with others:
>
> "I'm so proud to be part of a community that 'walks the talk' not only at home but in the streets! I wrote the following to my Global EcoVillage colleagues the day after the march, but then thought it would be fun to share it with my home community, too. I encourage others to share their stories ... what a remarkable day! We are very blessed to offer so many replicable examples of sustainable living."

Although it was genuinely encouraging to see the community working for a cause that was outside of EVI, it was revealing that only 11 EVI residents, including me, attended a local rally for social justice that did not require getting up at 5:00 a.m., and driving for 10 hours, and was in response to a deeply disturbing incident affecting youth of color in the Ithaca community. What counts as social and environmental sustainability? What happens when being green distracts from being just?

Instead of volunteering in the local community, serving on various community boards, EVI requires an incredible amount of time and energy. A brand-new village was created from scratch. Through emphasis on bioregionalism and deep ecology, US environmentalism actively removes itself from spaces that would require its proponents to confront race and class (Harvey 1996; Sarkar 1999). The green lifestyle in effect creates a boundary in which those engaged in it can create the criteria by which they will confront social and environmental degradation.

Although a participant identified the community as one that recycles, composts, and shares meals together, which made her feel good about living there, she did not herself participate in any of these "eco" activities; she was nonetheless proud to be part of a community that did. Another participant identified herself as being concerned for the environment by the fact that after moving to EVI, she was able to consume organic food thanks to the CSA just down the path; in fact, it was the CSA that was especially attractive to her and her family when deciding where to live.

Douglas and Isherwood (1979) argue that consumption is an important component to creating a unique lifestyle identity. They contend that specific items have social value because they allow households who own these meaningful objects to create stronger relationships with other households who possess the same value of objects. That is, objects carry with them distinct meaning that are used to create social identities (Appadurai 1986; Carrier and Heyman 1997; Miller 1995). This connection between valued objects and social relationships is also emphasized by Bourdieu's analysis of class and lifestyle in French social structure (Bourdieu 1984). Other scholars explore consumption through the lens of political economy. Carrier and Heyman (1997), in their frustration with the direction of consumption studies in anthropology, which they see as focusing too narrowly on the symbolism of consumption, argue that concentrating on mundane objects of consumption, such as organic foods versus non-organic foods, is merely identifying the symbolic values and not likely to make a significant impact. Carrier and Heyman argue that the focus symbolism neglects the political economic relationship of the process of production and consumption. The reorientation away from class to focus more specifically on consumption is related to a parallel emphasis on mass production and thus mass consumption (Carrier and Heyman 1997). Consumption of specific goods reflects the social and political forces that shape households who possess the objects in question. For residents, the unique identity of being a member of an ecovillage is achieved simply by purchasing a home in the community, yet it also carries with it the constraint of a larger social and political meaning for which households negotiate through their daily practice. The green lifestyle in EcoVillage extends further than the cheap consumable of sustainably harvested wooden furniture and into the realm of class distinction. Thus the green lifestyle identifies residents with a particular place and culture. For some residents, part of creating a sense of community is to establish strong roots in a particular location. Some of the residents envisioned their children growing up in EcoVillage and being part of the third or fourth neighborhoods, envisioning a village with an extended family. Yet, the broader impacts of consumption of a green lifestyle reinforce larger political and social divisions, namely race and class (Carrier and Heyman 1997). The consumption of a green lifestyle in EVI goes beyond the mere purchase of an energy-efficient home; it is an act that is embedded in a wider and more serious debate, for which residents are aware and struggle to negotiate.

By buying a home and living in EVI, residents have a lifestyle that automatically includes energy-saving, sharing resources, and access to nature. In turn, living in EcoVillage creates a green identity. According to Crawford, "consumption hierarchies, in which commodities define lifestyles, now furnish indications of status more visible than the economic relationship of class position" (1992: 11), that is, class distinction is represented through the consumption of specific commodities that are marketed as symbols of class status (Appadurai 1986; Crawford 1992). Residents in EcoVillage often describe themselves as being ecological by the fact that they live in EcoVillage and not in a typical suburban development. Even residents who did not move to EcoVillage for the environmental mission felt that by virtue of living in the community they were doing the right thing for the environment. Erickson (1997) makes the point that reducing consumption is difficult if it is the very means that environmentally conscious people use to define themselves.

In *Regarding Nature*, McLaughlin (1993) argues that a society that focuses on consumption is an "ecologically lethal" way to form personal identity. While Thoreau's "simplify simplify simplify" was a reoccurring theme in EcoVillage, reducing consumption of material goods was often limited to non-green items. Reminders of overfilling dumpsters led to informative discussions of waste and materialism, but eventually a larger dumpster was purchased (Walker 2005). Some residents responded that compared with the rest of the country, they were doing well on reducing their waste and materialism.

What is the significance of creating a green lifestyle in the United States? And what are the effects of creating such a lifestyle on the environment and environmentalism? The lifestyle option modeled in EcoVillage is not available to everyone. Over its development, so little data was collected, evaluated, debated, and corrected that it is unclear how EVI intended to carry out its educational mission without critical self-reflection of green living. The connection between the nonprofit and the neighborhoods clouds the responsibility and confuses the mission and goals of each. While consumption helps create a sense of community and facilitates innovative green technology, some scholars argue that it is consumption that has led to the breakdown of community going back to the Industrial Revolution and the expansion of a consumer culture (Sack 1990; Wachtel 1983).

Significance of a green lifestyle

One of the things which makes me feel really good about living here is telling other people about it and enlightening them about it …

(Sean)

> I think we have to be very careful not to act like we have so much to teach the rest of the world and oh couldn't they learn so much from us, cause it puts us on a pedestal even within Ithaca … we are already up on that hill, it's bad enough, but I just think we need to keep our egos kind of in check with reality in terms of what we have to teach.
>
> (Lela)

The significance of creating green lifestyles in general, and ecovillages in particular, is that they represent a growing trend not only in Western countries but also increasingly in non-Western countries (Fotopoulos 2000). As such, ecovillages and their members have the potential to influence public policy in a way that can address social justice as it relates to the environment. The model of creating green islands only for people who can afford them as a response to social and environmental degradation is unhelpful to the larger struggles of neighborhood health disparities. We have been down this road before; poor communities and people of color continue to be marginal to US environmentalism, and these new communities have yet to demonstrate that they are not following that path. As well-meaning and hard-working individuals and whole communities focus their environmental efforts on personal lifestyle choices, they risk actively ignoring or displacing local and global social and environmental concerns. Building and maintaining an ecovillage is not easy; there is little time to be civically engaged in the neighborhood and in the local community, so households have little choice but to focus inward on their small village, too exhausted to attend the Ithaca City Council meetings. When asked, "how engaged are you in social, political, or other activities in the town/city of Ithaca?" a resident responded:

> This is the hardest thing for me personally—I'm engaged at EVI, and I'm heavily engaged in the literary community nationally as part of my work, but I have had no time to develop ties in Ithaca. As a creative person, who needs contact with other creative people, I am trying to intentionally remedy that, but it adds to the feeling that I don't have enough time.
>
> (EVI resident 2014)

The EVI project is an opportunity to create an identity of environmental sustainability as an individual and as part of a village, a lifestyle that is comfortable, pioneering, and for many, desirable.

The desire to live in EVI is evident by the participants I interviewed who lamented the fact that many early members dropped out because they could not afford to live in the community, or didn't appreciate the exclusionary nature of that model of sustainable community. The EVI project excludes the larger community and creates its own community within the larger city of Ithaca. Some residents are perturbed by this and want it to be more integrated: "We really wanted to be part of a larger community outside of just the cohousing. That was really important to us; that it not be this insular group of people that never related to the outside world" (Lela).

Eco-exclusion and green flight

The exclusionary nature of creating a brand-new village outside an established city, that is, creating a private community, is a characteristic of green lifestyles.

> Although helpful in creating an alternative culture among small sections of the population and, at the same time, boosting morale for activists who wish to see an immediate change in their lives, this approach [of building ecovillages] does not have any chance of success—in the context of today's huge concentration of power—to create the democratic majority needed for systemic social change.
>
> (Fotopoulos 2000: 298)

The EVI project has perhaps inadvertently created another means by which upper-middle-class families in the United States can exodus undesired urban space and create exclusionary places, what might be considered *green flight*. Green flight might be compared with white flight; rather than stay and contribute to developing a diverse urban landscape, as people of color began buying homes in their neighborhoods, white homeowners moved into the rapidly expanding suburbs (Gregory 1998). Green flight involves moving to greener pastures rather than confront ecological degradation and its impact on the remaining community. In the archives of the community, EVI argues that the community is not an average suburban village, but rather a model of community development done right. Although the community is set up as a green theme park, its inward focus excludes confronting environmental and social degradation that remains in urban cities and in communities of the poor and often among non-Caucasian populations.

EVI works outside and apart from other groups who are trying to improve the environment, health, or community of all people (or especially those who are most disenfranchised) in the city, or working to preserve land for public use. While proclaiming to work for the environment, these new ecological cohousing communities help to redefine the solutions to environmental problems away from lobbying government to strengthen laws that protect all people, to lobbying city government to allow only a small population to benefit from a private green community. EVI chooses (consciously and perhaps unconsciously) to exclude social and environmental justice, preferring to focus on issues of personal choices, taste, and lifestyle. This choice led to, and continues to result in, many families leaving the project in frustration and disillusionment. A resident in FROG felt frustrated that no one else in the community seemed concerned about these larger issues.

> I feel selfish to … live up here, have all this land to ourselves. I don't really know how to … I do know that I feel alone in that concern.

In addition to the lack of an overarching mission to contribute to helping address social and environmental degradation in poor, polluted communities, the immediate, though what some called mundane, issues like whether pets should be allowed outside, or the role of the "Process Steering Committee" are overwhelming to residents who then lack the desire or energy to fight against Superfund sites or work to stop nuclear proliferation (issues that some residents had spent significant portions of their lives fighting against). Being part of the EVI community requires a lot of time and energy for making group decisions, participating in the large number of events, as well as providing basic needs for one's family.

EVI has become a politically correct way to live in suburbia. By design, the neighborhoods are excluded from the larger Ithaca community, preferring to construct new homes that are energy-efficient and comfortable. A SONG family that specialized in improving the energy efficiency of all houses moved out of EVI and into the community they serve. Several of the households in EVI are from outside of Ithaca and have only tangential connections to the local community, giving the EVI community an artificial park-like presence in Ithaca. Molly, a mother of two in her late thirties, felt that EVI was "superficial because most of the families were middle class … the working class is more honest and real."

Although Molly was active in the EVI community, she often found it difficult to get to know people well. A meeting of the SONG group reiterated this concern. During the meeting about making more of the homes affordable, a future resident announced that he preferred not to have a flip tax (where a percentage of the profit on a sold house is returned to the neighborhood in order to keep the house affordable for the next resident) because he wanted to build and sell homes for a living. He explained that "if cohousing really takes off, this could be really lucrative" (Martin).

At the same time another resident in her thirties cautioned the group against creating an isolated island in Ithaca: "it is extremely important for … my family not to feel isolated up here in this little weird enclave" (Trudy). These conversations revealed the tension of living in a capitalist economy that prioritizes the needs of the individual over that of the community, despite a desire people have to feel socially connected in meaningful ways.

I argue that creating a lifestyle that excludes a wide variety of people and concerns, in essence, masks issues of race, environmental racism, white flight, and unequal access to healthy environments. By focusing on creating a green lifestyle in EVI, the planners and residents have chosen to emphasize one type of nature and environmentalism over another. Specifically, residents focus on preserving only the immediate land around them, the land that primarily benefits them.

Although one participant told me that the EVI project was protecting the land on West Hill from development, she felt that her form of development was good for the environment and would show other families planning or able to build in suburbia a better way to create community. Yet if this particular EVI model was adopted, there would be nothing done for already polluted spaces (except perhaps the continued exodus of families who might have the resources to help solve the problems in the communities they left); our cities would be left dilapidated, our suburbs deserted, while new ones are built, and there would still be inadequate public transportation, increased use of fossil fuel, and increased loss of open land, and the poor would likely be further inundated by waste incinerators as we trade our gas cars for electric ones.

Residents frequently reminded me that their EVI lifestyle helped them improve recycling and to develop friendships they value. However, we need to ask bluntly, who, besides the residents, benefits from this miniature model of living in harmony with nature? We also need to question why this particular model might be preferable over other means of working for environmental sustainability. Further research can shed light on the approach of other countries like Germany, and their efforts at the city, state, and federal level, to ensure that all people benefit from environmental sustainability efforts. If we do not address social and environmental degradation that affects all communities, what should become of our cities and the most vulnerable people within them? In order to confront the real and imminent challenges we all face, we need environmental efforts that bring us together, rather than pull us further apart.

EcoVillage can be seen as successful in that the people who created the idea, and those who are living there and benefiting from this lifestyle, are happy; those who felt otherwise left, or remain but feel marginalized or disconnected within the community. Ironically, after separating from her longtime partner, one of the co-founders had to move out. She could not afford to remain in the community. She is happy living in her apartment building in downtown Ithaca.

EVI appealed to residents who were looking for accessible friendships and support in their efforts to be green. There are various reasons why families felt that the EVI lifestyle provided a better way to live than they experienced in the community they left. For example, residents felt that they benefited from collective pressure to recycle, share, and discuss the environment on an almost daily basis.

The juncture of consumption and environmentalism is most pronounced in the fact that EVI has a goal of creating more than one neighborhood. This trend is also reflected in the desire to purchase a large piece of land in order to develop it. While the mission of creating a village implies the addition of other neighbors, it also suggests a desire to have more over less. On an individual level, some residents in the second neighborhood chose to add an extra foot here, and two more feet there, in order to get more "house" for their money. One family built an apartment into their home with the good intent of renting the apartment to a low-income family as one way of addressing affordability in EVI. During a Village Association meeting, a participant had the idea of building a tennis court on the Village Crux, which lies between the three neighborhoods.

It is not surprising that the United States is home to the first cohousing community with more than one neighborhood. This fact demonstrates a fundamental concern within the larger US culture. In *Graceful Simplicity*, Segal (2003) reminds us that the signals we receive from our society about what the "good life" is include messages that "more is better" rather than "just enough is plenty." Like most people living in the United States, EVI and its residents are immersed within this culture of consumption, or over-consumption (Shove and Warde 2002). In order to work against the trend to take more than necessary, projects like EVI need to be critical, specifically of what presents itself as an easy solution, and generally, of long-held beliefs that capitalism, a system of endless production and consumption, is the most effective model to address ecological and social degradation. Once we are able to move beyond the temporality of eco/natural capitalism, we can begin to look for alternatives as a way of creating harmony in our communities and between the human and non-human environment that will have sustainable results.

Beyond a green lifestyle

> One of my biggest disappointments is that we're not talking as much as I had hoped we would, or think we should about what for me is the most urgent issue. Um ... which is, you know, reducing greenhouse gas pollution.
>
> (SONG resident 2014)

According to Trainer:

> much of the elements within [ecovillage movements] are politically apathetic, insufficiently socially responsible, sloppy, irrational and far too affluent, and not interested in structural changes. Much of it is quite self-indulgent, only concerned with establishing havens within capitalist society, in which people can go on consuming goods imported from Third World sweatshops.
>
> (Trainer 2002: 144)

Trainer is a supporter of what he characterizes as an ecovillage movement, arguing that modeling sustainable communities is the best way to change individual behavior from an unsustainable lifestyle to one that benefits both people and non-human nature. Yet, he admits that the current ecovillage movement has fallen short of being a useful model (Trainer 2002).

I often felt that the model of environmentalism and community-building that EVI is attempting to create was a "cover" for families who wanted a guilt-free upper-middle-class suburban lifestyle without highlighting their privilege and acknowledging that their lifestyle was contributing to sprawl. This is too cynical. But I have experienced the frustration of trying to address social injustice at a large scale and simply satisfying my own needs. I believe that all of the people I worked with at EVI genuinely want to find ways to balance our needs and the needs of the rest of the planet. (Imagine if all the EVI energy—meetings, process, conflict mediation, money—was applied to the greater Ithaca community.)

Accepting the message of green marketers, and to a large extent natural capitalism, means that social justice is replaced with buying organic meats and driving alternative fuel vehicles. The green lifestyle does little to change or raise awareness of fundamental, structural environmental and community problems like resource depletion, toxic pollutants in food and water, lack of adequate social policies, meaningful employment, adequate childcare and education, streets without sidewalks, and the lack of healthy grocery stores in low-income, minority neighborhoods. In addition to creating a green lifestyle and thereby overlooking the root causes of environmental and social degradation, I argue that EVI in particular has become another example of the way in which US communities are creating exclusionary spaces.

I make this argument based on two contradictions of the EVI project. First, in order to create a sense of community, the project emphasizes the creation of a new community separate from any established one, instead of supporting the creation of community in place. Residents in EVI moved away from their families or from places with established communities like San Francisco, Berkeley, New York City, and Ithaca.

Second, creating a sustainable community for many residents requires the acquisition of land (in this case farmland) and the construction of new homes. While it is clear that the project aims to demonstrate ways to construct more sustainable suburban development, it does not challenge the idea of sprawl, which many in the environmentalist circles, and in EcoVillage, have argued is one of the root causes of environmental and social degradation in the United States.

Although EVI aims to educate the broader public about living lightly and harmoniously with nature, the community project works through the current power structures. Specifically, as Fotopoulos argues, the power structures of the market fail to encourage social justice and equity, focusing more on consumption and individualism. EVI, Inc. contains an education component that aims to spread the word on the possible ways of designing communities. However, during my study, most of the people I characterized as falling into the "public education" category were university students and scholars. Other visitors were primarily tourists or potential residents. Only a couple of residents made their living from leading tours or by teaching seminars and workshops to students and visitors. It is not clear who is allowed to use the educational opportunities of the community to earn an income from visitors and students, especially when that income is not shared with all the community residents. Some households found it impossible or difficult to partake in hosting educational programs. Other residents resented being a laboratory and sometimes closed their windows or went inside when students or tourists walked through the community.

Natural capitalism argues that it is possible to create a higher standard of living and at the same time decrease the environmental impact (Hawken et al. 1999). A green lifestyle privileges wealthy families who can enjoy the luxury of being green: afford organic food, to live "close" to nature, and to drive alternative vehicles without needing to sacrifice. Producers of green commodities are designing new niches for consumption, which pushes people to change their lifestyle to meet those new niches, which in turn creates new needs and thus new markets. The green market, as the solution to environmental degradation, can only be true if social justice concerns are excluded from our environment and if only short-term solutions are sought. A green lifestyle only works when one defines nature and the environment as the non-human world, something many participants are painfully aware of and struggle to negotiate.

In summary, creating a new green lifestyle through ecovillages at first glance appears as a wonderful idea, yet on closer examination of the everyday reality, it is revealed to be a complex endeavor. Green lifestyles take our attention away from larger social, political, and economic concerns of the environment that many poor communities and communities of color have been working to correct (Bullard 1990; Di Chiro 1996; Fotopoulos 2000; Guha 2000). EcoVillage focuses the lens of environmentalism on personal behavior and choices that mainly benefit individuals. The EVI project emphasizes that environmental and community degradation can be alleviated by changing where and how homes are built, considering whether former farmland is redeveloped more sustainably and whether neighbors are recycling. However, as is evident from interviews with participants who felt disillusioned and subsequently left, less emphasis is placed on issues of clean drinking water for poor neighborhoods, demonstrating affordable living, and increasing the use of public transportation. At a town board meeting I attended, where permits were sought for the construction of the second neighborhood, a member of the town board raised a point that was ironic: while the EVI community was seeking permission to increase the number and size of houses, the project had not approached the town to increase public transportation along Route 79, the road that runs next to EVI.

While EcoVillage attempts to make protecting the environment effortless, it also demonstrates the difficulty faced by well-meaning residents to voluntarily simplify their lifestyle in a way that protects the environment. Bourdieu's idea that lifestyle is ingrained in us from a young age is reinforced by residents' inability to make sacrifices for the environment, like using public transportation. It also reveals a fundamental flaw in US environmental politics, the narrow definition of environmental problems and solutions in the US mindset such that, as Fotopoulos (2000) points out, even supporters of ecovillages admit that while "the Ecovillage Movement includes a wide diversity of initiatives ... many ecovillages simply involve people in trying to build better circumstances for themselves, often within the rich world in quite self-indulgent ways" (297). For ecovillages to become a useful tool in US environmentalism, they need to look beyond their intentional neighbors and into the larger community and the politics behind environmental and social degradation.

Notes

1 San Francisco State University is a smoke-free campus (www.sfsu.edu/~puboff/smokefree/).
2 I refer to the ability to spend income on green products and green purchases such as organic food, earth-friendly products, and green vacations such as eco-tourism, as belonging to a green class. This class is also one of the driving forces behind the influx of green commodities into the economic market.
3 The quality of the view one has from looking out from one's home.

References

Appadurai, Arjun. 1986. Introduction: Commodities and the Politics of Value. In: *The Social Life of Things: Commodities in Cultural Perspective*. A. Appadurai, ed. pp. 3–63. Cambridge: Cambridge University Press.

Applebaum, Kalman. 1998. The Sweetness of Salvation: Consumer Marketing and the Liberal-Bourgeois Theory of Needs. *Current Anthropology*, 39(3), 323–349.

Bourdieu, Pierre. 1984. *Distinction: A Social Critique of the Judgment of Taste*. Cambridge, MA: Harvard University Press.

Bullard, Robert D. 1990. *Dumping in Dixie: Race, Class, and Environmental Quality*. Boulder, CO: Westview Press.

Campbell, Colin. 1995. The Sociology of Consumption. In: *Acknowledging Consumption: A Review of New Studies*. D. Miller, ed. pp. 96–126. Material Cultures. London, New York: Routledge.

Carrier, James, and Josiah McC. Heyman. 1997. Consumption and Political Economy. *Journal of the Royal Anthropological Institute*, 3, 355–73.

Crawford, Margaret. 1992. The World in a Shopping Mall. In: *Variations on a Theme Park: The New American City and the End of Public Space*. M. Sorkin, ed. pp. 3–30. New York: Hill and Wang.

Davis, Mike. 1992. *City of Quartz: Excavating the Future in Los Angeles*. New York: Vintage Books.

Di Chiro, G. 1996. Nature as Community: The Convergence of Environment and Social Justice. In: *Uncommon Ground: Toward Reinventing Nature*. W. Cronon, ed. pp. 298–320. New York: W.W. Norton & Co.

Douglas, Mary, and Baron Isherwood. 1979. *The World of Goods*. New York: Routledge.

Erickson, Rita J. 1997. *"Paper or Plastic?": Energy, Environment, and Consumerism in Sweden and America*. Westport, CT: Praeger.

Featherstone, M. 1991. *Consumer Culture and Postmodernism*. London: Sage Publications.

Fishman, Robert. 1987. *Bourgeois Utopias: The Rise and Fall of Suburbia*. New York: Basic Books, Inc.

Fotopoulos, Takis. 2000. The Limitations of Life-style Strategies: the Ecovillage "Movement" is NOT the Way towards a New Democratic Society. *Democracy & Nature*, 6(2), 287–308.

Goldman, Michael, ed. 1998. *Privatizing Nature: Political Struggles for the Global Commons*. New Jersey: Rutgers University Press.

Goss, Jon. 1993. The "Magic of the Mall": An Analysis of Form, Function, and Meaning in the Contemporary Retail Built Environment. *Annals of the Association of American Geographers*, 83(1), 18–47.

Gregory, Steven. 1998. *Black Corona: Race and the Politics of Place in an Urban Community*. Princeton: Princeton University Press.

Guha, Ramachandra. 2000. *Environmentalism: A Global History*. New York: Longman.

Hardins, Garrett. 1968. The Tragedy of the Commons. *Science*, 162, 1243–1248.

Harvey, David. 1996. *Justice, Nature and the Geography of Difference*. Cambridge, MA: Blackwell.

Hawken, Paul, Amory L. Lovins, and Hunter Lovins. 1999. *Natural Capitalism: Creating the Next Industrial Revolution*. Boston, New York, London: Little, Brown, and Co.

Jackson, Kenneth T. 1996. All the World's a Mall: Reflections on the Social and Economic Consequences of the American Shopping Center. *American Historical Review*, 101(4), 1111–1121.

Katz-Gerro, and Yossi Shavit. 1998. The Stratification of Leisure and Taste: Classes and Lifestyles in Israel. *European Sociological Review*, 14(4), 369–386.

Kempton, Willett, James S. Boster, and Jennifer A. Hartley. 1996. *Environmental Values in American Culture*. Boston: Massachusetts Institute of Technology.

McLaughlin, Andrew. 1993. *Regarding Nature: Industrialism and Deep Ecology*. Albany: State University of New York Press.

Miller, Daniel. 1995. Consumption and Commodities. *Annual Review of Anthropology*, 24, 141–161.

Myers, Norman. 1997. Consumption: Challenge to Sustainable Development. *Science*, 276, 53–56.

Sack, Robert David. 1990. The Realm of Meaning: The Inadequacy of Human Nature Theory and the View of Mass Consumption. In: *The Earth as Transformed by Human Action*. B.L. Turner, ed. New York: Cambridge University Press.

Sarkar, Saral. 1999. *Eco-Socialism or Eco-Capitalism? A Critical Analysis of Humanity's Fundamental Choices*. New York: Zed Books.

Segal, J.M. 2003. *Graceful Simplicity: The Philosophy and Politics of the Alternative American Dream*. Berkeley, CA: University of California Press.

Shove, Elizabeth, and Alan Warde. 2002. Inconspicuous Consumption: The Sociology of Consumption, Lifestyles, and the Environment. In: *Sociological Theory and the Environment: Classical Foundations, Contemporary Insights*. R.E. Dunlap et al., eds. Oxford: Rowman & Littlefield Publishers.

Smith, Neil. 1996. The Production of Nature. In: *FutureNatural: Nature, Science, Culture*. G. Robertson, et al., eds. London and New York: Routledge.

Stein, Jeff. 2015. *New Lawsuit: Ithaca Police Racially Profiled Teens in 2014 Incident*. https://ithacavoice.com/2015/08/new-lawsuit-ithaca-police-racially-profiled-teens-in-2014-incident/.

Szasz, A. 2007. *Shopping Our Way to Safety: How We Changed from Protecting the Environment to Protecting Ourselves*. Minneapolis: University of Minnesota Press.

Trainer, Ted. 2002. Debating the Significance of the Global Eco-village Movement: A Reply to Takis Fotopoulos. *Democracy & Nature*, 8(1), 143–157.

Veblen, Thorstein. 1931. *Theory of the Leisure Class*. New York: The Viking Press, Inc.

Wachtel, Paul L. 1983. *The Poverty of Affluence: A Psychological Portrait of the American Way of Life*. New York: Free Press.

Walker, Liz. 2005. *EcoVillage at Ithaca: Pioneering a Sustainable Culture*. Gabriola Island, BC: New Society Publishers.

6 Conclusion

Arriving in the city of Ithaca is becoming an inspirational experience. The streets are lined with trees, park benches dot the sidewalks, and many homes have flowers and vegetables growing in their front yards. Since I began studying life in EcoVillage at Ithaca, the city of Ithaca has adopted a growing number of green efforts for its residents and those who visit. TCAT (Tompkins Country Area Transit) are public buses that buzz up and down the main arteries of the city and into some suburbs. The buses in the city wind their way through neighborhoods, making it easy to get around the city without a car, especially for those who cannot afford one. The downtown neighborhoods are alive and active. A new neighborhood design called a "pocket neighborhood" has sprung up. They are "clustered groups of neighboring houses or apartments gathered around a shared open space—a garden courtyard, a pedestrian street, a series of joined backyards, or a reclaimed alley—all of which have a clear sense of territory and shared stewardship" (Pocket-Neighborhoods.net). In recent years, the city began to install bicycle boulevards, designated streets that are optimized for traversing bicycles. These are not isolated innovative efforts of a small group of individuals. The city of Ithaca, like other cities around the United States, is proactive in its effort to bring all communities and neighborhoods the benefits of a sustainable future. It is hard not to compare these efforts with the ones in EVI.

This September morning, I'm meeting with a family who has decided to leave EVI. It is a bit sad as we reflect on our shared fond memories of hiking in the woods, playing with their now teenage children, and working on the farm in the early morning. It is also hard to reflect on the disappointments, missed opportunities, and hurt that is expressed. Although we agree that the project has a lot of wonderful aspects, living downtown feels connected. In fact, we are about to head into the streets of the Fall Creek and Northside neighborhood for Porchfest.[1]

Porchfest began in 2007 when two musical neighbors decided to organize a day of free porch music in their neighborhood; the idea has since spread to 60 other cities across the United States and Canada. Porchfest is reminiscent of sitting on the porch and engaging in random, spontaneous conversations with neighbors, just this time with a musical edge. We collect our schedule, a list of over 150 musicians of various genres performing on different people's porches and in front of people's houses, and head towards the growing masses. The streets are alive, crowded, and joyous. Within walking distance, people you may soon get to know are eager to share the space of community. The music is an eclectic mix of folk, rock, soul, reggae, and classical. Because these streets are public, you don't need to live in the community to join or feel that you belong. This is public space. If you want to maximize your experience, you could bike to the different porches, otherwise, a calm stroll around the community yields many rewards. We've arrived early at a very popular stop and the streets overflow with dancers; the Gunpoets draw one of the largest crowds at Porchfest with their family-friendly hip-hop beat and lyrics. I find myself in a crowd of people I've never met dancing and smiling. The children find each other and their parents watch from the corners of their eyes. No need to be panicked here: this is a safe, caring space. I see several EVI residents and former residents and I squeeze through the crowd to connect with them. Felipe, one of the early FROG residents, tells me he lives just around the corner, then informs me that his previous EVI neighbor lives a few doors down. This Fall Creek area has several EVI expatriates. It is not hard to see why. A lot is in walking distance: schools, downtown, libraries, grocery stores, diverse neighbors, and work. I look once more into the crowd before heading to meet some other former residents. The mass is slowly dissipating as the band wraps up. It feels good to be in this space, the middle of the road, in the middle of a crowd, in the heart of the Fall Creek neighborhood. The group is ethnically diverse and interracial. This is Ithaca at its best: the reinforcement of community and the celebration of diversity by reimagining the front porch. All this celebration and community began with two neighbors, a ukulele, and an idea.

The morning conversation with Nisa and her husband, who decided to move out of their SONG neighborhood and into this inclusive, buzzing, downtown environment, is easy to understand after Porchfest. Before it gets dark, Nisa and I walk a few blocks from her home, across the street, and up to the Fall Creek gorge. It's a beautiful nature walk in the city, just blocks from where she now lives. I had been surprised on my last visit to see that many of the households I had initially interviewed for this project had moved out. As I write this, two more families have left. When I return to Nisa's house, I am invited to join the second exit interview that two EVI residents conduct with the leaving household. Since time continues to be a valuable commodity inside and outside EVI, I agree and listen intently. As far as I know, there has never been a systematic collection of exit interviews at EVI; this new trend is both necessary and useful, especially for a project aimed at creating sustainable communities that can be models for other groups.

There are, however, environmental and community organizations, such as the Center for Environmental Health,[2] that are working hard to rid poor communities of toxic pollution. Other groups work to create healthy community gardens, and plant trees and other green plants in the city, such as Urban Ecology[3] and various eco-cities organizations. Environmentalists at Redefining Progress are critical of how national "progress" is often defined and insist on including the physical and mental health of all citizens, the health of the environment, and the quality of social justice.[4] In Ithaca, Sustainable Tompkins County[5] is "a citizen-based organization working towards the long-term well-being of our communities by integrating social equity, economic vitality, ecological stewardship, and shared responsibility." There is an emphasis on the need to work together to create healthful places in order to thrive in environments where people already live. The greater Ithaca community is determined to meet this goal and its success offers a modest model for other cities across the United States.

While I have attempted to describe the complex ways a concern for the environment and for a sense of community are negotiated through the medium of an ecovillage in the United States, concerns about equity and inclusion have weakened the influence of EVI to be an effective model outside its borders, and risks undermining the very valuable contributions of the project. Specifically, EVI might contribute to a growing and much-needed conversation about how communities in the United States can be powerful instruments for social and ecological change. Although sweeping generalizations based on one case study are not useful, this work sheds some light on the current discourse on ecovillages. Despite overwhelming positive reviews, these communities are complicated and deserve critical reflection if their proponents want to see them succeed. That EVI had not conducted an exit interview before 2014, after 22 years of existence, is a disservice for the incredible hard work that goes into the project. Finding or identifying weaknesses is not rejecting hopefulness, but creating a space for change and progression. As an experiment in sustainable living, we owe it to the process to see where we fall short in order to correct the course and move forward. Perhaps pride or fear stands in the way of acknowledging when we are wrong, making it hard to see where and how we need to effect change. This might avoid the perception of the "emperor's new clothes," specifically that the things EVI argues make it special are in fact adopted by other individuals and communities without the distinction of creating an innovative community—see, for example, solar panel installation, an organic farm, shared meal and laundry facilities, etc. What EVI is doing well is providing a space to critically study and understand the challenge of creating lifestyle changes that reduce our resource consumption while being deeply engrained in a capitalist consumer economy.

The research findings demonstrate the multiple ways environmentalism is expressed through the consumption of green commodities and through the creation of a new form of themed community that attempts to emulate the ideal of living in harmony with nature and with others. This analysis also suggests the possibility of why consumption has come to dominate US environmentalism. I specifically argue that an unwillingness to question green consumption and capitalism has resulted in maintaining the status quo by replacing products known to cause environmental or social degradation with greener ones, such as hybrid cars, instead of challenging our very dependence on cars through urban design. It attempts to broaden the discussion of environmentalism, consumption, and community to include political ecological questions that are directly and indirectly changing our local and global environments. My research challenges the notion that a green lifestyle in and of itself is a viable solution to ecological and social degradation, by questioning the sustainability of capitalism as expressed through green technology and its desirability as a means to achieve harmony between nature and community. Finally, I explored the role of ecovillages in designing communities that are at once good for people and nature. Not everyone can live in this kind of project based on the way they are currently designed, nor would it be sustainable if the remainder of US family farms were developed as "green sprawl." At the same time, ecological intentional communities can teach us much about how families and individuals are critically rethinking the current trend of constructing "McMansions," the development of new large homes in once open spaces with little or no opportunity for creating community cohesion. EVI raises questions about how we live and about our relationship to community and environmental degradation. Ecovillage communities emphasize the reality that changing our lifestyle to a less energy-intensive one will be the most significant way to create ecological and social sustainability. Finally, ecovillages demonstrate that it is possible to create one kind of alternative model of living that brings people together in an effort to improve the environment.

> I think, maybe over the last five years, we spent a lot of time taking the kids back and forth, and back and forth, and this place is all about face-time, you know, and being here. We didn't have meals with everybody in a long time and then when we re-entered meals, if you are not there right at six, it would end up being me and [my spouse] sitting by ourselves, we could do that at home, you know.
>
> (Rosario)

> I think for me, the mobility thing is the biggest factor and I think I've kind of taken that on as kind of my thing. You know, one of my missions in life is to try not to drive. It has just been a lot of work to do that here. A lot of cycling back and forth, TCAT [the local bus system], a lot of hitchhiking. It kind of works okay, but then you know like a couple of days ago was a typical example. I biked to work, then I tried to put my bike on the bus but there was already two bikes on the bus so I had to take the bus, but then call work and have them get the bike for me.
>
> (Johnny)

The couple goes on to describe the challenge of having two adults who work in town, and two children who attend the local public schools, maintain part-time jobs, and have sport practice after school. Their children need to be picked up: the constant juggling of time and mobility in a place that constantly requires a car.

The study of EcoVillage at Ithaca reveals a tension between creating a model of living that is good for the environment and using an economic framework that has been instrumental in creating social and ecological problems. For example, instead of supporting alternative transportation, like walking and biking, using "eco" and "natural" capitalism promotes the purchase and consumption of technologically "green" commodities. Richard Register, an advocate for eco-cities and outspoken against electric vehicles, argues the often over-looked reality that electric cars still require electricity. According to Register (1996), electric cars are not very useful in effecting social change. He argues that such technological alternatives are a diversion from confronting global environmental problems such as the rapidly diminishing natural resources caused by over-consumption. Register calls for social transformation that addresses the need to redesign the places where people live, and argues for the creation of green cities. What is needed, he argues, are eco-cities that reduce our dependence on the most environmentally and community-destructive product—the automobile. The EVI goal to create a community in harmony with nature by building in nature creates a tension between needing to be outside of the city, and developing the farmland in order to suggest a way to save it from development.

Possibilities of the eco-city

Many residents in EVI do not consider themselves environmentalists. They moved to the community not so much because they were dedicated to improving the environment, but rather, because they were frustrated with what they saw as the continuously unsustainable development of farmland and open space into single-family detached homes. Creating an ecovillage represents an opportunity to engage in a larger discussion about the future of US community and neighborhood development, especially during a time when some people are feeling alienated and disconnected from the community around them. Though it attempts to offer middle- and upper-class families a comfortable lifestyle that produces less damage to a vulnerable planet, EVI is an idea that might be best situated in an urban community where the current shortcomings—such as the lack of public transportation and public exclusion of the community—can be ameliorated. There are ecovillages that do this well, like the Los Angeles Eco-village (see Fosket and Mamo 2009). At the same time that EVI addresses, for residents, the need to have a sense of community, to feel safe in neighborhoods, to provide recreation space for children, and access to clean air, all families across the country—urban, suburban, and rural—would benefit greatly from safer neighborhoods and cleaner environments.

The vision of creating an ideal village with five neighborhoods, now reduced to three, and shared community services like recreation halls, education centers, and local cottage industries is an indication of the energy and enthusiasm of the people working on the project and is evident from the success of the project. What would be the impact of applying all the hours spent in EVI planning meetings to supporting city-wide efforts that spread the benefits of sustainable community design widely? Participants, in disagreement with the original EVI vision, complained that two neighborhoods were more than enough for EVI. TREE was making the community feel overwhelming to some, and the open land that they loved. Other contradictions included the fact that although the SONG intended to build smaller, more affordable homes than the FROG, they ended up designing larger and more expensive homes, mainly because they could afford to consume a larger house and the nonprofit needed their contribution to the project in order to pay back the land debt. The tension between creating models of sustainable living and enjoying private access to large pieces of land was hard to negotiate. What is needed is a model of urban living that reduces our need to consume farmland for houses, as well as local organizing to create safe neighborhoods that have green parks and community gardens, recycle old furniture, reuse cloth grocery bags, support Laundromats, and share the commodities that we already have. While this seems antithetical to a capitalist consumer culture, it will be one step to reducing our impact on the environment, leaving more resources for future generations. Furthermore, there are already several community organizations around the world working together to build green urban neighborhoods that spread the benefits to all.

In June 2005, San Francisco hosted the United Nations World Environment Day Conference with the theme of "green cities." A number of talks detailed the eco-city movement and the successful engagements of social justice and environment merging in the creation of green spaces in cities; it also included discussions on transportation, alternative energy, and smart growth of the city to preserve open space. The papers included discussions of African American imprisonment, unequal exposure of low-income communities to persistent chemicals such as estrogen mimics, and the need to encourage walking as one way to respond to the growing obesity epidemic in the United States. The green city (or eco-city) model was Mumford's vision of physically and psychologically healthful places to live. Now, more than ever, as most of the world's people live in cities, creating clean urban spaces and integrating nature with the built environment is essential for the health of all our communities.

EVI has invested vast amounts of energy to alter individual habits around community and environment. The everyday practices have few tangible connections to wider political and social forces that are improving or degrading the current state of the environment. Rather, EVI offers some families an alternative way to live comfortably while reducing their impact on further environmental degradation. The "eco" in ecovillage is a bonus feature of the community, as some residents told me that they had not recycled or composted in the cities they left, and that EVI made recycling and composting easy. EVI attempts to create harmony with nature and create a sense of community from within the current socio-economic realm of the United States. There is no effort to challenge the housing market in order to provide affordable housing to low-income families; instead EVI creates a green lifestyle within the boundaries of US middle- and upper-class expectations. By a resident's own admission, EVI falls short of reaching the expectation of creating a simpler way of life and reducing consumption. EVI is far from sustainable, not only because individual families find it difficult to give up certain luxuries, but also because there is not a consensus on the definition of sustainability and thus no way to measure the effects of sustainable practices at the community level. The reality for some residents was that their effort to simplify their lifestyle only happened when their financial situation required it.

We know from ethnographic studies of Western communities that having more energy-efficient appliances does not necessarily result in less energy used. Erickson's (1997) work in Foley and Munka, Sweden, found that residents believed they could have the luxuries they desire and reduce their impact on the environment; despite owning more eco-friendly products, residents of Munka still continued to engage in wasteful practices. Similarly, EVI suggests the ability to have a comfortable lifestyle and protect the environment, but I observed many residents behaving in ways they felt were unsustainable, like Josephine, who regularly used paper plates at home because she did not want to wash her dishes. Thanks to an aggressive green marketing campaign, the myth that technology will allow us to continue consuming at our current rate and protect the environment's limited resources is procured by well-meaning people who enthusiastically buy green commodities with the expectation that their purchase supports the sustainability of the earth. I have tried to argue that just the opposite is true. Buying green without questioning whether the product is necessary in the first place simply adds to waste. More directly, in order to make a significant ecological difference, we in Western countries need to reduce our consumption of commodities we have come to believe are essential, such as the automobile, be they green or not.

The failure of US environmentalism to question market forces and capital accumulation has meant that environmental causes can be greenwashed or simply ignored by redirecting solutions and redefining the problems away from the continuous polluting of certain environments and certain communities. The ecovillage movement, by constructing new green housing outside of the city, has moved away from addressing environmental degradation and instead focuses on developing spaces for private green-themed community parks. This paradox has helped to maintain the status quo that continues to construct the environment as wilderness, and that social justice concerns of poverty, exposure to toxic chemicals, and over-consumption are secondary to the preservation of green space, especially if that green space is part of one's backyard. Finally, the EVI community model falls short of challenging social structures that contribute to the model of capitalism that suggests continuous economic growth is a sustainable way to address the problem of resource depletion and tremendous waste generation.

At some level, most residents at EcoVillage want to protect the environment and have a connection with their neighbors (see Appendix C for a list of reasons why people joined EVI). At the same time, they are deeply conflicted about how to live a simpler lifestyle and to give up the freedom our US lifestyle has promised.

To live in EVI and participate in its culture, one purchases not just a home but a green lifestyle, a lifestyle that is supposed to make voluntary simplicity straightforward, easy, and require little or no sacrifice. At the same time, this green lifestyle is not accessible to everyone who wants to live in the community, nor does the green lifestyle necessarily mean it is sustainable. To this point, Mapes and Wolch (2011) rightly argue that there is a lack of clear indicators for what defines sustainability and, as a result, marketing of sustainable community has been employed by developers in order to attract buyers. Only families with both the social and economic capital can participate in the green lifestyle or are able to remain in the community. Erickson found that in Munka, Sweden, residents chose energy-saving practices such as drying clothes on a clothesline or biking, not because they were obvious sustainable options, but because "10-speed bicycles are part of the latest assemblages of status symbols rather than to save fuel or the environment" (Erickson 1997: 51). The implications of this dilemma for EVI, and the ecovillage movement in general, are that the efforts of the participants become ineffective in the search for environmentally sustainable practices. Instead, EVI becomes another suburban development project that uses the fashionable ideology of "being green" in much the same way that Celebration, Florida, uses the Disney theme to create a happy place to live. This conflict between voluntary simplicity and consuming a green lifestyle further alienates people who want to truly reduce their consumption and work towards a more just society. Almost all of the former residents or participants I spoke with felt that the community failed to address the elephant in the room: that there was little that made EcoVillage "eco." One active resident attempted to raise the idea of changing the name of EcoVillage at a community meeting; but this idea was not taken seriously or pursued.

Confronting green consumption

EVI situates environmental solutions within capitalism, by consuming open land, building new homes in nature, and consuming green commodities. The focus of environmental solutions falls on the individual (purchasing a hybrid car) and not on the community (advocating for public transportation). Contradictions embedded within historical and cultural values outside of EVI problematize capitalism as the solution to environmental degradation, and participants in EVI are less inclined to confront the incongruities. Despite the innovative and socially energetic communities created by ecovillages, the spontaneity, diversity, and complexity of cities and the city centers cannot be easily replaced with private, thematically constructed spaces that are accessible only to upper-middle-class households. This shifting of environmentalist focus away from the communal and on to the personal is not unique to EVI, but reflects larger trends in a market system that emphasizes technology as the environmental solution in a culture that values individualism. In EVI, concern for the environment is situated in personal lifestyle choices at the cost of overlooking larger concerns which participants told me they no longer had time to address.

What makes these choices challenging is our hesitancy to question consumption and using capitalism as the framework in which to solve social and ecological problems, when capitalism has been the cause of environmental degradation and social conflict around the world (Adams 1990; O'Connor 1994). Ironically, some forms of environmentalism in the United States, such as that represented in EVI, emphasize consumption, instead of greater public sharing. Without a critical eye to green consumption, we end up reproducing the very forms of degradation we aim to ameliorate. We need green vigilance. As an alternative to large single-family homes and gas-guzzling SUVs, EVI has offered an attractive solution, but as a model of how to reduce our impact on the planet, it has fallen short by co-opting a narrow and personal definition of the environment and environmental problems.

Although a clothesline is available just outside the laundry room, residents use the dryer, even on beautiful sunny days; one resident commented that she preferred using the dryer because her clothes were softer. By contrast, a SONG household reduced their planned house size when they ran out of money. Since involuntary simplicity helped families reduce their consumption, public policy that encourages reduced resource use may be the best tool we as a society can use to address over-consumption. The EVI project revealed the tension between the desire to live simply while being confronted with a powerful marketing industry that encourages the purchasing of commodities marketed as "good" for the environment (whether or not they are essential commodities). The magazine *Plenty* is an example of the marketing of the green lifestyle where they claimed:

> … green options … are pleasing to the eye but also require no sacrifice of comfort or design. You simply have to hunt a little harder to find them. There are hybrid cars that get unprecedented gas mileage, but still have most of the power we've come to enjoy and expect. Tasty organic foods, designer clothes, and elegant furniture made from sustainably harvested natural resources are available at competitive prices. There are even ways to build a beautiful house from ecologically friendly materials.[6]

What is needed is a critical discussion of green consumption, the marketing of green commodities, and the relationship between capitalism and environmentalism. A critique of capitalism is necessary before we use its framework to reverse the current social and ecological destruction it has caused.

Closing thoughts

By replicating some features of EVI, such as creating and sharing public spaces (community gardens, plazas, etc.), sharing resources (Laundromats, public libraries), supporting alternative transportation (walkability, bicycle corridors, public transportation, car-sharing), and getting to know our neighbors (pot-lucks, emergency preparedness, neighborhood night out), we can reduce our need to consume commodities and at the same time create community without building new neighborhoods. But we cannot do this at the expense of ignoring vulnerable communities. Our collective energy can transform abandoned build-ings into parks and gardens, support public schools, advocate for green public housing and jobs, lobby local and federal governments to clean up Superfund[7] sites, and bring nature into all communities. The energy in EVI to redesign the human habitat is inspiring and can be even more impressive when it is applied to improve all our communities, especially those spaces that need it most.

During both data collection periods, I was often asked if I would live in EVI. Several years later, I continue to find myself appreciating the opportunity to meet and live with many wonderful caring people, who in their small ways are trying to respond to social and ecological degradation. As a participant pointed out, EVI is a place you might go to while on vacation, and in many ways it resembles a theme park. One gets a special feeling driving along the dirt road, the surrounding beauty is breathtaking, and the everyday life, the comings and goings of neighbors, is pleasantly unique. I experienced neighbors to be welcom-ing and generous. Residents are friendly, yet the neighborhoods FROG, SONG, and TREE are geographically distant from the residents in the larger Ithaca community. It felt exclusive and to some degree escapist. There is a peaceful, yet inorganic feeling in EVI that has to do with the intentionality of the place. It was hard to know if the same welcome enthusiasm, care, and interest would be given to members of the larger community. I found this question reinforced when households who left fell out of contact with members of the community, feeling that they no longer belonged to the group inside the boundaries of EVI.

EcoVillage at Ithaca, and ecovillages in general, reflect beautiful ideas of healing the world and each other by merging nature with social cohesion. We need this spirit now more than ever as Donald Trump begins as the forty-fifth President of the United States, yet creating new cities in nature, isolating them from the larger community, and moving further away from public transportation and grocery stores doesn't seem wise. Rachel Carson sparked a call for the gov-ernment to protect the public from industrial toxic pollution, pointing out that persistent organic compounds know no boundaries as they spread through wind, water, and in the soil. We need to continue this demand for protecting all com-munities and all environments.

Although EVI has provided an opportunity for its residents to recycle easily, compost easily, meet and make friends, it has also demonstrated the ability of a small group of committed people to make significant change. If we are to stop the current consumption of natural resources, we need to broaden our actions away from ourselves and towards the general local and global community. We are rightly concerned that small islands will disappear as climate change causes sea levels to rise; this may be the same fate for islands of sustainable com-munities. There are not boundaries for environmental degradation and resource depletion. The need to be inclusive is urgent lest we risk ignoring social and environmental problems that are framed by large political ecological factors such as race and class, and that affect us all. A focus on confronting the root causes of environmental degradation and a restoration of social cohesion may be our best chance for sustaining life on earth. While the scope of this project did not include a detailed analysis of capitalism, it becomes clear that an open discussion of the logic of capitalism as a vehicle for environmentalism needs to be addressed if the future of our communities and the planet is to be rehabilitated. Such a discussion can begin the process of creative thinking about a real alternative, sustainable future for all people and the planet.

Finally, a growing number of former EVI residents have moved into downtown Ithaca neighborhoods like Fall Creek. In fact, there are several EVI expats who are part of a vibrant urban, social, and environmentally conscious community. Although the subject of future research, preliminary conversations with families who moved out of EVI and resettled within the larger community were positive and rejuvenating. Pocket neighborhoods, transition towns, and informal urban ecovillages are part of a new urbanism that aims at creating a sense of community and ecological health and well-being in the places people already live. A sense of community is contagious, especially when it is accessible. There are myriad ways individuals and groups of neighbors are confronting social and environmental degradation, modeling resilience, and confronting health disparities with social action. Despite the challenges facing new forms of community design—such as what Melissa Checker (2011) calls environmental gentrification, the displacement of lower-income households as new trendy spaces push rents and housing prices out of reach—the possibilities of celebrating, creating, and rebuilding a civically engaged, socially just, and environmentally sustainable way to live that does not depend on green consumerism, or structured intention, are real.

Notes

1 www.porchfest.org/.
2 www.cehca.org.
3 www.urbanecology.org.
4 www.redefiningprogress.org.
5 https://sustainabletompkins.org/.
6 www.plentymag.com/mission.
7 Superfund sites are lands in the United States that have been contaminated by toxic hazardous waste (abandoned mines, illegal dumping of wastes and toxic chemicals, or accidental spills). These sites have been identified by the US Environmental Protection Agency as the most hazardous and pose the highest risk to human health and the environment. Placing a site on the EPA's Superfund site list is one way to begin the process of cleaning it up and making the polluter accountable.

References

Adams, William Mark. 1990. *Green Development: Environment and Sustainability in the Third World.* New York: Routledge.

Checker, M. 2011. Wiped out by the "Greenwave": Environmental Gentrification and the Paradoxical Politics of Urban Sustainability. *City & Society*, 23(2), 210–229.

Erickson, Rita J. 1997. *"Paper or Plastic?" Energy, Environment, and Consumerism in Sweden and America.* Westport, CT: Praeger.

Fosket, J., and L. Mamo. 2009. *Living Green: Communities that Sustain.* Gabriola Island, BC: New Society Publishers.

Mapes, J., and J. Wolch. 2011. 'Living Green': The Promise and Pitfalls of New Sustainable Communities. *Journal of Urban Design*, 16(1), 105–126.

O'Connor, Martin, ed. 1994. *Is Capitalism Sustainable? Political Economy and the Politics of Ecology.* New York and London: The Guilford Press.

Register, Richard. 1996. An Encounter with Tomorrow's Auto-crats: Ecological Cities "Yes"; Electric Cars "No." In: *Culture Change.* www.culturechange.org/issue9/electric carsno.html: Auto-Free Times.

Appendices

Appendix A Resident-owned businesses at EcoVillage at Ithaca (from the EVI website)

Table A1

Name of business	Description
A Space to Sew	A fun place to sew (rent sewing machines, classes, studio space)
Alan Willett, Oxseeker Consulting	Organizational development and leadership training for the software industry
Beadwork	Suncatchers and off-loom woven jewelry, available at Handwork in Ithaca
Being Change	Weaving the Great Turning through circles, art, and story
blink digital graphics	We work closely with our clients and co-create designs that are appropriate, effective, and adaptable to change
Carpenter	Otto Ottoson
Chris White	Jazz, improvisational, and classical cellist, cello teacher, and founder-director of New Directions Cello Association and Festival
Consult-Design-Build	Homes and whole communities—Rod Lambert
Clear Light Communication	For photos, videos, and text with integrity, focus, and clarity
Dr. Deanna Hope Berman	Naturopathic doctor, certified midwife, natural health store
Entos Press	Publisher of Wayne Gustafson's novels, photographs, and original notecards
Finger Lakes Permaculture Institute	Finger Lakes Permaculture Institute—Education to connect people with the environment and each other
Frog's Way Bed & Breakfast	B&B at EcoVillage (in SONG)
Gourd Art—Hands on Gourds	Homegrown organic lamps and functional gourd art by Graham Ottoson

continued

Table A1 Continued

Name of business	Description
Home Green Home	Environmentally appropriate furnishings and retailer in downtown Ithaca
Hayabusa Ithaca	Karate, ju-jutsu, aiki-jutsu, and kobudo with Sensei James Entwood
Ithaca Piano	Piano lessons by Chieko Pipa
Jody Kessler	Singer/songwriter, interfaith minister
Jody Kessler Singing Heart Yoga	Yoga, chanting, and meditation: an inspirational body/mind/spirit experience!
Jonna Climie	Massage and certified Healing Touch energy work practitioner
Kestrel Perch Berries	U-pick CSA berry farm at EcoVillage Ithaca
LingoSite	Language and translation services: Spanish, Italian, French, German, Portuguese
Lorraine Faehndrich, Radiant Life Design	Mind body coaching and mentoring for women struggling with chronic pelvic and sexual pain
Muskrat Studio	Sculpture, mixed media, prints
Natural Investments, LLC	Sustainable/responsible investments and financial planning, formerly Ecolibrium Financial Planning
Port Bay Travel	Custom, escorted tours, and specializing in school trips
Rachael Shapiro	Therapist
SEED	Permaculture design consultation services and educational events helping people build skills to co-create a regenerative future
SOUNDSWELL	Audio and video production services
Sustena Life Club	Japanese language eco-tours and EcoVillage Ithaca homestays
Suzanne Kates, Sagework	Massage and Reiki, specializing in elders
Swallow's Nest Bed & Breakfast	An organic B&B at EcoVillage Ithaca (in SONG)
Sustainable Living Associates	Education, facilitation, consulting—Elan Shapiro
Tutoring in writing, reading, and the humanities	Valorie Rockney
West Haven Farm	Organic vegetable CSA farm at EcoVillage Ithaca
The Wildflower Room Bed & Breakfast at EcoVillage	Julia Morgan
Yoku Dekimashita	Japanese language summer day camp at EcoVillage Ithaca

Appendix B Mission statements of EcoVillage at Ithaca

1992

The purpose of EcoVillage at Ithaca is to redesign the human habitat by building a model village for up to 500 residents that will carefully integrate design for human needs (shelter, food production, social interaction, energy, work) with land and water conservation and ecosystem preservation. As a living laboratory associated with an internationally prestigious university, EcoVillage will become a teaching center with a global audience. As a national and international model, it will showcase systems and methods that are sustainable, practical, and replicable. (EcoVillage 1992)

2017

EcoVillage at Ithaca (EVI) is part of a growing global movement for a saner, more sustainable human culture. It is developing an alternative model for suburban living, which provides a satisfying, healthy, socially rich lifestyle, while minimizing ecological impacts.

EVI comprises both an intentional community, the EcoVillage Village Association (EVIVA), and a non-profit educational organization, Learn@EcoVillageIthaca. The residential portion of the project was initiated by the non-profit as a "living laboratory" to demonstrate and teach best practices of sustainable living.

Learn@EcoVillageIthaca, a project of the Center for Transformative Action, promotes experiential learning about ways of meeting human needs for shelter, food, energy, livelihood, and social connectedness that are aligned with the long-term health and viability of Earth and its inhabitants. Its primary teaching tool is the EcoVillage with its green buildings, renewable energy systems, cohousing communities, organic CSA farms, open space preservation, and social entrepreneurship. Increasingly, it includes collaborative partnerships with local organizations, and it is also part of national and international networks. (www.centerfortransformativeaction.org/ecovillage-center-for-sustainability-education.html).

Appendix C Why people joined EVI

Table A2

Response to why you joined EVI	Number of respondents
Interest in living in cohousing, in community, know my neighbors, desire to age-in-place	40
"with my husband traveling a lot, we felt it would be best for our family to live in a community context," "We wanted nice neighbors who wouldn't spray poisons on their lawns," "appealed to us to have an 'instant community' with our neighbors and the chance to interact at dinners."	
The location of the land and landscape, its place in nature, "beautiful surrounds," open space, pond, live close to nature, access to green space, fresh air, abundance of water.	23
City and Town of Ithaca	13
"I had decided to move to Ithaca, and realized I needed to be able to form community very quickly. Cohousing seemed like a good way to accomplish that goal," "Ithaca had a socialist mayor!"	
The length of time the project has existed. Households have lived there since 1996, homes were already built.	12
"Project [TREE] was relatively close to completion."	
The EVI mission/vision of 150 units, organic farm, commitment to education, welcoming to LGBT.	11
"[Wanted to] create a demonstration of a more sustainable way of living on a village-scale. I thought that by creating a living example it would be inspirational to others."	
Family, co-parent in village, near family.	6
Workshop, support the director, presentations about EVI, books and other media reports about EVI.	6
"A weeklong workshop at EVI made me think this was a place which would respect individuality while fostering community."	
Ecological/environmental values, promote sustainability, live more sustainably.	4
"Wanting to align environmental values with lifestyle."	
Raise children in community.	4
"A nice place for our kids to grow up."	
Affordable, in price range.	4
In response to divorce or separation.	3
Life changes, retirement.	3
Local and global events (9/11, hurricane, BP oil spill).	2
Desire for a high quality of life, personal growth.	2
"It just seemed like the only sensible way to live."	
Employment changes, job loss, job relocation.	2
Preferred downtown location.	1

Table A2 Continued

Response to why you joined EVI	Number of respondents
Place to continue social justice work.	1
"Desire to be part of creating a socially just, ecologically and economically sustainable community."	
Sharing resources.	1
Architecture of homes.	1

Appendix D Comments to social connections and EVI mission

Table A3 Comments to social connections and EVI mission

How well connected do you feel to residents in your immediate (FROG/SONG/TREE) neighbors?

Feeling of connection has diminished over time although I do appreciate having a shared history.

One friend, many acquaintances.

We know each other and can count on our neighbors to help us out. However, we have not had deep spiritual discussions with our immediate neighbors.

Much less connected than I expected. Everyone's attention is spread thin.

The connections I have here are amazing for how little time I have spent here.

Well connected in FROG/SONG, much less so in TREE.

Very caring, sharing group that functions like an extended family.

How well connected do you feel to residents in other EVI neighborhoods?
Much more to FROG than to TREE.

Not connected at all with most "new" residents of TREE.

Connected to specific members of other neighborhoods rather than the neighborhoods as a whole.

Many acquaintances, with a few closer ones.

There are still some neighbors whom we have not met.

This is by choice, I find the number of neighbors overwhelming.

Some neighbors have reached out and I have reached out—other folks are harder to meet and connect with.

It really depends on the person … am close to some, not at all to others.

Depends on who more so than in my own neighborhood.

Varies widely.

Many new FROGs/SONGs last year in addition to TREEs moving in.

Close to two families; involved in activities with several families.

Close connections with some people, overall closer with immediate neighbors.

continued

Table A3 Continued

How well do you feel you can share your personal needs with the community (disability, family concerns, need for privacy, etc.)?

Extremely difficult to discuss finances.

People have generally kind intentions and are willing to help but there is often a fear of judgment or of overstressing people.

I feel as though my needs are viewed with suspicion.

Again, by choice.

If I had to I feel strongly that my concerns would be heard. But, mostly I don't share really private things with many.

With individuals.

How well does EVI meet visible and invisible (mental illness, hearing loss, ADHD, chemical sensitivity, etc.) disability needs?

Some needs met beautifully; others not so well.

People are generally open minded and concerned but that doesn't always translate into useful action.

Ok with physical disabilities, but brain-based disabilities are handled very poorly.

These needs are on the table but realistic plans to meet these needs has been urged within the community.

There's not a lot of communication.

Better than most places.

Varies.

We try hard but we deal better with acute situations than with long term.

It's hard with so many people. Often disability needs conflict.

How well does consensus decision-making work at EVI?

Not very well. One or at most a few people can squelch almost any project, particularly in FROG.

Some people listen well but many do not.

We need to move to a more efficient system, such as dynamic governance.

I got burnt out and haven't been involved in community decision-making in a while.

It seems that sometimes individual viewpoints and agendas interfere with the consensus process.

Getting too big at village level for consensus.

There have been times when I have felt the group was held hostage by consensus.

It takes a looooong time to get anything done—years sometimes.

Most people don't understand how well it actually works. They focus on the few spots that are trouble and think we have a terminal illness.

I am suspect of the push to sociocracy as it seems to me that it would easily become hierarchical and much less participatory.

I'm in favor of moving toward dynamic governance model. From talking with folks who have been here and more involved longer, I think our decision-making by consensus gets stalled and ineffective.

Modified consensus in TREE but exploring dynamic governance.

Table A3 Continued

That seems to be in flux with addition of new neighborhood.

I'm happy that we are considering a more workable alternative.

Well somewhat. My impression is better on the village level than neighborhoods.

Fine until one person blocks!

Too slow, too cumbersome, an issue that's not so important can take months of time and energy.

How well do you understand the EVI mission?
I think pretty well, although the agenda of the new EVI, Inc., board is unclear to me.

I feel like growing up there allowed me to EMBODY the mission, but it's all dependent on perspective.

How well does EVI meet its mission?
The mission is outdated and much too grandiose! It needs to be updated.

The EVI mission has never been particularly important to me.

We need to find a way to shrink our footprint in regards to transportation. We have too many cars and not enough options for getting up and down West Hill.

There is an assumption that residents will jump on the bandwagon and support EVI's projects. This may not be what many residents want to do.

I checked this box because I believe the mission should evolve and be representative of those who live here, i.e., we should take time to look at our mission as we grow.

We're actually struggling quite a bit with some key principles (supporting and encouraging diversity and affordability).

Not sure—don't pay that much attention to it.

We are making a valiant attempt to do so, but with many obstacles and much ground yet to cover.

Except affordability.

? Not sure.

Don't know.

How well do you comprehend the various parts of the EVI project?
I still can't get ordinary, standard financial statements from either non-profit.

I am still confused about the parameters of the various village committees.

The disconnect between the non-profit, its various legalities and leadership continues to confuse me, though it's been somewhat clarified, still I do not feel connected to all entities.

Very complex set of interlocking parts.

I understand well what I am most interested in.

How well do you understand the goals/mission of EVI LEARN?
In a general way.

There are no goals, but I understand the mission well (if in fact you are considering the EVI mission and the Learn mission as the same thing).

LEARN is doing good work developing its vision and mission.

---

continued

Table A3 Continued

I think it is time for us to live in the most sustainable manner that we can. I think there has been enough publicity so that the world can find us and what life here is like by surfing the web. Perhaps experience weeks or longer 3 or 4 times/year could be a way that we teach others and have less invasive visits. This would also make less demand on "servicing" visitors.

I am very interested in this area and am learning quickly about the current status.

One of the major pieces of EVI for me.

It's ok if I don't understand that well, I trust and admire those working on it.

How satisfied are you overall with life at EVI?
I love it! It has many flaws, but I feel blessed to be able to live here!

I wish there were closer ties with individual neighbors/households and more time for small-group socialization.

In many ways I love living here, I feel frustrated though by how difficult decision-making and governance are, and also by the lack of cultural diversity. It may simply be that my community is elsewhere and I just don't have the available time to commit here.

Varies from day to day or week to week!

I think life here, from my perspective, is about as good as I could hope for.

I do not believe living here is economically sustainable for people without jobs.

Very well—well.

How engaged are you in social, political, or other activities in the town/city of Ithaca? Include the ways you are engaged below.
Quite engaged.

Vegan movement, Tompkins County compost educator (master composter), engage with and coordinate projects with permaculture specialists, etc.

Not a person with big social needs but in general my social and support needs are met outside EcoVillage and in Ithaca (homeschooling/unschooling, parent support, therapy).

Other ecovillage, SEEN, Sustainable Tompkins, Healthy Food for All, Food Donations Network, Seed Swap Network, new Roots Charter School.

We are active in our church and I am a member of the Dorothy Cotton Jubilee Singers.

Friends Meeting, Alternative to Violence Project, Talking Circles on Racism, Lifelong, other events as able.

This is the hardest thing for me personally—I'm engaged at EVI, and I'm heavily engaged in the literary community nationally as part of my work, but I have had no time to develop ties in Ithaca. As a creative person, who needs contact with other creative people, I am trying to intentionally remedy that, but it adds to the feeling that I don't have enough time.

Youth organizing. Tompkins County Youth Action Network. TCAT, other transportation groups. Get Your Greenback Tompkins. Energy Action Plan Advisory Committee. Tompkins Youth Services Department. Ithaca Youth Council. Ithaca Festival, Streets Alive! Other organizations and groups …

Unschooling parent groups; 12-step recovery groups.

Very active on Greensprings Boars. Music, crafts events and classes.

Friends, dance communities, some environmental groups.

Participate actively in social justice projects.

Table A3 Continued

Local government.

My social ties are almost exclusively with the larger community and I have few close ties within EVI itself.

Worked at Greenstar weekly for years, then monthly for years, then monthly for years more, further, until chemotherapy interrupted.

Was on parents group at LACS for years while our boys attended. Spent 2 years.

Helped a lot over 2 years to get New Roots School started.

Board HFDI, member AFCU, Greenstar, WASL.

Issues regarding all aspects of the aging experience.

Attending talks occasionally, as able.

Initiated creation of Disability Studies section for Alternatives Library; Participating in some GreenStar Co-op activities; Participating in local Living with Illness Group.

Participating in occasional rallies, as able; difficulty in participating in town/city activities because of disability access issues.

Initiated creation of disability studies section for Alternative Library at Cornell; Participate in Greenstar Co-op activities; Participating in Living with Illness group; Attend occasional talks as able.

Mostly work at Cornell and socialize at EVI, but some friends in city.

Have close ties to a group of Scottish Gaelic learners. I also teach ballet at a yoga studio in Ithaca.

I work full-time at Cornell. I sing with the Dorothy Cotton Jubilee Singers and perform around town. My sister and her family as well as close friends live in Ithaca. I'm involved with the Latino Civic Association. I attend festivals. I am also a landlord of two duplexes in Northside neighborhood.

School activities.

For just the few months that I have been in the area: growing connections with several local churches and with the local permaculture and small farm culture.

Quaker meeting.

Actively engaged in astronomy community and Friends meeting (Quakers).

Free income tax preparation program, native plant society.

Volunteer at Tompkins County Library 2 times/week, sing in 3 choirs.

Environmental (steering committee of interfaith climate action network); church (peace and justice committee); League of Women Voters; campaign for candidates.

Index

Page numbers in *italics* denote tables, those in **bold** denote figures.

Adams, William M. 12
affordability 57–8, 61, 85, 96, 97–101, **98**, 103, 115, 126, 127, 139
ageography 86–7
alternative energy 16, 106n2
anthropology 10, 22–3, 66–9, 75, 94; *see also* research methodology
Appadurai, Arjun 13
architecture 49, 52, 91–4
Athanasiou, Tom 14, 17
Austria 52
automobiles 82, 91, 112, **115**, 137; electric 137; sharing 82, 112, 115–16

bicycle boulevards 133
bioregionalism 122
bofællesskaber 11, 20
Boggs, Grace Lee 15
Bokaer, Joan 40–1, 62
Bourdieu, Pierre 13, 16–17, 116, 122, 130
building footprints 49
Bullard, Robert 15
buses *see* public transportation
businesses, resident-owned *145–6*

Campbell, Colin 118
capitalism 12, 14–15, 136, 140–1; natural 13, 14, 15–16, 105, 129–30, 137
Carrier, James 122
cars 82, 91, 112, **115**, 137; electric 137; sharing 82, 112, 115–16
Carson, Rachel 15, 142
Celebration, Florida 21, 85–6, 93, 94, 140
celebrations and rituals 9–10, 59–60, 92, 103–6
Center for Environmental Health 134–5

Center for Religion, Ethics and Social Policy (CRESP) **40**, 43, 78
Center for Transformative Action **41**, 43, 78
Checker, Melissa 143
Citizen's Network for Common Security **40**
city centers 18
civil rights 19
class distinction 13, 17, 58, 116–17, 118–19, 122–3
Clean Air Act 11, 109
Clean Water Act 11, 109
climate change 11, 121
cohousing communities 11, 20–1; *see also* First Resident Group (FROG); Second Neighborhood Group (SONG); Third Resident EcoVillage Experience (TREE)
commodity, community as 21, 117–18
Common Houses 44, 48, 49, 50–1, 52, 92, 94
communalism 11
community 11–12, 53, 58–62; as commodity 21, 117–18; and environmentalism 17–22; search for 11–13, 74–5
community boundaries, residents' views of **84**, 87
community LISTSERV 32, 43, 90–1
community organizations 134–5
community work 22, 53, 63, *63*, 69n9, 96, 103
community-supported agriculture (CSA) **41**, *42*, 43, 54–5, 62, 78, 122
composting toilets 51, 67, 113, 116
consumption 12–13, 14–15, 110, 111–12,

116; and environmentalism 15–17, 127–8, 135–6; and identity 13, 122–3; *see also* green consumption
Cornell University **40**, **41**, 43, 78
corporate environmentalism 17
Crawford, Margaret 123
CSA *see* community-supported agriculture (CSA)
cultural capital 116
curtains 91

Davis, Mike 81
deep ecology 122
deer 55
Denmark 11, 20, 45
Dequaire, X. 52
dirt road 8, 91, 112
disabilities 94
Disney, Walt 94
Disney theme *see* Celebration, Florida
Disney World 93, 94
diversity: environmental organizations 17; residents 55–8, 56, 57, 97–103, **98**, 99
Douglas, Mary 122
Durrett, Charles 20, 45

easements, land 21, 43, 78, 79
eco-capitalism 13, 105, 137
eco-centrics 15
eco-cities 137, 138
eco-exclusion 125–7, 129
ecological causes, residents' commitment to 76, 76
ecological disasters 19
eco-socialism 13
EcoVillage at Ithaca 1, 2–4, 75–85; architecture 49, 52, 91–4; as commodity 21, 117–18; community 11–12, 21–3, 53, 58–62; days in life of 8–10, 30–40; exclusionary nature of 94, 120–1, 125–7, 129; history and structure 40–55, **40**, **41**, *42*, *44*; location choice 78–80, 86–7; mission 43, 44, 46–7, 47, 147, *149–53*; perceptions of wider community 83–5, 102, 119; rituals and celebrations 9–10, 59–60, 92, 103–6; size 22, 45–6; tensions and negotiations 16, 44–5, 58–9, 95–103, 112–13; as themed community 85–95, 117–18; *see also* green lifestyles; residents of EcoVillage at Ithaca
EcoVillage at Ithaca Incorporated **40**, **41**, *42*, 43–7, 78, 89
ecovillage movement 11–13, 20–1, 128, 130, 136, 139, 140

edge cities 18, 81, 82
education centre **40**, 43, 82
electric vehicles 137
email *see* community LISTSERV
employment, residents' 82, 96–8, **97**, 103
endangered species 19
energy: alternative 16, 106n2; non-renewable 13, 16, 76, 111–12
energy efficiency 52, 126, 139
Enlightenment 12
environmental gentrification 143
environmental justice 11, 14, 19, 21, 61, 109
environmental movement 19, 109
environmental organizations 11, 17, 61, 134–5
Environmental Protection Agency 19, 109
environmental racism 15, 24, 121, 126
environmental studies programs 19
environmentalism 11, 12–13, 109, 120–2; and community 17–22; and consumption 15–17, 127–8, 135–6; corporate 17; personal 13–15, 111–12
Erickson, Rita J. 17, 123, 139, 140
Escobar, Arturo 12
ethnic/racial diversity: environmental organizations 17; residents 55–6, 56, 101
exclusionary spaces 94, 120–1, 125–7, 129
exit interviews 55, 134, 135, 136–7
exodus from cities 18, 81, 125–7

Fellowship for Intentional Community 20
feminist scholarship 12
financial resources of residents 97–8, **98**, 115, 116–17
First Resident Group (FROG) **40**, **41**, *42*, 43, 44, 46, 48–50, 51, 78, 91–2
fishing 92
Fishman, Robert 81
flip taxes 126
food, locally grown 1–2
food growing **41**, *42*, 43, 54–5, 62, 78, 122
footprints, building 49
Fotopoulos, Takis 21, 125, 129, 130
Friends of the Earth 61

garden cities 19, 78, 80–1, 82
Garreau, Joel 18, 81
gated communities 11, 18–19, 83
Geddes, Patrick 11
gender identity, residents' 57
gentrification, environmental 143
Germany 52, 127

Gibbs, Lois 15
Global Walk for a Livable Planet 40–1, **40**, 86
Goldberger, Paul 105
Gottdiener, Mark 93
green access 116–18
green cities 137, 138
green consumption 10, 15–17, 102, 105, 109, 116, 122–3, 135–6, 139, 140–1
green flight 125–7
green lifestyles 13, 109–30, 135–6, 137–40; constructing 109–10; eco-exclusion 125–7, 129; green access 116–18; green flight 125–7; green identity 118–23; green technology 10, 110, 113, *114*, 136, 137, 139; personal environmentalism 13–15, 111–12; resource sharing 115–16; significance of 123–4; theme of 94–5; *see also* green consumption
green marketing campaigns 139, 141
green sprawl 78–83, 136
green taxes 13
green technology 10, 110, 113, *114*, 136, 137, 139
greenwashing 2, 6n2, 112, 139
Guys Baking Pies ritual 103–4

habitus 13, 16–17
Hannigan, John 105
Harvest Festival 92
Harvey, David 61
Heyman, Josiah 122
house sizes *44*, 49, 51, 79, **80**, 138
Howard, Ebenezer 11, 78, 80–1

identity: and consumption 13, 122–3; green 118–23
incomes, residents' 97–8, **98**
inequality 14; *see also* class distinction
inheritances, residents' 97–8
intentional communities 11, 20, 93, 136
interviews: exit 55, 134, 135, 136–7; research 65–6
inverted quarantine 13–14, 111
involuntary simplicity 141
Isherwood, Baron 122
Ithaca 121, 124, 133–5
Ithaca Carshare 115–16

Jankins, Harvey 60

Kempton, Willett 109–10
Kestrel Perch Berry Farm **41**, *42*, 43, 54, 55, 78

land debt 43, 44, 51, 52, 61, 118–19, 138
land easements 21, 43, 78, 79
land purchase 21, *42*, 43, 44–5, *44*, 50, 52
landfills 21
landscape architecture 92–3
Learn@EcoVillageIthaca **41**, *42*, 147
lifestyle changes 110
LISTSERV, community 32, 43, 90–1
location choice 78–80, 86–7
Los Angeles Ecovillage 20, 78, 137
Love Canal 19
Low, Setha 18, 75McCamant, Kathryn 20, 45

McDonaldization 82
McLaughlin, Andrew 123
Mapes, J. 140
materialism 123
Mead, Margaret 75
meat eating 35, 105–6
methodology *see* research methodology
Miller, Daniel 13, 16
Milton, Kay 13
mission 43, 44, 46–7, *47*, 147, *149–53*
Mumford, Lewis 11, 81, 138
Myers, Norman 110

Nader, Laura 23, 62
National Environmental Policy Act 11, 109
natural capitalism 13, 14, 15–16, 105, 129–30, 137
nature 11, 12, 19, 21, 34, 61, 66, 75, 77–8, 87, 110; privatization of 118
Nature Company 105
non-renewable resources 13, 16, 76, 111–12

participant observation 62–3
passive house standard 52
Passivhaus Institut 52
Peoples Climate March 121
Pepper, David 15
personal environmentalism 13–15, 111–12
personal sharing 59–60
Plenty magazine 141
pocket neighborhoods 133
political affiliations, residents' 100
political ecology 12, 17, 136
pollution 14, 16, 19, 21, 134–5
pond 92
Porchfest 133–4
privacy 18, 51, 88–9
private-public spaces 21, 89, 93, 106n4, 112

property taxes 44–5
public health 19
public transportation 48, 89, 112, 115, 133

quarantine, inverted 13–14, 111

race and racism 18, 101; environmental
　racism 15, 24, 121, 126; racial profiling
　121; *see also* ethnic/racial diversity
Redefining Progress 135
Re-evaluative Counseling 60
Register, Richard 137
religious practice, residents' 56, 99
research methodology 62–9; anthropology
　10, 22–3, 66–9, 75, 94; archival data 64;
　interviews 65–6; participant observation
　62–3; survey 63–4
residents of EcoVillage at Ithaca:
　businesses *145–6*; class distinction 58,
　98–103, 116–17, 118–19, 122–3;
　commitment to social and ecological
　causes 76, *76*; community work 22, 53,
　63, *63*, 69n9, 96, 103; distribution **64**;
　diversity 55–8, *56*, *57*, 97–103, **98**, *99*;
　employment 82, 96–8, **97**, 103;
　financial resources 97–8, **98**, 115,
　116–17; gender identity *57*; leisure
　60–1; moving out 55, 119, 125, 127,
　133, 134, 135, 136–7, 143; origins of 86,
　86; political affiliations *100*; reasons for
　moving to 87, *148–9*; religious practice
　56, 99; schooling levels 99; sexual
　orientation *57*; social connections *47*,
　149–53; trust 58–9; vegetarianism 35,
　105–6; year born **45**
resource sharing 115–16
resources, non-renewable 13, 16, 76,
　111–12
rituals and celebrations 9–10, 59–60, 92,
　103–6
Ritzer, George 82
Rodwin, Lloyd 81

Sarkar, Saral 13
sauna 112
schooling levels, residents' 99
Second Neighborhood Group (SONG)
　40, **41**, *42*, 43, 44, 46, 47, 50–1, 92, 113
security 18; *see also* surveillance
Segal, J.M. 127–8
self-surveillance 90
sharing: car 82, 112, 115–16; personal
　59–60; resource 115–16
shopping malls 21, 81, 94, 112

Sierra Club 19, 61
simplicity: involuntary 141; voluntary 11,
　24, 140
Smith, Neil 109
smoking bans 110
social causes, residents' commitment to
　76, *76*
social connections, residents' *47*, *149–53*
social justice 2, 14, 15, 20, 120–2, 128–30,
　135
solar panels 48, 51, 113
Soper, Kate 75
Sorkin, Michael 85, 86, 88, 93
sprawl 10, 22, 24, 77, 78–83, 118, 136
straw bale insulation 51, 113
subsidized housing 100, 117, 119
suburban developments 18–19, 80–3
surveillance 88–91
sustainable development 12
Sustainable Tompkins County 135
Swan's Market, Oakland, California 20
Sweden 139, 140
symbolism 116, 122
Szasz, A. 13–14, 109, 111

talking sticks 59–60
taxes: flip 126; green 13; property 44–5
Taylor, D.E. 11, 17
TCAT (Tompkins Country Area Transit)
　133
techno cities 81
techno-centrics 15
technology, green 10, 110, 113, *114*, 136,
　137, 139
tensions and negotiations 16, 44–5, 58–9,
　95–103, 112–13
theme parks 21, 93–4, 112
themed communities 21, 85–95, 117–18;
　ageography 86–7; architecture 91–4;
　green living theme 94–5; growing trend
　in 93; surveillance 88–91
Third Resident EcoVillage Experience
　(TREE) **41**, *42*, 43, 44, 52, 92
Thoreau, Henry David 123
toilets, composting 51, 67, 113, 116
tours *42*, 44, 90, 129
Trainer, Ted 21, 128
transition towns 11
trust 58–9

United Nations World Environment Day
　Conference 138
U-pick berry farm **41**, *42*, 43, 54, 55, 78
Urban Ecology 135

urban renewal 21

Veblen, Thorstein 116
vegetarianism 35, 105–6
viewshed 48, 85, 119
Village Association **40**, **41**, 42, 43, 52–4, 127
visitors 88, 89–90, 129
voluntary simplicity 11, 24, 140

Walker, Liz 40, 55–6
Warren County 19
waste incinerators 21

water and sewer infrastructure 77–8
West Haven Farm **41**, 42, 43, 54–5, 62, 78, 122
wheelchair users 94
White, Richard 94, 97, 105
white flight 18, 81, 126
wilderness preservation 19
Wolch, J. 140
Women Goin' Swimmin' event 103–5
women's rights 19
World Wildlife Fund 19

Zehner, Ozzie 16

For Product Safety Concerns and Information please contact our EU
representative GPSR@taylorandfrancis.com
Taylor & Francis Verlag GmbH, Kaufingerstraße 24, 80331 München, Germany

* 9 7 8 0 3 6 7 1 9 2 9 2 1 *